Reforming American Education from the Bottom to the Top

Edited by
EVANS CLINCHY

H E I N E M A N N
Portsmouth, NH

To Blythe McVicker Clinchy
for her unending love and support

Heinemann
A division of Reed Elsevier Inc.
361 Hanover Street
Portsmouth, NH 03801–3912
http://www.heinemann.com

Offices and agents throughout the world

© 1999 by Heinemann

The author and publisher wish to thank those who have generously given permission to reprint borrowed material:

"Education for Political Life" by Alejandro Sanz de Santamaría. Copyright © by Alejandro Sanz de Santamaría. Reprinted by permission of the Author.

Excerpts from *The Boy Who Would be a Helicopter* by Vivian Paley, Cambridge, Mass.: Harvard University Press, Copyright © 1990 by the President and Fellows of Harvard College. Reprinted by permission of the Publisher.

"Reforming American Education from the Bottom to the Top: Escaping Academic Captivity" by Evans Clinchy; "Supposing That . . . " by Deborah Meier; "Is That Penguin Stuffed or Real?" by Susan Ohanian; and "Rethinking the Benefits of the College-Bound Curriculum" by Nel Noddings originally appeared in the December 1996 issue of *Phi Delta Kappan*. Reprinted by permission of the Publisher.

Library of Congress Cataloging-in-Publication Data
Reforming American education from the bottom to the top / edited by Evans Clinchy.
    p.   cm.
    Includes bibliographical references and index.
    ISBN 0-325-00174-X
    1. Educational change—United States.   2. Education—Aims and objectives—United States.
   3. Educational planning—United States.   I. Clinchy, Evans.
    LA210.R44 1999
    370'.973—dc21

    99-33274
    CIP

Editor: Lois Bridges
Production: Abigail M. Heim
Cover design: Jenny Jensen Greenleaf
Manufacturing: Louise Richardson

Printed in the United States of America on acid-free paper
03 02 01 00 99 DA 1 2 3 4 5

Contents

PART I — EDUCATION IN THE KINDERGARTEN TRADITION

PART II — SOME FURTHER PROBLEMS OF HIGHER EDUCATION

PART III	THE PROSPECTS FOR THE REFORM OF AMERICAN EDUCATION FROM KINDERGARTEN THROUGH GRADUATE SCHOOL

Editor's Note

This book is based upon two earlier books edited by the same editor that dealt with some of the major educational reform issues currently facing the American system of public education.

The first book, *Transforming Public Education: A New Course for America's Future,* was published in 1997 by Teachers College Press and set forth in general terms a new educational mission and a new organizational structure for U.S. public schools.

The second book, *New Schools, Old School Systems,* published by Teachers College Press in 1999, dealt in considerable detail with the creation in two of our major urban systems—those of New York City and Boston—of what we might hope to see as the wave of the future: a broad diversity of new, small, public, educationally autonomous schools created and chosen by parents, students, and a school system's professional staff. Some of these new schools can be public state charter schools independent of any local school district. But the bulk of them are—and should be—created *within* our local districts. These schools can be seen as the forerunners of an entirely new and much more democratic American public school system in which *every* school becomes an autonomous school of parent and professional choice.

The creation of these schools, however, requires massive changes in the way local districts are organized and operated. Indeed, these changes add up to a new organizational structure—a new *kind* of public school system. It is this new kind of system that the contributors to *Creating New Schools: How Small Schools Are Changing American Education* described in some detail.

The present book deals with the fact that such a new kind of public school system is not going to be created as long as our colleges and universities maintain their constrictive, authoritarian, and therefore anti-innovative, antidemocratic educational structure and practices, and most especially their constrictive, authoritarian admissions policies. It is simply not possible for our elementary and secondary schools to reform themselves as long as entrance into our colleges and universities—and thus access to the higher social and financial rewards this society confers on those who are college-educated—

is governed by the scholastically dictated straitjacket of a student's scores on the Scholastic Assessment Test (SAT) and College Board examinations, the number of Carnegie unit courses taken, and such numerical fabrications as grade point averages and rank in class.

Any true reform of our elementary and secondary schools thus depends upon the simultaneous, collaborative reform of our colleges and universities. It is such a process of coordinated reform from kindergarten through graduate school that this book advocates and attempts to describe.

Acknowledgments

I would like to acknowledge the longtime assistance and support of the people who have contributed to this book, and my colleagues, past and present, at the Institute for Responsive Education: Don Davies, Owen Heleen, Karen Mapp, Abby Weiss, and Jennifer Novak, and the mentors—Carl E. Lindstrom, Harold B. Gores, and William H. Ohrenberger—who made it all possible.

Introduction:
Preparing for an
Incalculable Future

American education is currently embroiled in a profound debate over the future shape of our system of public schooling from preschool through high school.

The immediate cause of this debate is the widely heralded standards-based juggernaut of educational "reform" and "restructuring" that was launched in 1983 with the publication of the U.S. Department of Education's *A Nation at Risk* report. That document accused the nation's system of public education of being awash in "a tide of mediocrity" and of being a severe threat to the present and future economic health of American society. If this country is to survive in the new viciously competitive global economy, and if all Americans are to have well-paying jobs in the future, the report said, there must be a major effort on the part of all local school districts, all state governments, and the federal education establishment to raise dramatically the academic standards and thus the academic achievement levels of all American students. It is this national reform agenda that has become the Clinton administration's Goals 2000 educational program now supported by several billion dollars of federal money.

This reputed failure of our public school system has been shown to be largely a myth.[1] Despite these refutations, the national education agenda sparked by *A Nation at Risk* is spreading inexorably throughout the land in two inevitably connected ways.

At the national, state, and local levels, a new set of "higher," "world-class" academic standards is being established in all of the traditional core academic disciplines of English, mathematics, science, history, economics, geography, civics, government, foreign languages, and the arts.

At the national level, these more demanding standards are called voluntary, but at the state and local levels, they are in almost every case being mandated for all local schools and thus for all teachers, principals, parents, and students. These new national standards are accompanied by "high-stakes" local, state, and perhaps eventually national tests to measure whether the standards are being met by all schools and all students all across the land. These are high-stakes tests because they will be used to determine whether students move from one grade level and one school level to the next, whether they will graduate from high school, and in conjunction with the SAT and College Board examinations, whether they will be admitted to colleges and universities.

Critics of this national agenda fear that the result is all too likely to increase the educational uniformity that has characterized the American educational system throughout most of this century. They fear that as the new standards are put into place, the traditional methods of teaching the established curriculum are also sustained and toughened. These are the methods by which many of us still remember quite well being taught. That is, the adult world in the form of the school and its professional staff decides what students should learn at each grade level in each subject (the standards that must be met), how the courses in each of those subjects will be organized and taught at each grade level, what the daily lessons will be, what the homework assignments will be, what tests will be administered, what grades will be given depending on the results of those tests, and whether a student will thus be able to graduate from each grade level to the next and eventually graduate from the school system itself.

In most cases, the method of teaching this standards-based traditional curriculum (often referred to as the information and skill transmission method) is that the teacher presents the material to be learned and the students are expected to understand and memorize that material, do the assigned homework, and pass the test on it. Critics of the new national agenda fear that while in the past some latitude was usually given to teachers in choosing and presenting what the students were expected to learn, the new demanding standards will significantly reduce any such latitude as teachers are increasingly compelled to cover all of the standards and to teach to the tests. It is those test results, after all, that will decide whether students are succeeding or failing, whether teachers (and their schools) are succeeding or failing, and whether teachers and administrators will be retained in their jobs or fired.

These critics also fear that these new strictures will make it even harder for schools to be innovative, to depart from the traditional model, and to try out new and better ways of educating children and young people.

The Decentralization Movement

At the same time as this traditional top-down national agenda is being put into place, we also have a much smaller but growing antithetical movement aimed at radically decentralizing and democratizing our public school systems. In matters of educational philosophy, curriculum, and teaching methods, this movement can trace its philosophical roots to the seventeenth- and eighteenth-century Enlightenment philosophers and to eighteenth- and nineteenth-century educational pioneers and experimenters such as Friedrich Froebel, Johann Herbart, Johann Pestalozzi, Robert Owen, and Alfred Russel Wallace.

A later version of this movement was promulgated by Maria Montessori and in the United States by John Dewey and the proponents of progressive education, a series of proposed reforms that have been systematically denigrated and ignored by the educational establishment that has dominated our schools since the turn of the twentieth century. It is a view that over the past several decades has gained significant scientific support from the work in human and cognitive developmental psychology by such researchers as Jean Piaget, Lev Vygotsky, Jerome Bruner, and Howard Gardner. This progressive approach has emphasized child- or learner-centered teaching, inquiry-based learning, and a broad, flexible curriculum tailored to the needs of individual children and aimed at developing each child's intellectual, social, and moral capacities and each child's ability to live and work in a democratic society.

This progressive movement has advocated placing the educational decision-making power in the hands of the people running and using individual schools—the school's professional staff and the parents who choose to have their children attend such a school. These schools need to have a degree of philosophical, curricular, organizational, staffing, and fiscal autonomy unheard of in the typical American public school system, a fact that may explain why so few truly progressive schools have ever been created or long sustained within our hierarchical, centrally bureaucratic public school systems.

This situation changed a bit in the 1960s, when many "alternative" and genuinely progressive schools were established within public school systems. This movement also brought about the creation of semiautonomous magnet schools all across the country as a result of the Supreme Court's 1954 *Brown* decision and the necessity to integrate unjustly segregated school systems. The alternative school and magnet school movement led to a slight broadening and democratization of the authoritarian structure of our local school systems through the creation of different kinds of schools and different approaches to schooling that began to match the enormous diversity of the nation's parents and students. These schools were (and often still are) granted at least a small degree of philosophical, curricular, staffing, and fiscal autonomy. They also pioneered the concept and the practice of parental and professional choice of public schools, both within and across school districts. While many of these magnet schools did not depart widely from the standard traditional model, a significant number were of the progressive persuasion.

The current version of this "bottom-up" movement is taking three different forms, two of them specifically designed as end runs around the inflexibly authoritarian and heavily bureaucratic local school districts. One of these is the push for *vouchers* that would allow parents to spend an allotment of public money to send their children to the public, private, or parochial school of their choice. The other is the creation of *charter schools*, public schools responsible not to a local school district but to the state.

The voucher movement is currently embroiled in legal and philosophical disputes about whether public money should go to the support of private, particularly religious, schools. But the charter school movement is flourishing, with charter schools now available in almost every state. There is in many quarters, however, concern that charter schools are taking money away from the regular district public schools and using it to create a system of essentially private schools for those parents who are informed enough to take advantage of them.

The third form of the antiauthoritarian movement is directly aimed at creating a radically different organizational structure for *all* of our local school systems. This is the effort to create in-district charter or pilot schools, a diversity of new, small schools that are created by or in collaboration with the local district authorities. In theory and increasingly in practice, these schools are blessed with the same philosophical, curricular, staffing, and fiscal autonomy that is enjoyed by the state-chartered schools. Ideally, this autonomy includes the ability to devise their own curricula and to establish their own standards and criteria for success or failure. These schools also operate on lump-sum budgets and in most cases are free of stultifying union staffing rules. They can either be new schools located in new facilities or new, small autonomous schools created by breaking down larger schools and housed in the old schools' buildings.

This movement is perhaps best exemplified by the work being done in two East Coast cities, New York and Boston (see Clinchy 1999). In New York the movement for new, small autonomous schools was pioneered in East Harlem's Community School District Four by such educators as Anthony Alvarado, the district's superintendent at the time, Seymour Fliegel, the deputy superintendent, and Deborah Meier, the creator of the renowned Central Park East Elementary and Secondary Schools. A recent study by researchers at the State University of New York at Stony Brook indicates that these free-choice schools and the free-choice system itself have assisted in dramatically improving the achievement of students in *all* schools in the district. (Teske 1997).

The movement originated in District Four is now being spread throughout the city by the New York City central school authorities with the support of the United Federation of Teachers, the local teachers union, and with the encouragement of two independent agencies, the Center for Collaborative Education and New Visions for Public Schools. Over one hundred such schools have been created or are being planned.

In Boston these new, small autonomous schools are called pilot schools, and there the movement is supported by the local school authorities, the Boston Teachers Union, and the Center for Collaborative Education–Metro Boston, modeled on the New York center.

There are now eleven such schools in Boston (with more being planned), including Fenway Middle College High School, based upon Theodore Sizer's Coalition of Essential Schools model; Boston Downtown Evening Academy, a competency-based, work-experience high school serving students who can attend school only in the late afternoon and evening hours; the Boston Arts Academy for students interested in the visual and performing arts; the Harbor Middle School, an Outward Bound, expeditionary learning school; a progressive K–3 Young Achievers Science and Math School; a Multi-Cultural High School, in which students design their own learning projects; a Health Careers Academy high school for students heading into the medical and health fields; two community-based schools, the K–3 Lyndon Pilot School and the Greater Egleston Community High School; and the Boston New School, a progressive, open-education K–8 school created and now being run by Deborah Meier.

While many of these schools are genuinely innovative attempts to explore new and better ways of educating young people, and while some of them could be called truly progressive, the basic point of the new system is to provide a democratic diversity of schools that will meet the educational needs and desires of any district's entire population of parents and students, and the full range of educational philosophies and pedagogical styles of any district's professional staff. This means that there will be schools that still hew to the traditional curriculum and teaching methods as well as schools that are attempting to break the traditional mold. From the point of view of advocates of the progressive approach, such as contributors to this book, this is as it should be. The new system at the very least guarantees that progressive schools can be created and flourish as permanent options within the district's system of educational choices. Since these advocates believe in a truly democratic American society and therefore a truly democratic American educational system, they do not believe that *any* single, one and only approach to schooling— including their own progressive model—should be imposed upon the American populace. They believe, rather, that their progressive approach should operate within a truly free marketplace of educational ideas and practices. If it proves eventually to be seen as the most effective and rewarding approach by the majority of the population, that is obviously to the good. If not, then it can be added to the boundless collection of wonderful lost causes that already litters the historical landscape.

A Slightly Different Take

While all of these discussions and attempts at reform are being conducted in our elementary and secondary schools, however, one major aspect of this entire picture is missing or simply being ignored.

This is the fact that *much of what goes on in our public schools—and most especially the current A Nation at Risk/Goals 2000 reform juggernaut with its traditional, standardized subject matter curriculum, its information transmission pedagogy, and its standardized testing leading to the student Armageddon of the SAT and the College Board admissions exams—is governed by what goes on in our colleges and universities.*

It is, after all, the higher education establishment that has always largely determined what will be taught in our elementary and secondary schools, how it will be taught, and how it will be tested so that a small portion of the student population can be admitted to the groves of higher academe.

Indeed, this book was born when some of those thoughtful and highly respected people who are actually working every day in, and attempting to reform, public elementary and secondary schools began asking some questions that went beyond simply criticizing the agenda of *A Nation at Risk*/Goals 2000. These people have begun to raise some profound issues not just about the reform agenda at the K–12 level but about the entire existing structure of American education, public and private, from elementary school through graduate school. And they are especially concerned about the role played in that structure, and therefore in the new national reform agenda, by U.S. colleges and universities.

These questions and issues run something like this. As a result of *A Nation at Risk* and now the federal government's Goals 2000 agenda, we in the elementary and secondary schools are being told that we must radically reform and restructure ourselves so that *all* of the students we educate are able to meet new world-class academic standards in the traditional academic disciplines of English, mathematics, science, history (or social studies), economics, geography, foreign languages, civics, government, and the arts. We are being required to do this, we are told, so that those students will be better prepared to function successfully in the world of the twenty-first century and especially so that they can get good, high-paying jobs and contribute to maintaining this country's leadership in the competitive global economy.

We are also informed that the twenty-first century world and the new global economy require us to broaden and deepen dramatically the education we offer our students. We need to make sure not only that our students improve all of their basic skills of reading, writing, and mathematics but also that they develop their "higher-order thinking skills" and become able to think through and solve complex problems out in the real world.

We are in addition told that we must make sure that more of our students (90 percent, if possible) graduate from high school and go on to post-secondary schooling to insure that they gain those higher-order thinking skills and all of the up-to-date knowledge they will need to survive and flourish.

However, at the very same time that we are being urged by our national leaders to implement this new national agenda from the top down, we are also experiencing a quite different set of pressures coming from the bottom up. These pressures arise from many of the same citizen dissatisfactions with public education that led to *A Nation at Risk* and from other concerns that are only peripherally related to—and in many instances are quite contrary to—the economic concerns underlying that report.

These demands are made by a broad array of unhappy parents, teachers, and grass-roots community people, especially people most directly concerned with helping poor and minority children and families trapped in neglected, underfunded, and decaying urban school systems. What these people are arguing for is a radical decentralization and democratization of their local school systems. These people want a genuine devolution of decision-making power down to the level of the parents and teachers in individual public schools. Parents want to be able to choose from a broad range the kind and the quality of the schools their children will attend. Teachers and other professional staff people want to be able to choose the different kinds of schooling they wish to practice. And they want the organizational autonomy to run those schools in the ways they and the school's parents believe will be best for the students in the school. While most of these parents and school people want these new, small autonomous schools to have high intellectual standards embedded in a demanding educational program, they want to be able to decide for themselves what the curriculum will contain and how it can best be taught to the students entrusted to their care.

And, these people are saying, if our local public school systems are incapable of providing such a radically revised system of public education, then we are quite willing, even eager, simply to abandon those systems and schools. Parents and community people are quite willing to agitate for vouchers that will allow parents to send their children to public, private, or parochial schools. Parents and teachers are willing to agitate for state-sanctioned charter schools that are, at least in theory, free of most of the bureaucratic and union restrictions that hobble their local district public schools.

Given these two conflicting sets of top-down and bottom-up pressures, elementary and secondary school people say, they find themselves caught in a mystifying dilemma, a double or triple bind that translates itself into a further series of very tough questions about the entire structure of education in the United States, at both the elementary and secondary and the higher education levels.

We are now being asked, they say, to make all of these Goals 2000 changes in our schools in order to prepare our students for a coming world that no one can even begin to describe, much less accurately predict. If this is so, why are we then being commanded to implement what looks like an even more rigid and restrictive version of the outmoded, nineteenth-century, heavily academic curriculum we have now? This is a curriculum that in both its old and new versions all too often has little or nothing to do with teaching higher-order thinking skills and often contains little first-hand, up-to-date knowledge about that unpredictable world out there.

One of things that most disturbs these elementary and secondary school people is that this new version of an archaic, heavily academic curriculum, based upon those "world-class" academic standards in all of those traditional core academic subjects, is called voluntary by the national educational authorities. But what these school people see happening is that those "voluntary" standards are being translated by state boards and state departments of education into state-mandated standards and state-mandated tests that prescribe and then test "what every student should know and be able to do" and therefore what every teacher should teach at every grade level from kindergarten through high school. By and large, this new de facto national curriculum is one that has been developed not by teachers and principals, who must deal with real students in the real, day-to-day world of the public schools, and especially our difficult urban schools. Instead, the new standards and tests are being developed primarily by college and university scholars and the central office subject matter curriculum specialists who are all members of the national associations in each of the traditional scholarly academic disciplines—the National Association of Teachers of Mathematics, English, the sciences, and so on.

It therefore appears to many school people that this national education agenda and its new de facto national curriculum are primarily aimed at preparing students to meet the entrance requirements of the major public and private colleges and universities. They are fully aware of the fact that what goes on in the elementary and secondary schools, most especially in the high schools, has traditionally been governed by the educational structure and the scholarly disciplines of higher education. They do not believe that it is an accident that the middle and secondary school curricula they are required to teach are made up of middle and secondary school versions of those traditional scholarly disciplines of English, math, the sciences, etc. This is brought home to them when they attempt to create and teach interdisciplinary courses and are told (as Joe Nathan points out in Chapter 3) that their students will not receive college admissions credit for such untraditional studies.

These school people also are deeply concerned by the college and university reliance upon numerical scores their students must somehow be able to obtain on the traditional pencil-and-paper and multiple-choice tests that are quite disconnected from and often quite irrelevant to what goes on in actual classrooms inhabited by real students and real teachers. Their students' futures depend on standardized achievement tests the school people are compelled to administer each year, on the SATs and the College Board exams, and on such slippery and often unfairly manipulated numerical fabrications as grade point averages and rank in class.

Perhaps what disturbs the school people most is that it is assumed that all students can and will achieve academic success with that scholarly curriculum and meet "world-class" academic standards, thus somehow becoming prepared for that quite uncertain and unpredictable world of the twenty-first century. The people promoting the new national agenda seem to assume that if all students are taught by means of this new curriculum, they will have experienced a broader and deeper education and developed their higher-order thinking skills, and will now be able to think for themselves and solve complex problems and be successful out in that real world. Given that the strictly academic subjects they are required to teach are almost always taught from second- or third-hand educational materials in school classrooms that are isolated from the real world, the elementary and secondary school people wonder if this set of beliefs is actually supported by the facts of contemporary public schooling.

These school people are fully aware, of course, that the world of higher education is also experiencing many of the same criticisms and pressures that the elementary and secondary schools are facing. Our colleges and universities are themselves being accused of being hopelessly antiquated and elitist, of being disconnected not only from the world of the elementary and secondary schools but from the larger society itself, and therefore of failing to serve that society well by failing to educate the enormous diversity of students that exist in that larger world.

These elementary and secondary school people are also somewhat aware—but by no means as aware as they should or would like to be—of the efforts being made by many people in the world of higher education to respond to the criticisms and pressures and therefore to change the way our colleges and universities operate. Indeed, what seems clear to these school people is that, in the immortal words of the film *Cool Hand Luke,* what we have here is a massive failure to communicate.

What they would like to see, they say, is a concerted, completely collaborative effort on the part of *everyone* involved in the educational enterprise from elementary through graduate school to rethink, to reconceive the entire process by which we attempt to educate our young people from their early childhood years to all of those various points at which they will be released from the educational system and turned loose on an innocent and unsuspecting society.

Changing the Direction of the Buck

Now, the traditional practice in American education—whenever it is suggested that the educational system is not working as it should—is to pass the buck simultaneously *down* and *up*. People in the graduate schools start passing the buck down by claiming that the undergraduate colleges send them students who are not by any stretch of the imagination adequately prepared to pursue their chosen professional fields. College and university people in their turn bemoan the inadequate preparation of students arriving at their cloistered doors from the country's high schools, those failing institutions that are clearly responsible for sending them immature teenyboppers. The high school people in their turn say that the fault lies with the middle and elementary schools that are not inculcating in students the basic intellectual and behavioral traits leading to academic achievement and success in high school. The middle and elementary school people in their turn suggest that if only the kindergarten and preschool people would start the children on basal readers and workbooks long before they get to first grade, the students would do much better all the way up the line.

On the other hand, the early childhood and kindergarten people start passing the buck upward when they complain that they are forced to abandon their proper developmental educational practices because of pressures to get children ready for the academic rigors of first grade and elementary school. The elementary school people say they must do what they do because of the stringent academic requirements of the middle schools, just as the middle schools blame the high schools for what they do, and the high schools blame the admissions requirements of the colleges and universities. And the colleges and universities, of course, claim that they must maintain the high academic integrity of their scholarly disciplines because such integrity is demanded by the graduate schools.

Given all of the questions raised by the elementary and secondary school people, given the need to escape the endless rounds of up and down buck passing, and given the need to begin a collaborative effort to reconceive our entire system of education, what we would like to do in this book is to begin that most necessary collaboration by conducting what Einstein called a thought experiment.

Einstein used his thought experiments to explore the concepts of special and general relativity. Our thought experiment will serve a more mundane purpose. It will ask the question, What might the result be if we simply started reconceiving the educational system by starting from the bottom and working our way up from there?

Deborah Meier, for instance, has stoutly maintained over the years, and does in Chapter 1, that the American educational system should be based not on the traditional scholarly disciplines and on the traditional information and skill transmission process but on the progressive, developmental educational principles by which most early childhood programs and kindergartens have been conducted when they have been allowed to do so. If we adopt this as a working hypothesis, the question then becomes, What might be the result if our elementary and secondary schools and then our colleges, universities, and graduate schools were *all* operated on those progressive, developmental principles by which our early childhood and kindergarten schooling is conducted?

We have therefore asked three elementary and secondary school people —Deborah Meier herself, Susan Ohanian, and Joe Nathan—to respond to this "Meierian Imperative" by spelling out the kinds of elementary and secondary schools they would run if they were released from the academic captivity they believe is imposed upon them at present by the admissions policies and the academic structure of our colleges and universities. What kind of schools would they run if they did not have to worry about their students being admitted to current institutions of higher education; if their graduates, certified by the schools' own educational standards as successful, were automatically admitted to whatever colleges they wished to attend; or if their students could attend more suitable institutions of postsecondary education that were actually based upon the developmental kindergarten tradition?

We also asked them to suggest some of the changes existing colleges and universities would have to make in their admissions procedures, organization, curricula, and the way they teach and assess students in order to provide those graduates from restructured elementary and secondary schools with a progressive, developmental education. In short, what would colleges and universities have to do in order to meet the radically new and different educational requirements and the new educational standards rising from truly reformed and restructured elementary and secondary schools? And what would those new postsecondary institutions look like?

We then asked a group of higher education people to perform at least one—or all, if they so chose—of three tasks. The first such task is to respond to the preceding contributions and spell out the changes *they* see as necessary to make colleges and universities responsive to the kind of radical reforms proposed here for elementary and secondary schools. A second task is to set forth their own criticisms of the effects that what Alejandro Sanz de Santamaria in his chapter calls the "conventional" model of higher education and its process of scholarly academic research have had on elementary and secondary education and on the students our colleges and universities are there to serve. A third task is to describe and assess the effects—good, bad, or indifferent—that our institutions of higher education have on their local communities and the larger American society that supports them. We also asked them to describe at least some of the efforts being undertaken at the higher education level to institute the radical reforms in higher education they may see as necessary and desirable. Their answers are in Parts II and III.

We then attempt, in Chapter 12, to sum up what all of the contributors have said and see if it begins to suggest what a new vision of both higher and elementary and secondary education in the coming century. We also put forth a most immodest proposal describing how one might go about demonstrating that such a new vision could actually work, how it might actually produce a vastly improved process of schooling.

It is perhaps only through such a thorough bottom-to-top reform, reorganization, restructuring, and revolutionizing of our *entire* system of education, public and private, from preschool through graduate school, that we will be able to create an educational system that is truly relevant to both the contemporary and future worlds that *all* of our students will perforce be living in.

Note

1. See Peter Shrag, "The Near Myth of Our Failing Schools," *Atlantic Monthly* (October 1997); David C. Berliner and Bruce J. Biddle, *The Manufactured Crisis: Myths, Fraud and the Attack on America's Public Schools* (New York: Addison-Wesley, 1996); and the many pieces by one of the country's leading educational researchers, Gerald Bracey, in *Phi Delta Kappan*.

References

Clinchy, Evans, ed. 1999. *Creating New Schools: How Small Schools Are Changing American Education*. New York: Teachers College Press.

Teske, Paul. 1997. "Evaluating the Effects of Public School Choice in District Four." Unpublished manuscript, State University of New York, Stony Brook, N.Y.

Introduction

Setting the Scene from the Front Lines

If we wish to begin our thought experiment of reforming the entire spectrum of education from kindergarten up, there is clearly no better place to start than from the embattled front lines of our elementary and secondary schools.

It could perhaps be said that the progressive educational approach of our early childhood programs and many of our kindergartens has so far managed to escape total annihilation at the hands of those who are imposing stricter academic standards and high-stakes tests on all of our schools. But this is most certainly not the case with our elementary and secondary schools.

As the three contributors in Part I make clear, the heavy hand of standardization of curriculum, teaching methods, and tests descends as soon as our children arrive at the doors of their first-grade classrooms. From there, the path is largely downhill.

It is this downward path that Debbie Meier, Susan Ohanian, and Joe Nathan describe for us in these first three chapters. The picture they give is not an attractive one. Meier's experiences of being forced to alter the educational programs at her New York City Central Park East schools, Ohanian's description of how she had to fight her often losing battles against uniformity in a variety of schools, and Nathan's tales of woe at the hands of the National Collegiate Athletic Association (NCAA) all testify to the destructive power of the established system of American public schooling.

But these three authors are not messengers of total despair. They offer some powerfully constructive suggestions about how to rescue the elementary and secondary schools of this country and how to make colleges and universities active agents of total educational reform.

1

Supposing That. . .

DEBORAH MEIER

In trying to imagine what schools might be like if we weren't thinking about what colleges want, I went back to beginnings, for perhaps the only other time I ever was able to ask this question in a pure fashion was in the first years of my own teaching.

The wonderful thing about being a kindergarten teacher—especially thirty years ago before the garden turned into a first-grade readiness program—was that no one much cared what you did. That can be depressing, I know. But it can also be liberating. You can fill it up with your heart's desire. And that's what I did. Of course, to do that successfully it turned out I needed to become a good observer of children's hearts and desires, as well as their families' and society's; I also had to either already know a lot about lots of things—because the curiosity of five-year-olds ranges rather widely—or enjoy finding out in the company of five-year-olds. It turned out to be just the job for me.

Ten years later I had an opportunity to start a school, which we called Central Park East Elementary School. We decided to build it around the simple proposition that children could best be educated from ages five to twelve in a school that sought to prolong kindergarten for six more years. The research on what happened to that rather typical population of youngsters is pretty conclusive: from any angle one might want to pass judgment, it was a roaring success.

We had, of course, some relatively clear goals, some of them implicit and some explicit. They were, in one form or another, the same ones, however, that I had had as a kindergarten teacher. I wanted to prepare them to be comfortable in the Big Conversations that grown-ups engaged in. I wanted them to feel confident that nothing, or anyway very little, was beyond their capacities; if it seemed important and worthwhile to them, then I wanted them to have a reasonable shot at being able to do it, or be it. That meant that they needed to be able to explore freely and pursue tenaciously without knowing for sure ahead of time where everything might lead, in a spirit of playful seriousness, with open minds. They needed to feel free to take intellectual and social risks, to ask silly and even outrageous questions, to make wild and improbable connections, to take on tasks that might require a long time to complete, and to take on tasks and abandon them in midstream as well.

When people tell me that skepticism is an advanced human trait, best left to college and doctoral students, I laugh. Teaching little children confirms the obvious—it's the natural state of the human species, and especially so in childhood. Skepticism is "merely" the intellectually serious name we give to children's play. Little ones take few things for granted; they don't mind uncertainty or ambiguity—they live with it all the time. If they're lucky, the only thing they take for granted is that their environment is organized so that they're usually pretty safe—someone is "looking out" for that while they explore. Safety helps.

Within the bounds of safety—hopefully rather wide bounds—young children can focus their attention on figuring the world out. They can turn everything inside out; they taste, touch, drop, bang every object they can get their hands on. Including people. They imagine being many different "others"; they think it reasonable to ask why, over and over again. Nothing is too outrageous to question—to our frequent embarrassment. And the right information, at the right time, feeds their curiosity. They are collectors of trivia that fit their current needs. They are naturally unbored. They have tenaciousness; little children have the most staggering attention spans. And it's very hard indeed to see the why and wherefore of what fascinates them. When first-grade teachers complained to me about the immaturity of one of my former students by commenting on his short span of attention, I was amazed: "Damien?" The kid I remembered was unwilling, nearly unable, to be dragged away from what he was involved in. Our attention spans, at least in school, seem in fact to run in reverse order to our age and "maturity."

Since I considered this kind of informed skepticism—a willing suspension of prior belief—to be at the heart of a democratic education, as a habit or disposition essential to an open society, my experience working with little children was rather fortunate. It confirmed for me my belief in the potential of all our children, and thus all our citizens. Unfortunately, in most human societies this quality of mind rarely outlasts childhood; and it is certainly not the hallmark of most schooling, at least as we know it. Could it be otherwise? The history of progressive schools suggested yes; and the history of the Central Park East schools and their ilk suggested that the answer was yes even for children deemed ordinary, at-risk, disadvantaged, and so on.

My experience in kindergarten suggested also that schooling could impact favorably upon another disposition central to a democratic society: informed empathy. Democratic society depends not only on our openness to other ideas, our willingness to suspend belief long enough to entertain ideas contrary to our own, the expectation that our ideas are forever "in progress," unfinished, incomplete. It also depends on our developing the habit of stepping into the shoes of others, both intellectually and emotionally: to literally "feel," if even for a very short time, the ideas, feelings, pains, and mind-set of others, even when doing so creates some discomfort. In fact, only if it becomes a habit are we likely to do it when most needed, which is when it creates such discomfort. Such a disposition is increasingly critical to democracy, at least in part because our natural inclination to empathize seems not to go very far. It stops long before we are required to experience much unease. We empathize best, of course, with those most like ourselves, those with whom we have natural ties and shared self-interest. But in the modern world our long-range self-interest depends upon our going way beyond this, and to do so will require rigorous and continuous schooling toward precisely such an end. Imagining how the world might look if seen from a different position, physically or mentally, requires information, training, and practice. It lies at the heart of great literature, mythology, history, and art, and, lo and behold, of science and math as well. It is not a "soft" subject but the hardest one of all. It must marry imagination and scholarship.

My kindergarten classroom was an interesting place to explore the ways in which we can encourage or discourage such empathy, and the ways in which human beings both pursue and back off from such experiencing of others. The dramatic play of children is a way of widening their horizons, the reading of stories and imagining ourselves as other people and even other species is part of all good storytelling. The morning sharing circle is designed to help us hear and see each other in our diversity. But it is modeled also by the way we respond to children's joys and hurts. When a child is injured, we can model empathy by our quick response to the wounded one rather than by an immediate search to find who's at fault. What we praise, what we attend to, and what we announce as valuable helps predispose children in one way or another. If differences are seen as threatening, if kindness is seen as a scarce commodity to be hoarded, we have furthered one kind of disposition rather than another.

The moral code of kindergarten was not unimportant. Too often children assume that to be good in school refers only to acts of compliance and that the adults in their world are more interested in whether we "make trouble" than whether we display virtues of kindliness, generosity, and sympathy. Being bad is too often merely synonymous with "causing the teacher trouble," not causing harm to one's peers. In fact, the various cruel forms of inclusion and exclusion that even very young children practice are often ignored by school adults; their consequences are thus unmediated by adult moral concerns. Vivian Paley's astute stories (Paley 1992) are a painful reminder of the moral lessons conveyed in the routine practices of schooling. There are so many small and unintended ways in which we communicate that "fitting in" matters most. School after all is an institution that depends on some fairly complex and unnatural forms of compliance. We naturally elevate in importance those behaviors that make such institutional arrangements run more smoothly. For little ones new to the demands necessary for the organization of very large groups, this makes for some difficult adjustments. We speak of these new necessities in tones normally reserved for very holy virtues. Raising one's hand, not fidgeting, staying in line become not merely convenient habits but moral imperatives. The intentions that lie behind children's noncompliance are purposely ignored, but in doing so we have missed a golden opportunity to teach higher-order moral thinking, as it is called in some of the latest cognitive moral theories.

In imagining how to organize schooling otherwise, we need to rethink the nature of the institutions we have created. The sheer size of our schools, for example. In creating huge bureaucratic institutions we have exacerbated these moral issues, reduced the opportunities for empathetic thinking, and stripped the environment of those spaces where imaginative experience can more easily take place. In creating schools in which teachers rarely get to know each other, their pupils, and the families deeply, in creating spaces too small for children, too cramped and too highly monitored to carry out imaginative play, we limit the opportunities for both open-ended and empathetic learnings.

The kindergarten comes closest to encouraging such open-ended and empathetic learning, and each year thereafter schools strip away, one by one, all those kindergarten-like features that help sustain such qualities.

Each year the room looks barer than the year before, less connected to the children's own interests and possible passions, less social and collaborative in nature, and less kind to individual differences. The adults in charge are less and less likely to know the child or his or her family well, and the presentation of material is less and less likely to require children's active imaginations and concerns. Children are more and more judged in competition with each other, and displays of generosity and affection are increasingly seen as divisive and inappropriate. Flights of fancy are now frills, and those aspects of the arts that most speak to our capacity for empathy are more and more classified as frills. We increasingly glorify objectivity over subjectivity, the impersonal over the personal, external standardization over the development of internal standards, certainties over ambiguities, the one right answer over possible alternative paths.

Our reasons for doing so are a combination of ideology and convenience, with both mutually reinforcing each other and making it hard to escape their clutches.

But suppose it were otherwise. Suppose that we could keep the kindergarten mentality going all the way through. Suppose we took a step beyond the Central Park East Elementary School, where for years we felt constrained to prepare kids, even if not immediately, for the harsher realities of junior and senior high?

That's why we created Central Park East Secondary School—to allow us to keep it going for another six years. And we did. We continued the practice of keeping kids in multiage classrooms with the same teacher or teachers for at least two years. We continued to create schedules and curriculum that had room for personal preferences, flexibility, overlapping of disciplines, and sustained work individually or in collaboration with others. We found ways to organize space so that youngsters had room to build over a period of time, to have their work valued and analyzed before real audiences, and to make choices in terms of when and how they pursued a topic.

We even created a system of graduation that depended neither on credit hours in traditional disciplines nor on the passing of standardized tests covering a prescribed curriculum. We built a system of graduation around a series of intense doctoral-dissertation-like committee meetings in which students presented their work for review by the faculty and their peers. Each student, with the assistance of her advisor, could design these Graduation Committee portfolio reviews in distinctive ways, although the parameters had been set by the faculty. While all students had to present their work in ways that demonstrated competence both orally and in writing, some rested their case more on one form than another and some even focused on alternative modes—their capacity to communicate through video, visual arts, music, and so on. Some built their portfolios largely out of evidence accumulated through off-campus experiences, while others rested it almost entirely on fairly traditional academic course work. Some relied more than others on the attestation of employers, coworkers, and others in the larger world.

But, for all that, we kept a careful eye on how it would look to colleges. Running through every discussion was that Question: Will it meet the approval of teachers of freshman English, math, science, and history? Not to mention its impact on College Boards, the SAT, the CUNY entrance tests, and the mindset of a typical college admissions office.

"Is it fair," we'd ask ourselves, "to send them out into the world in ways that will set them up for failure in the eyes of important others?"

No, we said. Of course not.

We hoped that their strengths would make up for some possible weaknesses. We hoped that we could justify our deviations on the grounds that only because of them had so many kids stuck it out at all rather than dropping out as so many of their peers had done in other more traditional schools. Granted, they'd not be quite as prepared for college freshman math. But if we had stuck with the traditional curriculum, many would never have gotten a shot at a college freshman math class at all but would have dropped out along the way. As it is, they'll need to know how to get the extra help they will on occasion need; they'll need more than the usual perseverance when things don't make sense, and more self-confidence in their basic capacities as learners. So if we've given them these skills, maybe we can forgive ourselves for not having always quite accomplished the other—preparing them with what the college freshman math class sees as the essential bits and pieces of prior knowledge and skills.

But we are not easy about these answers. The compromises may lose students on both ends—those who cannot enter into even our academically focused decontextualized frameworks and those who seek entry into the most rigid traditional schools. We look good statistically, but only we know the price paid.

If we have precious few huge lecture classes, and only an occasional multiple-choice or short-answer quiz, if we offer kids lots of opportunities to consult with others, to rewrite their papers, to get a second, third, and fourth chance, will they know how to deal with settings in which all these are absent? The most sophisticated and well-prepared of our graduates were, in fact, the most likely to get into small, elite private schools whose structures more closely resemble Central Park East Secondary School (CPESS)—small seminars, intimate tutorials, and so on. It was precisely those who most needed CPESS and who had most benefited by its unorthodox practices who would be in for the greatest shock in their post-CPESS academic life, exposed to large underfunded public urban and state colleges, whose structures most closely resembled the worst of America's high schools—large, impersonal, and mindless. Horace's compromise between good teaching and curricular and organizational imposition, as described in Ted Sizer's book of that name (1984), is a reflection of the horrors of contemporary public two- and four-year colleges.

How paradoxical; worse—how tragic.

What should we do?

How rarely, then, did we have the luxury of just asking, But is this kind of schooling good for them? Will it stand them in good stead *after* they get out of college, after they've gotten the many certificates of merit that stand between them and the larger world itself?

We felt more confident, oddly enough, in our capacity to prepare kids well for the world of hard knocks than for the protected world of academia.

In fact, the intellectual habits and disposition—focused as they are on the development of informed skepticism and empathy—would have their roughest and toughest survival test on the college campus, not in life itself.

We at CPESS compromised right and left. We never challenged the New York State Regents' categories of knowledge. We required kids to demonstrate their habits of mind in fourteen different fields, most of them precisely those designated by the Regents. And we required them to include the traditional four majors in the seven for which they would be most intensively required to present and defend their work. We challenged the state's definition of coverage and opted for depth, for habits of mind rather than for retention of information. But . . .

While we knew for a fact that even in our own ranks were intelligent teachers who were mathematically illiterate and who had suffered only mildly for this defect, we still insisted that our graduates had to display their intelligence in each and every field to a level of competence that not all of us any longer could master.

We were too often unable to spend the time and energy that had seemed so natural in elementary school to promote young people's personal passions, especially those that would take them into nonacademic domains. We put "first things first"—getting kids into college. The arts suffered, although we regularly decried this. Kids with oddball passions or with strong traditional vocational interests were largely left to feel a little inadequate, a little bit like failures.

Since we counted our success in terms of the number of graduates, as well as the number who went on to college, and within that the number who got into four-year colleges, and the number who survived college long enough to get degrees, this was natural enough. The kids knew it, and it set a value system for them. They didn't want to let us or the school down. But it had its price.

But just suppose . . . Just suppose the world itself celebrated what a good kindergarten seeks to accomplish as the fitting criterion for schooling itself—at any age, at any stage.

Suppose we acknowledged that all life educates but that for a mere one-sixth of every child's life, from age five to age eighteen, we would publicly join together to formally inculcate what we think is most important. First and foremost, we would join around what we share: our citizenship, our capacity to join in the civic life of our nation. Suppose our public precollegiate schools were to be judged only on this criterion, without regard for whether they prepared kids for particular postgraduate vocational programs, of which college is, after all, merely one possibility. If we deemed all such post–high school possibilities of equal merit, we might think more about what dispositions, habits, skills, and knowledge cross over all such postgraduate activities. We might ask whether all such students didn't need certain habits, dispositions, skills, and knowledge to responsibly take on one enormous shared task: voting for public offices, serving on a jury, deciding on the nation's collective future?

Then we'd look at the full range of vocations and occupations that adults participate in—friend, neighbor, family member, parent, citizen, and producer of goods and services. Who might the "experts" be in designing such tasks? They'd be precisely these same people: neighbors, friends, family members, employers, and fellow citizens. We'd need to develop some consensus on how public funds would be used to meet some commonly agreed-upon societally accepted tasks, as well as ways to allow for acceptable levels of disagreement around the same issues.

Some schools then might teach calculus, in part because it's an example of a human invention of great beauty, wonder, and utility, in much the same way as is a sonata or Impressionism or cathedral architecture; and in part because it serves a particularly important role in the most critical of our modern sciences. But another school might not place calculus in its major course offerings or call it essential knowledge for a well-educated person, but would place music or visual arts or another subject in such a position, and for much the same set of reasons.

What would *not* predispose schools or students to choose one or the other or neither would be the requirements for a high school diploma based upon the requirements of college admissions offices based upon the latest traditions designed by the academic communities of U.S. universities. At present, each existing academic discipline (and subdiscipline) struggles to ensure that the particulars that distinguish the field at its highest level be presented in appropriate forms in the tracks leading up to the peaks. Thus, if one does not want to cut off at the pass a student who might one day seek to be an esteemed academic historian, literary critic, scientist, or pure mathematician, one must pass the hurdles such disciplines design along the way. For it is such hurdles that help select from the largest possible pool the choicest few. The number needed at the end, however, remains a precious few. As Mark Kishlansky (1996) explains in describing his passion for teaching, of a thousand students who begin graduate study in history only about sixty will do productive work in the field. He designs his work with them in mind. It's for those sixty that Kishlansky mightily strives, not with an eye to his effect on the habits of mind of all those who pass through Harvard University. Is he so different from the best and brightest of our current high school history teachers?

Instead, we are proposing that the justification for requiring that a particular subject, discipline, or competency be included in the high school leaving certificate must rest upon its equal importance to all vocations and all occupations, with particular importance to those that are public in nature—our tasks as citizens. The training of specialists would not be the task of our public high schools.

It would thus be left to post–high school education—be it education sponsored by the public, by private institutions of learning, or by private industries—to train people for specific disciplines necessary for the conduct of their specialty. If we believe that citizens need more than these required thirteen years (K–12) of public education to conduct society's business, then the *publicly required* part should be extended for everyone at public expense. If this seems futile, as it does to me, perhaps more sensible would be to provide a "voucher," much like the G.I. Bill, that would allow all citizens at any desired period of their lives to pursue such a common liberal education, in the tradition of the Norwegian folk schools. Eighteen seems a good time to get down to the serious business of preparation for specific roles in life—even if only for the *next* role. Where there are "trades" of public importance that the market is unprepared to fund—as may be the case with varied scholarly pursuits—public subsidies should encourage students with such dispositions to pursue such fields and even be highly rewarded for doing so where a shortage might otherwise impede socially desired ends.

But the primary public debate should focus—over and over, at various levels of social discourse—on what it is that's so important to know that we must require every single American to spend thirteen years at the task. The argument put forth on behalf of the "kindergarten tradition" of skepticism and empathy would thus be placed before the public as one possible organizing principle, but not the only one and quite likely not the winner, at least under present circumstances. And whether we can organize the debate so as to permit different answers, even allowing for some shared common core, will itself be part of the debate.

But only when we change the terms of the debate can the debate be an authentic one. Since the number of Harvard freshmen will not change appreciably no matter how we resolve the debate, Harvard's admission policy should not set the ground rules for what constitutes the educated person, as it has since the late nineteenth century. For reformers the problem is to maximize the benefit for all our children. That requires changing the way the score is kept. We're looking to find a definition of "well educated" that allows us to judge our students on a basis that could be universally achieved. Rather than seeing education as a sorting machine for later rungs on the ladder, such definition of success would describe traits that could be universally held by all citizens and that could underlie their successfully carrying out the whole range of occupations that society requires of them. Thus, the cosmetologist and the cosmologist would both need a first-class basic education. As citizens, their tasks are identical; as "trades people," they differ, and only at that point should their future goals be critical to the nature of the expectations we hold for them. Both need to know how to think about complex matters, both need to care about others, both need to know how to learn new things to keep up vocationally.

What might such a redefinition do to post–high school education? It might make the current system completely unnecessary. A wide range of quite different kinds of new institutions might arise, including schools organized by particular trades and industries to fill specific needs. Such institutions would probably be tuition-free or even pay stipends for on-the-job training and apprentice-like status. Others might be organized for students directly interested in specific academic disciplines preparatory for vocations that required high-level disciplinary specialization. Some of these would require heavy public subsidization; some would function more like vocational schools— preparing their students for accountancy, law, medicine, or teaching in tandem with practicing professional colleagues.

Still other institutions would develop as halfway houses for young people interested in exploring future options in a setting of general education, with the aim of leading them into one of the other paths or directly into fields that do not require highly specialized talents. Some of these choices would offer appropriate parental-like supervision and opportunities for students to test out their life skills in new campuslike settings. Some would combine important public service work with various forms of general education and some specific field-oriented education: forestry, child care, recreation, and so on. The range of possibilities is enormous. But no one would be taking a course in mathematics or Western civilization just because the credits are required in order to get the "damn certificate." We would reduce the hordes of young talented people sitting through years in expensive colleges without any interest in their courses of study. Most of these new schools would be open and accessible to people of all ages, part of a general national effort to upgrade the skills and mental habits not only of eight-year-olds but of its older citizens as they shift into new fields at various points in their life.

Side-by-side with this there might be a thriving industry of general education programs and courses offered to Americans of all ages and inclinations—both basic and advanced—so that our general curiosity, and our search for knowledge and truth, would remain a subsidized human activity. These would be the most prestigious of schools, filled with eager and enthusiastic citizens driven by their own curiosity and ambition. As mentioned earlier, upon successful completion of what we now call high school each graduate might receive a certain number of lifetime vouchers to such an assortment of free or inexpensive courses and programs. We could even stack the deck in favor of *not* using the vouchers until one is older and wiser.

Wouldn't it be fun to approach the question of educating the young in a more commonsensical way, one not imposed upon us by decades and centuries of academic and vocational rituals? There's not a country in the world where the members of college faculties think their students come "properly" prepared. Prepared for what? For them. Employers always complain, too, although when one gets right down to it, they're mostly upset not about new employees' lack of academic expertise but about their unwillingness or inability to pick up new skills and new aptitudes, plus their bad attitudes and poor work habits. But we feel obliged to pretend otherwise.

Academic has become a code word, signifying many different things to many different people. It's time we talked in ordinary language so that *academic* can revert to its time-honored meaning and not be a stand-in for everything else we happen to be in favor of. Lately, some critics of the teaching establishment use *academic* simply to mean teaching the ABCs and rote arithmetic, which were traditionally preacademic. *Academic* can be insult or the highest praise; it can mean "pointless" or "important," but usually it also means "dry" and "not inherently interesting."

Precollegiate education is primarily about raising children; there's no getting away from the fact that teachers share this task with parents. It makes good sense to raise them to conduct themselves in ways compatible with democratic life, which includes some describable set of habits of heart, mind, and work. And it makes good sense to raise them in ways that keep them safe from harm to themselves and others. After that, grown-ups have many different tasks, and we should not presort the young by trying to predict who might best fit which task. Instead we should create the widest possible range of options from which the young can freely choose at the age when they are fit to do so, according to their merits and inclinations, or their willingness to work hard at something for which they don't have a natural talent.

In a way, what we're proposing might get back to what it meant to raise children prior to the invention of modern schooling, but with a far more complex and ambitious agenda given the far more complex role citizens of a modern democratic society must all be prepared to play.

The horse-and-buggy was not at fault for not being able to go sixty miles an hour. Exhorting the driver and horse to go faster, or blaming them for having insufficiently high expectations, would have been futile. What was needed was to invent the car. We decided that everyone deserved the best and forgot to redefine that best, for fear we'd look like we were cheating. But once we wanted everyone to get "the best," we in effect told the horse-and-buggy to do the impossible. Rather than chugging along as though we hoped no one would notice the sleight of hand, it's time to ask, What's it all about?

References

Kishlansky, M. 1996. "Serendipity and Skepticism." *Harvard Magazine* 98, no. 3 (January-February): 31–35.

Paley, V. 1992. *You Can't Say You Can't Play*. Cambridge, Mass.: Harvard University Press.

Sizer, T. 1984. *Horace's Compromise*. Boston, Mass.: Houghton-Mifflin Company.

2

Is That Penguin Stuffed or Real?

SUSAN OHANIAN

Essayist Will Cuppy once pointed out that penguins are dignified, they get their names in the newspaper, and only an expert can tell a live penguin from a stuffed one. I feel the same way about plans for revamping the schools. Curriculum reform must be at the heart of any substantive change, but too many people who talk the talk of reform can't tell a live curriculum from a stuffed one. And, as every teacher knows, it would be easier to move a graveyard than to change a district's existing curriculum. For people who plan school curriculum, God is in charge of the SATs and Santa Claus presides over Chapter 1. Now, with the chancellor of the New York City Schools joining the crowd that declares every third grader *will* read on grade level and every twelfth grader *will* take calculus, schools need a direct line to the fairy godmother, too.

Because I'm the kind of teacher who focuses on what I'm doing this minute with this kid, when curriculum reform stalks the corridors, I try to duck, but more often than not I weep. My husband asks how anybody can possibly cry over curriculum, but he's never tried to obey the mandate of teaching *Silas Marner* to ninth graders. Nor has he ever tried to convince a primary-grade teacher not to teach the comma in apposition. Saying she had "no time for supplementary reading" when I offered to lend her my collection of rhyming books, my colleague insisted that to "maintain standards" and "get students ready" for the rigors of third grade (well, every third grade but mine) she had to teach commas in all their exotica. I was no greenhorn; I knew that in the schoolhouse mythical standards invariably win out over sensibility. Nonetheless, I somehow became involved in this comma confrontation. My colleague stood safe and secure behind her teacher's manual. I ended up in tears.

My husband did get involved in a curricular dispute that cuts to the heart of the university territorialism that undermines every attempt to bring about significant reform to schools. He was teaching physics at a liberal arts college and when the English department suggested revamping Freshman English, he volunteered to teach a new course in which students would fulfill the composition requirement in the department of their major instead of in the English department. My husband and I prepared a great reading list for science majors. "Oh, no," protested the English department. "We still want everybody to read Plato and *Gulliver's Travels*. We just want *you* to teach it."

Why was I surprised? I guess I thought professors might be collegial toward their colleagues, even though, when dealing with teachers, they typically make all the choices from the safety of Plato's Cave (where there are few teachers and no children). Then, the choices made, the mandates passed, the certifications issued, they'll leave us to teach the kids. I once spent several years being retrained as part of a big National Endowment for the Humanities grant administered by a prestigious university. I'm a dutiful, even good, student: I do all the reading, write the papers. And so I was considered an asset to the course. The only problem was I taught the wrong kind of kids. The good professors did not regard seventh- and eighth-grade rotten readers as worthy of being included in a sophisticated NEH project. And so, caught up in the esoteric intellectualism of the endeavor, early in the morning before our school began I went next door and taught humanities to a ninth-grade honors class.

I loved that honors class, but I loved my rotten readers, too, and after a while I was troubled by the exclusionary zone imposed by the university. If a humanities approach to teaching literature was good for honors kids, why wasn't it good for rotten readers? So I began working on ways to make the university scheme meaningful to my own students.

Michael was one of those students, and Michael already knew about some of the humanities material because an eleventh-grade history teacher used material I had developed and Michael's brother talked about it at the dinner table. The fact that Michael was dumbfounded, impressed, and pleased that his teacher's work was being used at the high school should remind us that remedial kids, so often relegated to the academic slag heap, think their teachers must be remedial rejects, too.

If such a thing as dyslexia exists, Michael had it in spades. He also had wit, humor, and a very real charm that made it easy to forgive his whining and wheedling to get out of work. The students and I had a daily note exchange, which Michael complained about every day. When I asked students to fill in an open-ended statement "I'd rather read than . . . I'd rather write than . . ." Michael wrote that he'd rather read than die and he'd rather write than read.

All winter my notes were filled with complaints about the snow and ice. Michael counseled me, "I just take the months as they come." I began to write about the first signs of spring, and I wrote my students that I looked forward to asparagus ads in the newspaper as a sure sign winter was ending. They thought this was hysterical—only a teacher would come up with asparagus. They also began to scan the paper for asparagus ads and leave them on my desk.

One day Michael came in and went straight for the typewriter. He left this letter on my desk:

Dear Mrs. O,

As you no I went to Boston firday. It was a lot fo fun. Wen I first got to Boston we drov aron looking for a parking plas. We fond one and then we got out of the car. We walkt to a fance markit and had a bite to aet.

Then we went to the aquarium and that was eciting. Thar was a shoe with dolphins and seals. Wan we got out we went by a fruit markt. I thot of yoou and chekt the pric of asprgus. It is $1.00 a lb in Boston and 3 heds of letis for $1.00. Boston is a long way to go for asprgus tho.

Your freind,
Michael

Michael asked me how to spell *aquarium.* Thinking at last I could show the university professor why my work was so important to me, I was feeling proud when I gave him Michael's letter. He looked at it and then turned to me with a sad face. "Sue, when are you going to stop wasting your life with these kids, join our doctoral program, and get on with something worthy of your talents?" That professor had observed me teach the honors class, but he never set foot in the seventh/eighth-grade classroom for rotten readers. I say that anyone who cannot see past the awful spelling, and recognize that Michael's letter has structure and voice as well as humor and charm, should find himself another job. Certainly he shouldn't be setting standards for teachers or restructuring schools.

I'd been struggling with the university course for three years. I was challenged and captivated by the rigor of the intellectual model. What I couldn't stand was the professors' refusal to entertain any discussion about the day-to-day needs of students. I'm the kind of teacher who's not particularly interested in getting kids ready for tomorrow, not directly, anyway. I believe that if I teach them well today, this minute, tomorrow will take care of itself.

As science writer and maple-syrup maker Roger Swain (1994) tells us, even where the sap flows best "the drops form one at a time." Sugaring and teaching are not projects for the impatient. Even in these days of instant everything, you can't hurry maple syrup—or third graders or seventh graders. Swain goes on to say that in boiling the sap "the change from colorless sap to a light amber syrup is impressively slow." So, too, third-grade Chris' transformation from an intransigent, reluctant reader, the child who only scowled at books, to the boy who insisted on copying *Peter Rabbit* in longhand because he "just liked the way the words feel." So, too, Michael's appreciation of the written word. When he graduated from elementary school, Michael's mother wrote me a note: "I was going to phone and thank you for everything you have done, but Michael insisted that I must write you a letter. He said people know you really mean something when you write a letter." Over the years I received half a dozen such letters from parents. "My child told me to write." Half a dozen letters may seem insignificant to the number crunchers, but for a teacher, half a dozen letters sustain the spirit in a way that a stack of SATs cannot match.

I learned recently that Michael is now a noted chef at a prestigious restaurant. I wonder if I can take any credit. I did, after all, spark his interest in asparagus.

Poet-farmer-teacher Wendell Berry (1981) points out that "Good teaching is an investment in the minds of the young, as obscure in result, as remote from immediate proof as planting a chestnut seedling." Teaching is a rigorous act of faith. We must be guided by the present lives of children, not by the shadow of the college admissions officer lurking in the corner.

Although college entrance requirements must bear a share of the blame for the inappropriate curriculum content imposed on the nation's third graders (fourth graders, fifth graders...), there's plenty of blame to go around. Whose hands are bloodier: The Harvard admissions office or Fortune 500 CEOs who collect 250 times the wages of the middle managers they downsize into poverty (while proclaiming something is wrong with the work ethic taught in schools)? Two presidents with their Goals 2000 hot air balloon or the media muckrakers who are convinced their high school graduating class contained the last students who knew anything? Ineffectual and out of touch professors of education who wouldn't last twelve minutes in today's urban classrooms or parents who have abrogated their ethical and moral responsibilities? Gutless schoolmarms who go along with curriculum status quo or rabid change agents who insist they've found the one true path? So many to blame, so little time.

The trouble is, as a teacher, I must be ever aware that whenever I point one finger at somebody else, three more point back at me. Norman Maclean (1997) says that when how you define yourself no longer haunts you, this should tell you that you are dead. I can't think of a profession that could be more haunting than teaching. Every new student we encounter must cause us to redefine ourselves.

Does it really matter to most people how many quadratic equations can fit on the head of a pin? Has anybody noticed that at the same time school folk worry about how much Dickens a high schooler needs, the real world out there is putting Danielle Steele on the best-seller list? Isn't it out of kilter that the nation that wants all kids to take calculus can't figure out that credit card debt is ruining it? Are school uniforms, the Internet, the V chip, and calculus really the answers to our balance of trade, crime rate, health care crisis, or divorce statistics?

What I want to know is what the chancellor of the New York City schools and all the other education bureaucrats drafting standards across the land are going to do with the kids who don't measure up to their Olympian goals. What happens to the third grader who doesn't read on grade level? Or the twelfth grader who cannot master calculus? As Claude Brown asked thirty years ago, "Where do you go when you're already in the promised land?"

I was my school's third-grade representative on a district language arts committee. Our charge was to come up with grade-level guidelines. So we polled the teachers in our schools, asking what the minimum language arts expectations should be for students in each grade. Surprise, surprise. Second-grade teachers said entering students should read on second-grade level; third-grade teachers said students should read on third-grade level, and so on. We committee members looked at the list, and because we were teachers and not bureaucrats, we did not put forth these grade-level requirements as standards or even guidelines. Instead, we laughed.

We laughed and then we did what good teachers always do: we tried to figure out how to teach the kids we have. Not ideal kids, maybe, but definitely the kids we have. School, after all, is now, and should remain, the place where, when you come, they have to teach you. We primary teachers broke away from the rest of the committee and decided that instead of blaming the victim, we'd take a look at ourselves. We asked ourselves what we could do to become better language arts teachers. For starters, we asked that instead of spending hundreds of thousands of dollars on language arts textbooks, the district should give each teacher a package of resources: professional books, journal subscriptions, and so on. It was a truly revolutionary act: a group of teachers giving up texts of busy work (or, in the lingo of the trade, "seatwork") and committing themselves to learning more about how language works.

Of course, we didn't get away with it. On various pretexts, the assistant superintendent in charge of curriculum called our committee back to vote again. And again. First it was because one school's representative was absent from the first meeting; another time we were told the board of education felt our vote should be by secret ballot. Finally, we caught on that we were going to be asked to keep voting until we got it right. The assistant superintendent in charge of curriculum insisted that the public would perceive the lack of language arts texts as a lack of standards. Never mind that nobody was taking away the children's reading texts, spelling texts, handwriting texts, math texts, social studies texts, health texts, science texts.

You can bring textbooks to a teacher, but you can't make her use them. That same assistant superintendent in charge of curriculum once sent me a curriculum by pickup truck. Without ever setting foot in our storefront school, which had been set up to accommodate high schoolers with drug, crime, and social problems, kids who had been excluded from the regular campus, this administrator decreed that what the students needed was fourth- and fifth-grade math and grammar skills. So without seeing the students or talking with the teachers, this administrator had copies of fourth- and fifth-grade math and grammar books reproduced for every student at our school.

Unfortunately, the paper was copied on both sides, so we couldn't even use it for scrap. In addition to being illegal, those pages were pointless. It is typical of an education bureaucrat to assume that students who hate school must be behind in something called basic skills. Those high schoolers didn't hate school because they couldn't do it. They hated school because it was conducted in a language and pattern that excluded them. My job was to help the students find a curriculum with meaning, intrigue, and consequence. And so I chose *Mathematics, A Human Endeavor* by Harold Jacobs (1994) for their text. These high school failures, law breakers, social misfits, and general malcontents were pleased and excited to be doing something difficult. They groaned and bragged at the same time as they struggled with algebra, geometry, statistics, probability.

So am I contradicting myself? Should every high schooler learn calculus, French, and Dickens? No. Some of the students at our very small school could not handle Jacobs' sophisticated text. They did different math. Easy to do when your school houses just forty students but impossible when it numbers in the thousands? I don't know why. The first school I taught in was a Queens, New York, high school larger than my northern California hometown. When one of my students refused to read *Johnny Tremain,* I asked the department chairman for advice. And the man who had also told me that every teacher should have the experience of teaching *Silas Marner* (now, decades later, I think he must have been employing irony, but at the time I was too green to detect it) told me to ask the kid what he *would* read, to get him another book. It's probably the best teaching advice I ever received. Certainly a school that can't change the curriculum for a child is a school that is too large, a school that must be dismantled. We need to remind ourselves that schools should exist only to help children.

I have no quarrel with the entrance requirements of Harvard or any other institution of higher learning. My quarrel is with all the school folk who insist on the thirteen-year curriculum that aspires to get all students ready for Harvard. I say that if Harvard wants its students to write research papers, then let Harvard train them. I refuse to "get third graders ready" for the research rigors of fourth grade. After all, fourth-grade teachers are only inflicting the research paper on their students to "get them ready for" the rigors of fifth grade, and so on.

Obviously, our august institutions of higher learning can set any standards they want. But does anyone really believe that if tomorrow first-grade teachers bowed to sanity and stopped teaching the apostrophe, if third-grade teachers stopped teaching cursive, and fifth-grade teachers stopped intoning "invert and multiply," and high school teachers stopped teaching English literature from *Beowulf* to Wordsworth, that the number of college admissions would drop? The truth of the matter is that the number of freshman university admissions is based not on Carnegie units or SAT scores or other things that go bump in the night but on the number of bodies the institutions of higher learning can squeeze in. If students refused to take the SATs for the next four years, Harvard would not close its doors. It would find some other way of separating the wheat from the chaff.

Proof of the pudding? When I taught GED courses for the Neighborhood Youth Corps, one of my students was brilliant. He quickly got his GED and then we began looking for a university that would accept him without Carnegie units. Someone knew someone who was a Harlem Globetrotter and an alumnus of a prestigious Ivy League school. He said if our student was at least 6′4″ tall, he could get him into the university. Alas, Jared was just 5′11″, five inches short of the university's admissions standards.

Truth in disclosure: I couldn't come close to passing the ambitious standards approaching final draft at the education department of a large state with a multicultural student population. Here's a brief sampling: In science, all ninth graders are expected to understand the structure of atomic nuclei and to explain the fusion process in stars. In math, students must be able to use trigonometric ratios and to solve linear and quadratic equations. In social studies, students must explain "how processes of spatial change have affected history" and analyze trends in world demographics. Ninth graders are also expected to lead discussion groups and to prepare a research report in a foreign language. (Primary graders are expected to "make inferences based on information in print media available" in the foreign language. How many primary graders do you know who can make inferences in their mother tongue?) In the fine arts, ninth graders must "analyze and evaluate the distinguishing musical characters of works representing historical periods." And finally, in physical education, ninth graders must "achieve improved health-related fitness" through a physical fitness program they design.

Does this mean fatsos won't be eligible for a high school diploma? Pardon me, "the weight-challenged."

Of late, there have been several press stories noting that Chelsea Clinton sometimes gets help with her algebra homework from Alan Blinder, an economics professor at Princeton and vice chairman of the Federal Reserve Board. Chelsea's dad confesses he's finding it increasingly difficult to cope with her complex homework. Certainly a case can be made for our future presidents as well as other dads and moms to know algebra. A competency test for all candidates. What a delicious thought.

But before we scurry around to set up the requirements, we'd better take a careful look at what doors we are willing to shut on those who don't take to algebra or music theory or a physical fitness regimen. Interesting, isn't it, that the politicians and business leaders who are quick to denounce the present lack of rigor in school curriculums were themselves educated in the days when the only required courses were driver's ed and home economics? They seem oblivious to the glaring contradictions inherent in the fact that while governmental bodies pass laws that demean residents who are already fluent in a language other than English, some state boards of education insist that any student who wants a high school diploma had better be fluent enough in a second language to lead seminars and do independent research.

I want to know who's going to pay for all this excellence. Where's the money for the foreign language teachers in elementary school, for the computers, for the electrophoretic and other sophisticated scientific equipment required to study the new curriculum? Point out to a bureaucrat calling for curriculum reform that his state is eliminating librarians and fine arts teachers while passing standards to increase the emphasis on student research and artistic performance, and he will shrug his shoulders. The fellows standing guard at the exit gates don't communicate with the fellows who control the purse strings. Ask, "What happens to the kids who cannot master these skills?" and you'll get a pep talk about Jaime Escalante.

You could say I taught without standards for nearly twenty years. I worked in a district that never saw a government grant it wouldn't grab, and so I have taught everything from high school to first-grade remedial reading, with K–6 science, ninth-grade honors, and high school dropouts in between. I've taught third graders who hated reading, seventh graders who hated everything, and high schoolers in school only because the alternative was jail. Am I revealing a failure to appreciate my students' potential when I admit that I was too busy taking students to Planned Parenthood and court, as well as trying to find them shelter, to spend any time looking over my shoulder for college admissions officers? We short-change students when we give them the message that they can't find success and happiness without going to college.

Instead of asking university admissions officers how many Carnegie units need to be delivered, schools would do well to ask their graduates how often they read to their children, take them to libraries, museums, concerts, and parks. Do they have hobbies? Friends? Meaningful jobs? How often do they call their parents, perform community service, vote, recycle their refuse, and refrain from running red lights? Everett Reimer (1977) cut to the heart of the matter years ago when he asserted that "unless people enjoy, in the main, good human relationships, they can neither be educated nor educate themselves."

Schools can't improve themselves if they ignore the students. It seems such a simple matter to ask our students what they really dislike about school and talk about what we might do to change it. Without exception, students at our alternative high school agreed that what they hated most about regular school was the bells. "Just when you'd get interested in something, a bell would ring and you'd have to go start something else." At our school they knew the requirements for graduation. They could work on them in any order they chose, and at any speed. Typically, a student would work on, say, social studies for several weeks. Then she'd switch to science for a while. Okay, so this isn't practical in a big school of three thousand students, but other monolithic institutions have figured out ways to change time-honored schedules and procedures. With large industries throwing out the factory model as counterproductive, it is long past time for schools to do the same. I wonder how many adults would do well at dealing with different job requirements and a different boss every forty-seven minutes.

Too many schools are designed to encourage kids to fall between the cracks. When I taught in a junior high newly built to house eleven hundred seventh and eighth graders, we were put on a crazy six-day cycle, a cycle ruled necessary to accommodate half-time "special" subjects such as art, music, and physical education. Students came to my reading tutorial for three days and then went to regular English class for three days. This meant when a student's third day was on a Wednesday, I wouldn't see her again until the following Tuesday. It was an extraordinarily idiotic plan: it put the worst readers into literature classes for half as much time as "regular" readers. Surprise, surprise. Those discipline-problem rotten readers piled up in the principal's office.

On the first day of school I discovered I was sharing a room with the eighth-grade reading tutor. Not knowing each other, we divided the room with a couple of bedspreads hung on a rope stretching across the middle of the room. After one semester, we took down the rope and went to the principal with a proposal. "Give us the worst readers in the school, but give them to us for double-time, not half-time." We wanted these rotten readers for two periods a day. "It will be their best last chance to become readers before they're lost in high school."

The principal immediately grasped the benefits that would accrue from getting the school's worst discipline problems out of his office and into the classroom of teachers who did not send students to the office. Nonetheless, the principal fell back on the old excuse: "It's a scheduling impossibility. There's no room in the day for an extra period of reading."

We were ready for that one. "Let students choose a class to drop from their schedule," we proposed. We'd done a little digging in state education department rules and regulations and discovered that although math and English were mandated in both seventh and eighth grades, science and social studies were not. "Why not let these kids choose whether they want to skip social studies or science? This will lighten the academic load of kids who are nonreaders and failing their courses. It will also give them a feeling of autonomy." A revolutionary thought, that: letting a seventh grader make some decisions about the subjects he studies. The principal talked about making the dropped class a nonessential such as art or shop, but we pushed for letting twelve-year-old nonreaders have at least one class a day that wasn't reading-intensive. He warmed to the notion that it's better to let a kid skip social studies altogether than to have him spend it in the principal's office.

Somehow, reason prevailed and students were allowed to choose. We had a good success rate. Some students scored well enough after one year to go into regular English in eighth grade. All students had individual programs. Separate, individual spelling tests may have been a slightly loony idea, but those brief encounters every Friday gave me a chance to talk about the way language works with each student, as well as to get them to accept responsibility for learning their words. Parents were especially grateful for the decrease in stress, grateful for the fact that their children had two periods a day where the classwork was tailored to fit their needs. People who advocate wholesale mainstreaming don't ask children how it feels to be the dumbest one in the class year after year. I remember Dan's mother hugging me and saying, "It's the first year he's been successful in school."

But all this happened more than a decade ago. Our program lasted for six years, actually a longevity record in my district. I can't imagine such a radical proposal as helping a fifteen-year-old read his way through Dr. Seuss' *Hop on Pop*—the first book he ever read in his life—getting heard in today's climate of world-class schools hoopla. Nobody talks about what happens to the kids who don't read on grade level.

Of late, I have been looking at the different ways students are treated in college prep and non-college prep math classrooms. Recently I sat in on some quite wonderful Interactive Mathematics Program college prep classrooms. IMP is an innovative, problem-based high school mathematics curriculum that emphasizes communication skills and integrates such traditional math topics as algebra, geometry, trigonometry, and precalculus as well as incorporating topics from statistics, matrix algebra, linear programming, and finite math. Working in teams, students work on a real-world problem that may take six weeks to solve. There is a lot of talk in an IMP classroom: teasing, roasting, and peer coaching commingle with quiet, concentrated thinking. A student will withdraw from the group, struggle with a problem, and then come back to the group for confirmation that she's on the right track. These students could tell me what they were studying and why it was important to study it. They were articulate about how and why their work differed from that of traditional college prep math. Unsolicited, students were quick to assure me that things may look relaxed and full of fun, but IMP students score just as high on their SATs as those enrolled in traditional college prep math courses. No matter how you justify your innovations, the bottom line stays the same: for college prep kids, those SATs had better be good.

I sat in on skills math in the same schools where I saw the innovative IMP. In a school where a knowledgeable, enthusiastic, and proud vice principal in charge of curriculum talked to me for an hour, expressing her enthusiasm and pride in IMP, the skills courses were never mentioned. When I saw the skills class, my worst fears were realized: it could have been my own fifth-grade math class; it could have been the seventh-grade teacher across the hall from me twenty-five years ago. Skills math has a content frozen in time. On this day it was, "Do all the odd ones on page 146 in class; do all the odd ones on 147 for homework."

"We do the odd ones because the even ones have the answers in the back of the book," a girl in my group confided. It's the only explanation I could pry out of students for why they were doing what they were doing. Was I nuts or stupid or what? They were doing what they were doing because that's where they were in the book. Forty problems calling for division of fractions for seatwork in class. Forty more for homework. *Ours is not to reason why. Ours is to invert and multiply.* Students write out the problems for homework because there aren't enough books for every student to have one, never mind to allow books to go home. (When all students are present, the teacher borrows from a colleague—if some of *her* students are absent.) This is predominantly a middle-class school, not a place one would think to choose to portray the horrors and injustice of our educational system.

Students in college prep math are treated like intelligent, reasoning, social human beings. Kids in skills math are treated like inmates. Here's one small example: In each class I joined a group of four. In IMP, the college prep classes, I was interviewed by the group I sat with, who then introduced me to the rest of the class. (The students were given free rein to exercise their humor, asking me, among other things, my favorite vegetable and my favorite joke about Rush Limbaugh.) In the skills class, student desks were clumped into groups of four, but the clusters must have been left over from the previous class. In skills math, anybody who talked was sent off to a corner. When a boy nodded toward me and asked the teacher, "Who's that?" the teacher singled him out for ridicule, sneering, "It's none of your business. You have enough trouble looking out for yourself, never mind worrying about other people." The teacher didn't say anything to me except to mention that he looks forward to retiring in fifteen years.

In the March 1996 issue of the *Washington Monthly,* the Rev. Al Hicks, the principal of the Nativity Preparatory School in Roxbury, Massachusetts, pointed out that we know what to do to make the schools right. "It's just a matter of *doing* it." Reverend Hicks and I might well disagree on a number of points, but he and I agree that we don't need a blue-ribbon panel or some longitudinal research to tell us that the students in the IMP class are getting a much better break than the students in the skills class, and I'm not talking about algebra. Of course, it's not enough to bring in a good curriculum and get good teachers. Money enters the equation. The IMP teachers are trying to change fundamentally the way mathematics is taught, and change doesn't come cheaply. Teachers who are trying to change need time. IMP teachers receive an extra preparation period, time to consult each other, bolster each other, plan strategies, figure out how to grade nonconventional problems, and so on. But we might question why the skills teacher should get any prep time.

Time to be thoughtful is what few schools give teachers. When an editor at a large publishing conglomerate once asked me, "If you could draw up a language arts curriculum for your school, what would it be?" I realized I had been teaching in public schools eight years—in no fewer than five different language arts programs, each one hailed as "innovative" and "creative." It's easier for a district to switch to a new, creative program than to dig down and be truly thoughtful about the one it already has.

For me, drawing up the plans for an ideal school isn't a matter of basics vs. electives, phonics vs. whole language, new math vs. old, tracking vs. heterogeneous grouping, Aztecs vs. Inuits. No matter what side one takes, it always has to be amended with a "yes, but." The woman with whom I team-taught for six years and I were polar opposites: personality, pedagogy, procedures—we did things differently. She believed in the sixteen rules of syllabification, and I don't know what a schwa is. But somehow, on the things that really matter—putting kids first, working hard, and being able to learn new things—we were aligned. People numbed by TV talk shows and ritualized news forums of point-counterpoint want definitive, thirty-second answers. They want to know if syllabification is more important in the curriculum than riddle books, and they don't have the patience to stay around for the "yes, but" complications. People committed to reforming schools must insist that real life is not *Crossfire*.

Instead of posing polar opposites—big schools vs. small, cooperative learning vs. individual responsibility, we must learn to create environments that do not expect the worst of children and teachers. Allowing children to choose the books they read will not create anarchy and illiteracy. Kids who use calculators *do* learn math facts. Teachers who are given free access to phones do not call their psychics in Las Vegas. Kids whom the buses drop off at 7:55 A.M. in ten-degree weather will not trash the school if the doors are opened before the official bell at 8:30. I don't have the statistics here, but I really wonder if depriving middle and high schoolers of lockers (and thus forcing them to carry around all their books, musical instruments, coats, and lunches all day long) reduces drug use in the schools. What I do know is that taking away the lockers shows kids that you expect the worst, and kids have a way of living up to our expectations.

One image by William Ayers (1989) continues to resonate. When a young child makes a choice between riding in a wagon or walking, we see the careful, thoughtful planning of a teacher who is helping her students learn about choice and responsibility. Ironically, because schools are structured to expect the worst, those preschool choices are the last real choices many children will make in their school careers.

I got involved in school reform very early in my career. Just eight months after I started teaching high school in Queens, I received a fellowship to study new techniques in urban education at Princeton University. In those days teachers were paid to take summer courses. Having married a graduate student the day before the course started, I was excited to learn that teachers were even paid a stipend for their dependents. So teacher trainees met at the university, and black teenagers were bused to the idyllic sylvan setting from Trenton. The curriculum was movies, not the stiff and static education junk but high-quality Hollywood movies. Every day we'd hand the kids a paperback book and show them a full-length movie based on that book. The idea was that teachers would learn about the power of film to lure reluctant readers into books.

I learned something important from that course. I learned about the power of the book. Those kids couldn't believe we were giving them all those books. Every day they'd carry in every book. You could see that they enjoyed the books' tactile qualities. They'd run their hands over the smooth, shiny covers. They'd brag about the weight of all their books. "Not another one!" they'd laugh, groaning as they clutched each new book possessively. And while, say, *On the Waterfront* was playing on the screen, the students would crouch over *The Red Pony* or *To Kill a Mockingbird*, trying to read by the light from the projector. Every day we saw the professors proved wrong once again. The books definitely had much more power than the movies. But no one ever said a word about this. Not one word. The professors just kept handing out the books and showing the movies. And we teachers who were being retrained just sat there watching the kids struggle to read in the dark.

I don't know if other teachers learned from that course what I did. As a teacher I now know that what a teacher thinks she teaches often has little to do with what students learn. Since this was in the days before chairs in a circle or in clusters of four, the other teachers and I never talked about what we were learning. All I know is that it's a good thing I learned what I did, because I have never worked in a school that had the money to make high-quality Hollywood films a part of the curriculum. Ever since, when an ed-whiz-biz consultant comes in with a plan to improve our school—reading through typing, reading through art, reading through transcendental meditation, reading through basketball, reading through pizza—I think of those kids from Trenton reading in the dark.

Kids want to learn. They don't have to be bribed, threatened, or shamed into learning. They need to be given a reason to learn. Not pie-in-the-sky promises that if students will just learn calculus they'll be guaranteed lifetime employment. Such claims are a disgrace and serve only the bureaucrats who make them. Students need benefit right now. Today. The wonderful thing is that children will come in tomorrow and give us a chance to do better.

If I may be permitted one last personal story, I learned this aphorism about tomorrow's being a new day from a big, mean seventh-grade girl with a wicked tongue. I was devastated the day she called me a white M-F. I was apprehensive the next day. How would she act? How would I act? She came to class cheerful, energetic, and expecting me to teach her. And I did. She taught me to keep my eye on today, not yesterday. I don't much believe in planning for tomorrow. Do good today, and tomorrow will take care of itself.

Recommending reform to others is easy. Blue-ribbon committees do it all the time. The language of reform is global, grandiose, and gutless. By the time I got out of graduate school I had some sympathy with the fellow who didn't like the way the English department was run. The semester before I arrived, he walked into the building and started shooting. I'm not recommending wholesale slaughter in the ivory towers, but professors do need to look at their students through different lenses. A professor friend of mine had one of these telling moments a few years back. After major surgery, he awoke from the anesthetic to see someone in hospital garb fiddling with his tubing. The caregiver mentioned that he'd been a student in the professor's course. The professor made the mistake of asking, "How'd you do?"

"I failed."

Finding that your life is in the hands of a person who failed your course offers a clarifying moment few academics experience. If we are ever to have any hope of reforming schools, we can't, of course, put all professors under the scalpel, but we can look for ways to help them understand schools better. I offer just two modest proposals for reform. First, require that professors teach regularly in public schools. I don't mean a demonstration lesson here and there. I mean a full schedule for a semester, say, every three years. If that's too onerous, I'd settle for one full semester every five years. Or ten. The teacher whose class is being taken over can teach practicums at the university for that same time period. This practice will not only open eyes and reform practice, it will remove dead wood.

Second, require recertification every five years of anybody who works in schools or makes policy about schools, at all levels, pre-K through graduate school. The recertification should take place in a public meeting where someone is willing to stand with the candidate and bear witness that the candidate is loved. This testifier may be a student or a colleague. It may be a relative. But it must be a different person every five years. This practice will demonstrate that competency alone is not enough.

My favorite story about teaching and learning and standards and values appeared in the *New York Times* Metropolitan Diary, November 1, 1989. A woman driving in midtown Manhattan made an illegal right turn and was pulled over by a stern-looking cop, who took her license and registration numbers and explained the error of her ways. Then he let her go with a warning. As she started to drive off, the police officer queried, "Aren't you going to ask why I didn't give you a ticket?" When she nodded, he grinned, "You were my first-grade teacher."

Surely no teacher can read that without both jubilation and terror. I spent three days making lists of students I thought would have let me off and students who would have (gleefully) thrown the book at me. If we could go into our classrooms every day with the thought that these kids are tomorrow's traffic cops, the world would be a better place.

References

Ayers, William. 1989. *The Good Preschool Teacher: Six Teachers Reflect on Their Lives.* New York: Teachers College Press.

Berry, Wendell. 1981. *Recollected Essays.* San Francisco: North Point Press.

Jacobs, Harold R. 1970; 1994. *Mathematics, A Human Endeavor: A Book for Those Who Think They Don't Like the Subject.* New York: W. H. Freeman.

MacLean, Norman. 1997. *A River Runs Through It.* New York: Pocket Books.

Reimer, Edward. 1977. *School Is Dead.* New York: Anchor Books.

Swain, Roger. 1994. *Earthly Pleasures.* Boston: Houghton-Mifflin Company.

3

Changing College Admissions Requirements Will Help Change High Schools

JOE NATHAN

Here are two often overlooked keys to high school reform: change college admission requirements, and change the backward standards and processes of the National Collegiate Athletic Association.

Recent action by the NCAA has challenged high schools that are seeking to be more effective by offering innovative, interdisciplinary, and applied courses. People urging high schools to improve need to understand the barriers created all too often by colleges and the NCAA.

The NCAA's actions are startling. Excellent students like Jenny Bruun, Winny Brodt, Amber Hofstad, and Kelly Cherwien have good reasons to feel betrayed. Despite their hard work, academic honors, and good grades, the NCAA blocked participation in college sports for months because one or two of their high school courses don't meet new, questionable NCAA standards.

Hofstad is a National Merit Scholar and one of those many honor students the NCAA delayed from participating in college sports. Getting very high grades and test scores, being a National Merit Scholar, being a class valedictorian isn't enough for the NCAA. Hofstad, for example, had her participation in cross country at Michigan Tech University delayed for months because the NCAA questioned a couple of her courses that had been taken, as Minnesota law permits, at a college. As Hofstad's father noted, "Einstein would have problems with the NCAA."

The NCAA routinely allows athletes to attend universities with, to put it mildly, marginal academic skills. Many universities hire tutors to help these athletes stay eligible. Do Bruun, Brodt, and Cherwien fall into this category: young people with strong athletic but modest academic skills? Bruun recently graduated from Crookston High School with a 3.93 grade point average (4.0

31

is straight A). Brodt graduated from Roseville High School with a 3.5, and Cherwien graduated from Hopkins with a 3.4.

So what's the problem? After heavy criticism for permitting unprepared students to accept athletic scholarships, the NCAA began asking high schools to submit a brief description of their courses. On the basis of these descriptions and criteria it developed, the NCAA decided which courses would be acceptable preparation for college.

Two years ago, Brodt and other Roseville High School students now attending Carleton, Colorado College, the University of Minnesota's Institute of Technology, the University of Chicago, the University of Wisconsin, and the Air Force Academy took Critical Reading. Roseville officials say the course is "taught at an honors level." The NCAA turned it down.

Bruun and Cherwien plus students from Elk River and St. Louis Park were denied scholarships because they took courses combining rigorous work on writing, research, and speech with community study, i.e., interviewing business people or writing a local history. Parents and educators had to spend months before the NCAA reconsidered. The Elk River superintendent, David Flannery, calls the NCAA "the most obstinate, frustrating, arrogant group I've dealt with in more than thirty years in public education.

Chris Schuemann, director of athletic eligibility at the University of Minnesota, has found that the NCAA committee "doesn't like interdisciplinary courses," which combine several subjects, helping students see the connections between, for example, history and English. A recent report by the National Association of Secondary School Principals and the Carnegie Foundation urged high schools to connect curriculum "to real-life applications of knowledge and skills to help students link their education to the future." Many high schools are trying to do that.

People disagree about the best approaches to teaching. That's why the driver's license program is a good model: the state doesn't specify what courses a person has taken—in school, out of school, from a friend or relative. The central question is, Does the prospective driver have the necessary skills and knowledge? That's what the NCAA should ask.

The NCAA should rethink its approach to athletic eligibility, measuring what young people know. We should honor, not penalize, young people's hard work and responsible behavior. As Roseville principal Bob Rygh notes, "These are excellent students who are being unjustly denied what they've worked hard to earn."

The NCAA's activities also are discouraging school improvement efforts. Nick Olsen, principal of Elk River High School, shared a three-sentence memo the NCAA sent describing an Essential Communication course as "too vocational" and unacceptable as a core English course. This short memo has three errors. "Thank you for you fax," it begins. It then substitutes the word *do* for *due*, and concludes that "the decision remains unchange for student named above." As Olsen says, "Perhaps NCAA staff should take this course before deciding it's not good preparation for college."

David Flannery, superintendent of Elk River, praised the teachers who developed the course, noting that it was designed to improve students' writing skills, which Minnesota includes in new high school graduation requirements. Sadly, two Elk River honor students who took Essential Communication spent months in limbo. One of them was Minnesota's 1996 state AA girls' Nordic cross country ski champion and received a scholarship from the University of Wisconsin, Green Bay. The other has a basketball scholarship at the University of Tennessee.

Lloyd Styrwoll, principal at Grand Rapids High School, is another of the many principals frustrated with the NCAA. A 1995 graduate of Grand Rapids, who earned a B average at the school, was not allowed to accept a hockey scholarship at Colorado College or at North Dakota State because of a dispute over one math class. The NCAA insisted that the student was half a credit short in math, though he had taken four years of math. Styrwoll writes, "The NCAA refused to listen to us. They were rude and dismissive." The student and the high school are still battling with the NCAA about whether he can accept a scholarship offered by the University of Minnesota, Duluth.

Humphrey Institute student Marguerethe Jaede has learned that outstanding high school students in North Dakota, Colorado, Illinois, New York, and Washington State have similar problems. Parents like Bill Rohe, Julie Linder, Ronna Zien, and Sue Braga can't understand the treatment their children are getting from the NCAA. Neither can I. Despite criticism from all over the country about its treatment of strong student athletes, the NCAA says its process is working. You judge.

There are hundreds of other examples from all over the country and the problem has been apparent for months. (See Nathan 1998 for additional examples of students and schools frustrated by the NCAA.) Yet the NCAA's director, Cedric Dempsey, still defends their acceptance or rejection of courses, insisting in a *USA Today* column that the NCAA is "insuring the integrity of our academic standards" (Dempsey 1996). The paper's editorial page disagreed: "Kids are losing a chance at college because of the NCAA's arrogance" (*USA Today* 1996). *Sports Illustrated* called the NCAA "a politically jumbled mess."

Judy Conger, Dean of Community High in Ann Arbor, calls the NCAA "out of date, out of touch." The NCAA has confused becoming rigorous with being rigid. Educators are furious. Parents are dismayed. Youngsters are losing a chance to attend college and play sports they love. How many hardworking kids will be victims before the NCAA listens?

Under heavy pressure, the NCAA then changed a bit, saying principals could recommend which courses met NCAA standards. But the NCAA still insists on setting the standards, and insists on the right to overrule principals. Among other standards, the NCAA insists that acceptable social studies courses may not spend more than 25 percent of their time on current issues, criminal justice, community service, or humanities. Who is the NCAA to dictate such standards to high schools?

Minnesota Governor Arne Carlson and Senator Paul Wellstone are working on this. Carlson, a Republican, wrote a letter to every state governor urging them to "join me in an effort to prevent this NCAA micromanagement from continuing" (Carlson 1996a). Carlson also wrote a letter to the *New York Times* explaining the concern of governors: "As the leaders of education policy, we have serious concerns about the ability of an independent entity to strike down courses we encourage students to take. . . . Do we really want some bureaucracy in Overland Park, Kansas, the NCAA's base, telling public and private high schools around the nation how to teach our children?" (Carlson 1996b)

Senator Wellstone, a Democrat, wrote to the NCAA, "After talking with principals, teachers, high school counselors, students and parents, it appears that the NCAA is not familiar with some of the exciting changes occurring in high school curriculum" (Wellstone 1996).

The NCAA is discouraging good teachers who are redesigning courses to improve students' skills. And the NCAA's treatment of these outstanding students? It's disgraceful. As a *New York Times* editorial pointed out, "The NCAA should be promoting educational innovation, not obstructing it" (*New York Times*, December 1997).

But the NCAA is not alone in discouraging innovations in high schools. For more than fifty years high school change advocates have confronted college entrance requirements that push high school courses toward credits, grades, and traditional academic disciplines. Over the years, a few high schools have been bold enough to break out of that pattern. Their encouraging experiences are described later in this chapter. But the vast majority of high schools have retained 50–60-minute courses, courses based on academic disciplines, credits, and grades because of convenience and a concern that acting otherwise would make it more difficult for their graduates to gain admission to college.

A 1995 study surveyed high schools around the United States that were trying to shift toward graduation based on demonstration of skill and knowledge, toward at least some interdisciplinary courses, and toward combining more classroom work with community research and service. The study found that the most frequently cited barrier retarding this work was the attitude of college admissions offices (Nathan, Power, and Bruce 1995). Some high schools proceeded anyway, but many felt bound by the expectations of credits in disciplinary courses and grades, which are cited in the materials distributed by college and university admissions offices. Parents read this material and, in many cases, demand that high schools prepare their youngsters for admission to these postsecondary institutions. So, changing the message from postsecondary institutions is critical.

One high school that has encouraged colleges and universities to change admissions criteria has been working on this issue for twenty-five years. In 1971 a new K–12 inner-city St. Paul public school at which I worked examined the meaning of high school graduation. The school wanted to insure that graduates would have strong skills and knowledge, not just take courses. We formed a committee, including parents, students, educators, and community members. Students wrote to more than six hundred businesses, community agencies, universities, and advocacy groups, asking what skills and knowledge they should master before graduating from high school.

Several hundred people answered the students' letters. Businesses, colleges, and advocates generally agreed: students should have strong verbal and written communication skills. Students also should have strong mathematics skills. And they wanted students to be able to work with others in a group to complete various tasks and responsibilities. The school expanded those expectations. Before graduating, students were required to demonstrate skills not only in mathematics, communication, and working with others but also in information finding, career awareness, school and community service, consumer protection, cultural awareness, and maintaining a healthy body. Students had to obtain validations from teachers, employers, parents, and other competent adults showing how the young person had demonstrated each skill. These validations were bound and sent to universities throughout the nation. We had many team-taught, interdisciplinary courses. We gave no grades or class ranks and had no required courses. Since 1973 students from this inner city St. Paul public school have been admitted to colleges and universities throughout the United States. They've won scholarships, including National Merit. The U.S. Department of Education gave the school an award, concluding it was "a carefully evaluated, proven innovation worthy of national replication." Students from the school have obtained a vast array of jobs. A survey of graduates two years out of high school found these youngsters were significantly more satisfied with their high school than those from a traditional, well-regarded high school in the same city (see Nathan 1989).

Students from the experimenting school learned that the credit system of graduation is not based on research about learning, it's based on an attempt to improve the status of college professors. In the early 1900s the Carnegie

Foundation for the Advancement of Teaching decided to give grants for pensions, hoping to making teaching at universities a more attractive career. It had to determine what a postsecondary institution was.

The Carnegie Foundation surveyed secondary schools, discovering that on average they offered year-long classes lasting 120 sixty-minute hours. The foundation called this time period a standard unit (soon known as a Carnegie unit). In order to receive grants from the Carnegie Foundation, a college or university had to require for admission successful completion of fourteen standard units (Carnegie units). This system was almost universally adopted.

Students studying high school graduation also found that grades don't necessarily predict success outside of school. A 1974 American College Test study studied students who earned high grades in high school, high grades in college, high scores on their ACT admissions test, or were in extracurricular activities such as debate, drama, music, journalism, and speech. Only extracurricular success predicted success in adulthood (Munday and Davis 1974).

A study of the Scholastic Aptitude Test found it "offered virtually no clue to capacity for significant intellectual or creative contributions in mature life" (Wallach 1972). The best predictor of adult creativity was a person's performance during youth in independent sustained ventures.

While there does appear to be a relationship between high school and college grades, other studies found little correlation between college grades and later success in fields such as medicine, law, education, and engineering. Nevertheless, grades and credits are used, in part because they are a convenient way to make difficult decisions.

Ten years ago Ted Sizer made "exhibition of mastery" a central element of his high school reform plan. A few award-winning high schools, such as Central Park East in New York City and Walden III in Racine, Wisconsin, moved in the direction Sizer urged. Yet many Coalition of Essential Schools faculty have told me they're reluctant to move away from credits, clock hours, and grades because of the pressure to meet college admissions expectations.

Sizer (1996) concluded that college admissions "drive the kind of high school programs millions of students attend." He believes that changing college admissions is "one of the central issues of high school reform." In 1993 presidents and admissions directors from twenty-four private colleges signed a Coalition-developed statement of support for high schools trying to make major changes. The colleges, including Amherst, Brown, Columbia, Dartmouth, Johns Hopkins, MIT, Smith, Wellesley, and Williams, "applauded those schools involved in endeavors which emphasize rigorous independent thinking and the direct engagement of students in serious work." They agreed to "welcome applications from students at such schools" (see Houghton 1993, 24).

What about large public universities, which must deal with thousands of applications? These universities also sometimes must justify their admissions decisions to parents and state legislators. While college admissions officers often acknowledge that an A from one school is not the same as an A from another school . . . indeed an A from one classroom often is different than one granted next door, or down the hall in the same school, the traditional transcript, with its one-page list of grades, courses, and class ranks is convenient.

Nevertheless, some public universities are rethinking entrance requirements:

- Wisconsin college admissions officials and high school reformers have been meeting for several years. The state university system is trying to respond to changes in high school programs. Beth Weckmueller, admissions director at the University of Wisconsin, Milwaukee, and a member of the statewide committee, told me, "Universities must reexamine admissions policies. We're asking a great deal from high schools. We must ask more of ourselves." (Weckmueller 1993).

- Dr. Nils Hasselmo, president of the University of Minnesota, wrote recently that "as elementary and secondary schools change, colleges and universities are obligated, in my view, to be flexible and creative in developing revised or optional systems for making admissions decisions." The university is talking with the State Department of Education, high schools, and assessment specialists about its response to proposed new high school graduation requirements (Hasselmo 1993).

- According to the National Governors Association, college officials in Wyoming and Nebraska are developing new performance-based admissions requirements that schools may use as an alternative to the traditional credit system. The NGA recently produced an excellent booklet, *College Admission Standards and School Reform* (Houghton 1993).

- In laying out his 1994–1995 agenda, Roy Romer, Education Commissioner of the States and Colorado Governor, noted that colleges and universities "have been slow to support K–12 changes and reflect these in entrance requirements." He urged action to do so. (Roemer 1994)

While these actions are encouraging, the details are daunting. How exactly will colleges deal with thousands of portfolios? Are there simpler forms of performance assessment valid and reliable enough to help admissions officers make decisions? Will colleges and universities tell parents that they need not insist on four years of English or three years of history to have skilled, competent children? Will we be able to find convenient alternatives to grades?

We can learn from a remarkable Eight-Year Study conducted during the late 1930s and early 1940s. Thousands of youngsters attended about thirty high schools that had been given the opportunity to create programs quite different from the 50 – 60 minute class schedule. Three hundred colleges agreed to exempt graduates of these high schools from traditional grade, class rank, required course, and credit requirements.

The study paired about fifteen hundred students from experimental high schools with fifteen hundred students from similar but nonexperimental schools. It matched students by sex, age, intelligence, family background, race, and other factors. The students from experimenting high schools did better in college in grades, participation, critical thinking, aesthetic judgment, knowledge of contemporary affairs, and student leadership. Graduates of the two most experimental schools, which featured extensive learning in the community, students tutoring other students, and interdisciplinary problem-solving curricula, were "strikingly more successful" in college than the students from traditional schools. (Aikin 1942)

Unfortunately, this major study has been mostly lost in U.S. educational research. It's time to learn from it. Michael Timpane, former president of Teachers College, Columbia, is right when he says, "If the colleges and universities were willing to create some new entrance requirements, you'd see real, valuable changes in high schools." (Timpane 1995)

Here are a few strategies to increase student achievement and promote a smoother transition from high school to colleges and universities:

- Governors and chief state school officers should ask universities in their states to develop new, optional admission requirements. Rather than totally discard the admissions system based on grades and credits, there could be several ways to enter universities.

- Colleges and universities should issue public statements (such as the one developed by the Coalition of Essential Schools) supportive of thoughtful innovation and should revise materials sent out to prospective students. The materials should clarify the universities' support for high school innovation.

- College presidents, mindful of the need for better-educated students, should ask their admissions officers to develop new options for admission.

- Foundations and the federal government should commission new studies, based on the Eight-Year Study, that examine what happens to youngsters from different kinds of high schools in postsecondary institutions and in later life. This kind of research is expensive. But it's important. (See Chapter 12.)

- The NCAA should end its efforts to tell high schools and colleges which courses are and are not appropriate preparation for college. And the NCAA should expand the range of tests it accepts, looking, for example, at writing samples and other "applied performance" examinations that have been nationally validated.

Thousands of high school educators are eager to create new models of secondary education, featuring the best research about learning and teaching. But they need help from postsecondary institutions. New admission options are a vital part of creating more effective high schools and, most important, more skilled, competent high school graduates.

References

Aikin, Wilford. 1942. *Story of the Eight-Year Study.* New York: Harper & Brothers.

Applebome, Peter. 1996. "Effort to Raise Academic Standards Leaves Many Top Students on Sidelines." *New York Times,* October 23, p. B12.

Carlson, Arne. 1996a. Letter to the Honorable Fob James, Governor of Alabama. October 24.

———. 1996b. "NCAA Should Play High School Principal." *New York Times,* November 10, p. B14.

Dempsey, Cedric W. 1996. "NCAA Program Works." *USA Today,* October 29, p. 12A.

Hasselmo, Nils. 1993. Letter to the author, December 2.

Houghton, Mary J. 1993. *College Admissions Standards and School Reform.* Washington, D.C.: National Governors' Association.

Munday, L. A., and J. C. Davis. 1974. *Varieties of Accomplishment After College: Perspectives on the Meaning of Academic Talent.* Iowa City, Iowa: American College Testing Program.

Nathan, Joe. 1989. *Free to Teach: Achieving Equity and Excellence in Schools.* Cleveland: Pilgrim Press.

———. 1998. "Major Barrier to High School Reform." *Phi Delta Kappan* (June): 764–768.

Nathan, Joe, Jennifer Power, and Maureen Bruce. 1995. *Deserved, Defensible Diplomas: High Schools with Competency-Based Graduation Requirements.* Minneapolis: University of Minnesota, Humphrey Institute, Center for School Change.

New York Times. 1997. "The N.C.A.A.'s Eligibility Standards." December 23, p. 23.

Roemer, Roy. 1994. "Agenda for Action." Denver: Education Commission of the States.

Sizer, Theodore. 1996. Conversation with the author, November.

Timpane, Michael. 1995. Conversation with the author.

USA Today. 1996. "NCAA's Too-Tight Rules Hurt Deserving Students." Editorial. October 29, p. 12A.

Wallach, Michael. 1972. "Psychology of Talent and Graduate Education." Paper presented at International Conference on Cognitive Styles and Creativity in Higher Education, sponsored by the Graduate Record Examination Board. Montreal, Canada. November.

Weckmueller, Beth. 1993. Conversation with the author, November.

Wellstone, Paul. 1996. "Letter to Gene Corrigan." October 5.

Introduction

The Problems of Context and Authoritarianism

Meier, Ohanian, and Nathan have set a general scene and raised some profound questions about the nature and organization of our systems of elementary, secondary, and higher education.

Certainly one of the basic points they make about both of these systems is that their organizational structure and their traditional curricular and instructional practices render it extremely difficult for teachers to treat students as individual human beings who arrive at their doors with an enormous diversity of histories and outlooks—with that immense variety of intellectual, social, ethnic, and economic backgrounds that are all too often ignored or denigrated by both the elementary and secondary and the higher educational systems.

But those three contributors also raise questions about the role and purposes of these educational systems, or rather, the one system of schooling running from kindergarten through graduate school. It is these questions that we continue to explore in Part II.

Alejandro Sanz de Santamaria asks, Given their present authoritarian structure, are our schools, colleges, and universities—which claim to possess our culture's important knowledge and pass that knowledge on to students and communities who "know nothing"—adequately educating our young people for political life in a democracy?

William Coplin raises roughly the same question in a slightly different fashion: Are our schools, colleges, and universities training our young people to be concerned only with themselves rather than with society as a whole, on which the very survival of the human species depends?

In Chapter 6, I then briefly describe some of the historical reasons why our schools, and in particular our colleges and universities, have become institutions intellectually and functionally decontextualized and dangerously disconnected from the larger society that supports them, a society of which they are a part and which they are supposed to serve.

And finally, Patrick Shannon raises the equally disturbing question of whether our schools, colleges, and universities are not, in fact, inadvertently supporting and promoting an American society that is economically, socially, and politically lacking in elementary justice for the vast majority of its citizens—indeed, a society that is not only economically but morally outmoded. Given the drastically altered economic situation in which the rich few are getting richer and the majority is getting poorer, Shannon sees the task of the educational system to be revolutionizing itself in order to support the dreams and vastly improve the economic status of the many rather than maintaining the economic status quo that unjustly rewards the privileged few.

4

Education for Political Life

ALEJANDRO SANZ DE SANTAMARIA

As a university professor, I am involved in two main activities. I teach (economics and management) and I undertake research (mainly in economics). And I now find myself deeply concerned about the kind of education for political life we provide through our teaching and research activities. I suspect that through these activities we are not educating people to take their place in a democracy.

For me, the central question is this: What is urgent and important if we are to provide people with a better education for political life? Should we generate additional educational activities—additional to those being practiced in formal educational institutions—that are directly concerned? Or should we radically transform the current forms in which we carry out our educational practices in all subjects so that they effect a different, better political education? The truth is that I'd be reluctant to argue against any of the efforts being made outside the formal educational institutions to improve education for political life. Yet I have a strong sense that these efforts consume immense energies merely to counterbalance the *damaging* effects that formal education, as it is provided in all subjects through existing academic institutions, is having on political life in our society. Thus my hypothesis that it is more urgent and important to work as hard as possible to transform current formal educational practices in certain new directions than it is to create additional activities to improve people's education for political life. I think a transformation in the conventional social forms of education has to take place in the classrooms at schools and universities.

Just over a decade ago, I was invited to analyze the way in which local laborers' migration patterns, in the Colombian peasant community of Garcia

Rovira, were affecting regional economic development, and to make appropriate recommendations on an economic policy that the government could enforce in connection with migration. More recently, I have been engaged in evaluating the impact of a government economic development program that has been under way in the region for more than eight years.

A central feature of these two experiences was that the recommendations I was to produce had to be constructed from primary information collected through in-depth fieldwork and surveys. Thus in both projects the knowledge production process comprised, schematically, four "conventional" steps: a thorough analysis of available literature on this rural community; fieldwork in which different constitutive social agents of the community—peasants, landowners, merchants, state functionaries, local politicians, religious and military authorities—were interviewed at length; a survey, designed and implemented in the light of the fieldwork; and finally, the knowledge construction process itself, using all the information made thus available.

The experience was traumatic.

The available literature on Garcia Rovira when I started the first project was overwhelming: there was information on the agrological characteristics of the soil (soil qualities, steepness, altitudes over sea level), on local weather conditions (rainfall, humidity, winds), on water availability (rivers, streams, dams, and other irrigation facilities), on the regional population's size, growth rate, and structure (urban, rural, age groups), on the most important crops grown in the region and the different labor processes practiced to cultivate each of them (amount of labor time required, constitutive tasks of labor processes, production inputs needed) on the main characteristics of the markets within which the different products circulated (local, regional, national, international markets), on prices per product, on rural development programs that had been enforced and were being enforced by the state and other institutions, on land ownership distribution, on productivity and levels of production per product, and so on.

The abundance of this information meant that it was impossible for me to use it all in my own production of knowledge; yet, at the same time, I knew this information would have to be taken into account by any research that proved effective in procuring economic development in this community. A troubling contradiction indeed.

Then, as I came into direct and close contact with many individuals and households in the second step of my conventional knowledge production process—the in-depth fieldwork—this contradiction became not only increasingly evident but also increasingly problematic. The richness and complexity of the innumerable natural and social conditions under which each of the individuals and households interviewed reproduced themselves over time, as well as the impressive differences (the heterogeneity) of such conditions among social units—which are often "homogenized" under the concept of "peasant"—progressively undermined the possibility of producing a conclusion that I could legitimately claim to be a sound basis for any kind of recommendation.

Recommendations could be formally constructed, of course. But I felt a moral impediment to doing so: in the name of what golden rule was I to make the abstraction necessary to produce my knowledge and make my recommendations about what ought to be done to attain this community's economic development?

But I had to do it: there was a legal contract to which I had to respond. Thus, I had to select a principle of organization—a theoretical framework, a symbolic space—with which I could select and relate my story about Garcia Rovira. And so I did.

The complexity of the scenario I gradually perceived—of the numerous intermingled social and natural processes in which the different individuals and households interviewed participated—turned the experience of the third step of my work (the survey) into the most forceful and valuable evidence of the arbitrariness of the abstractions economists have to make. The design of the sample, the painful process of constructing the survey questionnaire, the even more painful process of collecting the information—the pain one feels in this kind of research is, I think, directly proportionate to how deeply concerned one is, as a researcher, about the future of the community under study, about the real social effects that the knowledge production process itself will have on the community. How was I to design a sample survey of approximately five hundred households that would be representative of this community as a totality? I didn't have an answer then, and I still don't have it today.

But the sample was designed, the questionnaire was constructed, the survey was carried out, and the collected information was ordered in several computer files to be used as raw material to construct new knowledge about the community. I proceeded then with the fourth and final step of this conventional knowledge production process: to use all of this information, collected in the three preceding steps, for the construction of new knowledge and corresponding recommendations. But the only firm conclusions I could draw from this exercise were confirmation of my own technical incapacity unilaterally to determine what policies would actually be effective in enhancing the development of these households. This strongly reinforced the moral impediment I had felt in making such policy recommendations. How could I unilaterally construct knowledge on such a complex totality, or recommend anything to do in order to procure its development? On what grounds could I claim that the specific options I had taken throughout this long and cumbersome abstraction process were the correct options to procure such development effectively?

In the light of this experience, I found myself asking how was I, as a protagonist of this social process of producing knowledge, to ensure that the specific knowledge I was to produce was adequate for, and would be effectively and successfully used in, procuring its stated beneficial ends? The radical separation in space and time between the economic knowledge production process and the social uses made of the resulting knowledge allows for the social agents producing the knowledge to be different from the social agents responsible for taking action based on it (in this case the state). Further, there is a still more radical separation between both of these two social agents and the people directly and radically affected by the production and use of knowledge—the investigated community itself (in my case, the rural community of Garcia Rovira).

It was clear to me that in these social forms of producing and using economic, scientific knowledge there was no communication whatsoever between science (myself as an academic economist) and society (the rural community of Garcia Rovira).

The question of the political legitimacy of conventional social forms of producing and using economic knowledge is, to me, strikingly similar to the question Paulo Freire, the well-known Brazilian educator, had to face when he called into question the legitimacy of conventional forms of education. For Freire (1970) the conventional forms of education, which he called "banking" education, "become an act of depositing, in which the students are the depositories and the teacher is the depositor. Instead of communicating, the teacher issues communiqués and makes deposits which the students patiently receive, memorize, and repeat. . . . Knowledge is a gift bestowed by those who consider themselves knowledgeable upon those whom they consider to know nothing. Projecting an absolute ignorance onto others, a characteristic of the ideology of oppression, negates education and knowledge as processes of inquiry."

Similarly, the conventional social forms in which economists—unilaterally, not dialogically—construct knowledge, and the separation between the production and use of economic knowledge, transform knowledge into a fetished commodity whose production, circulation, and use can be separated in space and time. In the conventional forms of producing and using economic knowledge, the economists isolate themselves from the communities they investigate; communication between science and society is obstructed. In the conventional forms of producing and using economic knowledge the investigated community's perceptions of its realities is always abstracted by the economist. And such crucial abstraction is legitimized in the name of objective, scientific knowledge.

This separation in turn produces a political effect of the utmost importance: an authoritarian power is consistently exerted by social science researchers on their investigated communities. Feyerabend (1987) was right when he denounced the intellectuals—in this case, economists—as people who "have so far succeeded . . . in preventing a more direct democracy where problems are solved and solutions judged by those who suffer from the problems and have to live with the solutions. . . . [They] have fattened themselves on the funds thus diverted in their direction. It is time to realize that they [the intellectuals] are just one special and rather greedy group held together by a special and rather aggressive tradition. . . ." (85–86)

To develop alternative social forms for producing and using economic knowledge, in which these separations are superseded, has meant for me in my more recent work, among other things, that my responsibility as a developmental economist in front of a community could not be limited to the conventional academic task of producing economic knowledge and making a set of formal recommendations. I had to be responsible for the use, or misuse, that would be made of this knowledge, and for the concrete social effects that the knowledge I was to produce would have (or would not have) on the community over time. In other words, my responsibilities as a developmental economist comprise the *political* problem (in the broadest sense) of how my activities as a social researcher will ultimately affect the living conditions of the community, not just the academic or technical problem of constructing knowledge to justify—in front of social agents different from the investigated community (the state, for example)—a set of formal economic policy recommendations. It has meant abandoning the comfortable position of being accountable only for analyzing and recommending, to be held responsible—in front of the real individuals and households that constitute the community—for the concrete social effects that my produced knowledge might have on their living conditions.

But I could not assume this new responsibility unilaterally. I had to develop radically new forms of knowledge production and use. I had to start a collective reflection process to identify and thoroughly analyze (understand) a few concrete problems; to start a communication between the academic economist (science) and the community (society); to achieve a collective and integrated process of knowledge production. The crucial contribution of this process has been to provide us—and by *us* I mean the *new* community of peasants and academic economists that this process has been progressively engendering—with a collective experience, within which a collective knowledge of the numberless complexities of concrete problems has been constructed (by reflection) and used (in action). New channels of communication between science (academic economists) and society (the communities with which economists are doing impact evaluations of government development programs) are being constructed, out of which new pieces of knowledge are being produced. The conventional separation between subject and object in the production and use of knowledge has been superseded; thus no totalitarian power is being exerted by science on society. And the knowledge itself that is being produced is not any more a commodity, a finished product; it is now a permanently changing process that is increasingly becoming a constitutive element of the daily life of this new community.

The broader, most profound implication of this research experience as I have lived it, and made sense of it, is political: it has revealed to me the totalitarian nature of the exercise of social power that is ingrained in the conventional forms of producing and using economic knowledge. This pattern in the exercising of social power is embedded in the radical separation between, on the one hand, the few individuals who participate in the production and use of economic knowledge and, on the other, the masses of people who, in spite of being the most deeply affected by these processes, are maintained as nonparticipants in the production and use of this knowledge.

A second crucial matter I have learned has to do with the importance of collective participation in the process of production and use of economic knowledge that will affect the living conditions of the communities. Attaining this participation requires tremendous efforts in the construction of communication channels between science (economists) and society (the investigated communities). These communication channels can be constructed only if economists are willing to stop ignoring (abstracting), in their research practices, the cultural complexity of how the communities they investigate perceive their own realities. Communication between economic science and society will not be possible unless economists understand and fully accept in their research practices Feyerabend's striking proposition (1978): "I am not looking for new theories of science. I am asking if the search for such theories is a reasonable undertaking and I conclude that it is not. The knowledge we need to understand and to advance the sciences does not come from theories, it comes from participation."

As for the role of the academic economist, this experience has taught me that it cannot be any more than that of an external agent in charge of the limited and comfortable task of producing knowledge to justify recommendations. Such a role leads only to undesirable scenarios: the production and circulation of useless knowledge and recommendations that nobody takes seriously; or the use of knowledge and recommendations as weapons to exert subtle but violent forms of social power through science. This second scenario—the worse of the two—is eloquently described by Michael Foucault (1980): "In fact we know from experience that the claim to escape from the system of contemporary reality so as to produce the overall programs of another society, of another way of thinking, another culture, another vision of the world, has led only to the return of the most dangerous conditions." (46)

Alan Watts observes,

> Government is simply an abandonment of responsibility on the assumption that there are people, other than ourselves, who can really know how to manage things. But the government, run ostensibly for the good of the people, becomes a self-serving corporation. To keep things under control it proliferates laws of ever-increasing complexity and unintelligibility, and hinders productive work by demanding so much accounting on paper that the record of what has been done becomes more important than what has actually been done. (1975, 81–82)

In my long and intense research experience with economic development programs in so-called underdeveloped rural areas, I could clearly see happening what Watts describes. The well-intended efforts by the government's central offices to direct and control the actions of all the social agents involved in these programs—direction and control functions that are always exerted in the name of certain preconceived objectives—led inexorably to the development of rules, norms, and policies of "ever-increasing complexity and unintelligibility" that suffocated everyone, including the government institutions responsible for the development programs.

But these programs generated even more serious problems at the social and political levels. One that I could see very clearly was how government actions, as they are generally conceived and implemented in these development programs, engendered profound paternalistic relationships that, paradoxically, reproduced and deepened human underdevelopment in those communities that were supposed to be the beneficiaries, as they were led (by these programs) to systematically expect others (e.g., governments, experts) to solve their problems because they were led to see themselves as "ones who do not know."

Today, I can see no essential difference between this expanded reproduction of human underdevelopment through paternalism in the government's development programs and what we do in the classroom when we teach as we usually do. The interaction of the development experts with the communities on which they carry out their research is, in this sense, very similar to the interaction of the teachers and their students. In both cases, the relationship is governed by the alienating assumption that one has the knowledge the other lacks and has to learn. This is why the concept of knowledge, and the use we make of it in both our teaching and research activities, has become a significant political problem for me.

Again, Watts writes,

> The game of Western philosophy and science is to trap the universe in networks of words and numbers, so that there is always the temptation to confuse rules, or laws, of grammar and mathematics with the actual operations of nature. We must not, however, overlook the fact that human calculation is also an operation of nature; but just as trees do not represent or symbolize rocks, our thoughts—even if intended to do so—do not necessarily represent rocks and trees. (1975, 42)

My conviction is that in our educational and social research practices we are permanently treating the concepts and ideas we teach and use as if they were "the actual operations of nature." Since in our educational institutions and research projects it is always assumed—even in many of those institutions that theoretically reject this assumption—that the teachers or researchers know and the students or investigated communities don't know, the students and communities are never given the opportunity to express and describe their own experiences and knowledge in their own ways and their own words. The education/research process' objective is rather the opposite: to teach the students and the communities to express themselves in the professors' and researchers' ways and words, since they are, by assumption, "the ones who know."

Since the fall of 1988, I have been experimenting with different teaching formats trying to create conditions in which students can express themselves authentically. This has posed a serious challenge to my own capacity to listen to them. Both tasks—to create the conditions for them to be able to express themselves authentically and to develop my own capacity to listen to, and understand, what they want to express—have proved to be much more difficult and revealing than I could have expected. It has demanded a tremendous effort on my part to understand and transform my own biases, prejudices, and mental preconceptions as a professor, in both the content and the process of my teaching—biases, prejudices, and preconceptions that, as I have gradually discovered, pervasively obstruct communication with my students and their own personal development.

Thus, embedded in and hidden behind these concrete day-to-day human relationships—teacher-student, researcher-researched, boss-subordinate, government–civil society—there is a deep, tough, invisible, political education process that we usually ignore or overlook. I call this invisible education process in which people learn so thoroughly, though mostly unconsciously, "political education by experience." I want to draw a sharp distinction between this invisible political education by experience and what I would call a "visible process of political education" (to refer to what we usually do in the classroom—teaching as usual): *there* we take given, already constructed knowledge ("networks of words and numbers") about politics, contained in books, articles, or in professors' heads, and teach it to our students. This kind of visible education process (and the same is true of research) is, I think, starkly separated from concrete, day-to-day human experiences; and it is my feeling that because of that dichotomy, this kind of education (or research) does more harm than good. It is inevitable that together with this visible process of political education—intended to affect students' (or community members') intellects—there is also invisible political education by experience, which affects students' real lives in the classroom (or the community's real life in the research experience).

I want to underscore that this invisible political education process is not explicitly and openly acknowledged as a constituent part of education or research. But life and mind *are* thus separated in the classroom and in research practices; and this separation carries with it profound and harmful contradictions. For example, we often teach democratic theories in the classroom ("networks of words and numbers") while practicing, at the experiential level of teacher-student relationships ("actual operations of nature") the nondemocratic exercise of power that is generally embedded in teaching. In other words, we teach one type of politics at the discursive level and we practice a different type of politics in the classroom. Because of this profound dichotomy between discourse and practice we lead our students to learn a very sophisticated discourse on democracy that they reproduce eloquently without changing anything at all in their day-to-day lives to practice the democratic theories they are knowledgeable about. This is how, at the university, we end up producing tyrants who are intellectual experts on democracy.

Does it make sense for me to conceive, as one of my tasks, the education of others for political life? I find the notion of educating others problematic when the process of education is conceived and practiced in the conventional way—teaching as usual—of transferring a given, structured knowledge to other people through discursive means. An increasing number of experiences have shown me that when I practice this kind of education I alienate people, kill individual creativity, and bury extremely valuable knowledge and personal motivations. These kinds of educational practices operate on the assumption that the processes of production and circulation of knowledge, and then the use of this knowledge, are tasks that have to occupy separated moments in space and time, and be performed by different people. By doing so, by transforming knowledge into commodities, we separate the knowledgeable people from the unknowledgeable people and thus create the conditions under which our teaching and research practices become, in themselves, non-democratic practices in a totalitarian exercise of power systematically exerted by the knowledgeable on the unknowledgeable.

I am more convinced every day that it is only through my own personal self-education for political life—conceiving self-education not as a process of accumulating discursive knowledge ("networks of words and numbers") but as a continuous practice in exploring new specific ways to relate to people in the classroom, in my research, and so on ("actual operations of nature")—that I can effectively recruit others—my students, my peers, my bosses, my research assistants, the members of the communities I do my research with—to join me in a collective, continuous, and open process of educating ourselves for political life.

My work as a teacher and as a social researcher is profoundly political. I may not deal with politics and political life as subjects to be studied in my courses or in my research projects: there are no readings assigned on this topic, no questions on the exams that require my students to use any formal knowledge of politics and political life. Yet, in the very process of teaching and constructing knowledge, when I give a class, coordinate a meeting, collect a survey, and so on, I am teaching my students and the investigated communities—teaching them in a profound way, through the experience they live out in the classroom and in the research activities—much more about politics and political life than I would if these topics were dealt with as subjects of study in the conventional way.

References

Feyerabend, P. K. 1978. *Science in a Free Society.* London: Verso Editions.

———. 1987. *Farewell to Reason.* London: Verso Editions.

Foucault, M. 1980. *Power/Knowledge,* ed. and trans. C. Gordon. New York: Pantheon Books.

Freire, P. 1970. *Pedagogy of the Oppressed.* New York: Continuum Press.

Watts, A. 1975. *Tao: The Watercourse Way.* New York: Pantheon Books.

5

Higher Education Against the Public Good

How Future Generations Are Conditioned to Serve Only Themselves

WILLIAM D. COPLIN

Many of the problems we Americans face today can be attributed to our failure to balance our own self-interest with the needs of society; that is, to pursue personal freedom as an end in itself. This "foolish freedom" can be seen in smokers who use the sidewalk as their ashtray, drivers who fail to wear seat belts, youth who can't wait to have babies, parents who don't have the time to discipline their children, voters who oppose higher taxes but want more services, business people who call simultaneously for the free market and government subsidies, and politicians who put their political survival first.

The unwillingness to accept the need for individual and collective investments in the public good can be traced to many factors. Our history began with people coming to America to be free, and our culture embraces individualism as its primary, if not only, universal value. Technological developments and our advantageous geography have helped that individualism to grow into an obsession. We are a nation short on "informed empathy," as Deborah Meier says.

Unfortunately, our educational system is doing little to encourage "informed empathy," but much to prevent it. Children may enter school with the desire to contribute some of their time and energy to society, but by the time they become young adults, they are so obsessed with economic survival and unlimited consumption that they have little room in their lives for the public good.

This should not be surprising because educational institutions reflect the norms of society. We cannot fix society only by improving education. Reform is an interactive process among all societal institutions, so changes in our social, economic, and political institutions must accompany changes in our educational system.

However, our educational system is pushing our citizens in the wrong direction and higher education shares much of the blame. What happens in K–12 is shaped by higher education's role in setting curriculum goals for our students. Higher education also affects collective and personal finances in the United States and educates its students in a way that heightens self-interest and diminishes social consciousness.

Before presenting my argument, I need to register a caveat. I am not saying that higher education makes no contribution to the public good. Our colleges and universities do contribute to the public good. They help increase the number of skilled professional and educated citizens, support some research that makes society better, and often encourage some commitment to the public interest among students. However, given the enormous resources these institutions consume and the leadership roles they have in our society, they could do much more to promote the public good and damage our society much less.

Money

For better or for worse, money is the organizing force of U.S. society, as it is in all modern industrialized societies. Therefore, one needs to begin the examination of the impact of higher education and our willingness to work for the public good by looking at money.

Of the $560 billion spent on education in 1996–1997, more than 40% ($225 billion) was spent on higher education according to estimates from the National Center for Education Statistics publication entitled *Mini-Digest of Statistics 1997*. With about 52 million students in grades K–12 and 15 million full-time equivalent college students (U.S. Bureau of The Census 1997, 154), per pupil cost is about $6,400 for K–12 students and $15,000 for college students. We spend more than twice as much on our adult and near-adult population as on younger age groups where education is likely to have the largest impact. This gap has not diminished and most likely has increased since 1995, given the increase in tuition charges by most institutions of higher education. It will continue to increase as higher education becomes more expensive, greater numbers of students and parents are willing to borrow to chase the dream it offers, and support for increased funding of K–12 education diminishes.

College administrators are quick to point out that higher education is expensive and that the United States has the best system of higher education in the world. They also point out that a major mission of higher education is the accumulation of knowledge, which is very expensive. These contentions raise several interesting questions. What does *best* mean? Hopefully, not the production of Ph.D.s in fields like philosophy or history whose viable job options all too frequently are driving cabs or working as temps. Would we still be "best" if we reduced expenditures 50 percent?

By investing three times as much per pupil in higher education, our society is putting resources into the top of the pyramid rather than the base. Given this pattern of public allocation, we have created a system similar to the one that exists for basketball players. Millions of wanna-be Michael Jordans spend their youth on basketball courts so that a few hundred can win coveted National Basketball Association positions. Today, millions of our youth compete in venues, some of which are no better than the cement basketball courts of inner-city playgrounds, to go to colleges and universities to become lawyers and doctors. Not surprisingly, 50 percent who go to college fail to graduate, and very few make it into these professions or into careers that meet the expectations raised by college brochures. Because public expenditures are top-heavy, students in the K–12 system are expected to compete among themselves to get into four-year colleges, where unrealized dreams are the norm. This overfunding of college education and the relative underfunding of K–12 is a recipe for a competitive and uncaring adult population.

It is also a recipe for the growing class warfare in our society. Higher education disproportionately benefits the rich because they are more likely to have the background and resources to take advantage of it. The small percentage of poor who make it into professional careers provide the rich with justification for a system designed to serve them. The majority of poor who do not make it end up with anger at themselves and at society.

Money drives representatives of higher education to act like narrow special-interest groups rather than protectors of the public good. They travel to Washington, D.C., and state capitols, begging for dollars. Arguing in public-interest terms, our college presidents and their lobbyists seek subsidies in every way, shape, and form. While many of these subsidies serve the public good, many are little more than payoffs to feed an industry that cares only for itself. For example, the American Association of Higher Education's Educational Trust program, which seeks to improve K–12 education, publishes a newsletter called *Thinking K–16*, which indicates that the AAHE wants federal and private funding to make K–12 education generate more and better college students, regardless of the value to students. The institutions of higher education act too much like self-serving lobby groups and not enough like Common Cause.

At the individual level, the monetary impact of college is more direct and more destructive of the public good. The debt that many students incur makes greed and lack of concern for the public good almost inevitable. In 1993 about 50 percent of all college graduates started off with a ten-year debt averaging $8,474 (TERI 1996, 12). Each doctor had on average a cumulative debt (including college) of $64,059, and each dentist of $67,772, while each lawyer owed on average $40,300 on law school expenses (TERI 1996, 12). The consequence is that students face a future in which paying off college loans saps both their willingness and resources to serve the public good. Law graduates who choose to work for public legal services average 27 percent of their income in law school loan repayments (TERI 1996, 44).

Is it any wonder most of our college graduates care little about serving others or voting for candidates who serve more than their own interests, when they are preoccupied with a future burdened by debt? Is it any wonder that the time they might spend working for the public good is spent on a second job? Is it any wonder that students who would like to take a job with a nonprofit organization to help their community choose not to? Is it any wonder they tend to distrust all societal institutions? Is it any wonder they have even less inclination than they would otherwise to pay more taxes? Is it any wonder our doctors pursue lucrative and oversupplied specialties and our lawyers search for jobs in large corporate law firms?

K–12 Education Diminished

As if it were not enough that institutions of higher education take huge amounts of money from our society and our students, they have had a devastating impact on K–12 education in the United States.

Susan Ohanian and Deborah Meier spell out many of the constraints imposed on K–12 education. They discuss the role a traditional four-year college plays in motivating students and in the shaping of curriculum. Ohanian explains how the impact of K–12 education has limited the educational opportunity for many students by requiring a universal curriculum that colleges value. Meier's message is more mixed but raises the issue. A more comprehensive treatment is provided by Evans Clinchy in an article entitled, "Higher Education: The Albatross Around the Neck of Our Public Schools" (1994).

For the purpose of my argument, I need to demonstrate how higher education, through its emphasis on four-year degree programs, shapes K–12 education and destroys, or at least significantly reduces, our future citizens' willingness to hold self-interest in check for the public good. Throughout the following discussion, I use the term *college education* to refer to the traditional four-year college program that the vast majority of students undertake. There are many postsecondary programs that prepare students for specific vocations, which are not subject to the same criticisms.

Too many students, parents, and school staff see a college education as the best path to economic success for everyone. As students move from elementary school to high school, the curriculum emphasis changes. In the early years, the skills necessary for work, play, and citizenship are emphasized. As students enter junior high school, the curriculum requires students to jump through a series of what Clinchy calls decontextualized content hoops that have little application except to help students get into and do well in college.

Those who have trouble jumping through the content hoops become discouraged. Pressured to take forms of mathematics and science that are highly abstract and theoretical, when they lack basic reading and mathematics skills, students are threatened with the prospect of not being admitted to a good college. Being forced to learn what they do not value as useful and then threatened by a diminished capacity for economic opportunity, students disengage from the system.

Those who can jump through the hoops become cynical, not only about education but also about society in general. The highly academic nature of the material covered in most high school programs is frequently above the heads of all but those most facile with abstraction and memorization. Typical "A" students achieve high grades by memorizing, parroting, cramming, and occasionally cheating their way through high school. They feel that their high grades are not a true reflection of what they know, and they resent being forced to play a game they do not believe in. Moreover, with the crush of extracurricular activities, part-time jobs, and family responsibilities, education becomes an exercise of getting the highest grade with the least amount of work. Those that are good at it succeed, and their success makes them cynical about the public good.

Because alternatives to the traditional four-year college education continue to be devalued, students who would pursue other paths are not given a viable escape. Education that aims at vocational and life skills is considered to be trivial, not just by many educators but also by politicians, parents, and students. Vocational education has a bad name in the United States because it is viewed as a place for those who cannot make it. This view is becoming more pronounced. In 1972, 18 percent of high school seniors said they expected to attend postsecondary vocational schools, compared to 10 percent in 1992. A third of all high school seniors said they expected to go to graduate or professional schools (Mansnerus 1994, 160). Compared to other industrialized countries, we have done very little to recruit and train skilled workers. Someone interested in motors and fixing things is encouraged to become an engineer rather than a mechanic, even if he or she barely passed ninth-grade algebra.

The opponents of vocational education, or real-world education, are not just those protecting the elite. A crucial source of opposition comes from those who say they care about the disadvantaged. The reality of this opposition struck me when I attended a lecture by Jonathan Kozol who is an ardent spokesperson for giving the poorest kids an equal chance. I was predisposed to the arguments Kozol made in his lecture. However, in the question-and-answer period, I found out that he bought the elitism of higher education. He saw little value to vocational or life skills education, and he stated as his measure of success an educational system wherein children from every economic level or social status would be able to reach their potential as great poets. As he spoke passionately about a pervasive attitude that did not allow students to develop their full talents and potential, I thought to myself how demeaning his view is to the inner-city youths who are working their butts off to become nurses and marines.

We fail to prepare the majority of students for the kinds of jobs they are likely to get. Kenneth B. Hoyt heads a research action project housed at Kansas State University and heavily funded by the DeWitt Wallace–Reader's Digest Fund called Counseling for High Skills. He states that between 1994 and 2005, "77 percent of the expected new job openings will not require a bachelor's degree or more formal education" (1996, 2). As James Comer (1980), a college professor who has exposed himself to the trenches, writes, "Most occupations are not as intellectually demanding as they are generally thought to be. It is estimated that 65 percent of today's and tomorrow's jobs can be held by people with average (or slightly less) intelligence and a good ninth-grade education" (17). He continues by arguing that people in the workforce today "require greater frustration tolerance, personal discipline, organization, management, and interpersonal skills than were required" in the past (17). Learning modern mathematics up to the level of calculus, developing abstract reasoning, or mastering facts that college professors think are important does not lead to the kinds of personal attributes Hoyt and Comer argue the majority of our students need.

The reality of this overemphasis on college was brought home to me by one of my students, who went to an alternative high school that incorporates many of the ideas of Deborah Meier. This student was very strong on teamwork skills, had a first-rate work ethic, and wanted to learn so that he could get a job that was both interesting and well-paying. However, he lacked strong analytical skills. He enrolled in my major, which is an interdisciplinary policy studies program that provides Arts and Sciences students with the skills they will need to succeed in a variety of careers. He saw himself working for the public good as a research analyst in some think tank, or working in research for a socially oriented lobbying agency. After receiving a low grade from me in his methods course, which was based primarily on a community research project, he talked to me about why he had difficulty. I finally said in the gentlest way possible that I thought his talents lay elsewhere than in social science research.

He should take a job working with people rather than with numbers and research. If he accepts my advice, I know he will have a well-paying job, and he will have the opportunity to serve the public good as a citizen. I thought about the conversation and shuddered to think what would have happened to this student if he had been in a more academically oriented program. I also thought the student probably would have been better off going to some more vocationally oriented postsecondary program in the first place. The fact that an alternative school program could not direct this student into an educational path more suited to his abilities, and probably interests, is a testimony to the power of higher education, even for those who should know better. Finally, I thought about the criticism that my advising would receive by those in higher education and elsewhere who push the self-serving myth that you "can be anything you want to be." This myth is another way of saying "go to college." "Be all that you can be," is a much more humane slogan even though it is the recruiting slogan of the U.S. military.

The content of the curriculum taught in secondary schools does enough damage in alienating students from the educational process, but the methods of testing make matters worse. Encouraged, if not demanded, by the higher education establishment, standardized tests and particularly the SAT and ACT have an additional negative effect on stimulating people to put a place in their hearts for the public good. They reward students who can figure out, for example, how a paddle is to a canoe as an engine is to a car. Why would we expect to have a ready supply of high-quality carpenters, child care workers, or even caring professors, if such exercises in intellectual gymnastics are considered by the authorities in our society to be a measure of an individual's academic potential?

Standardized multiple-choice tests strip individuals of their self-confidence if they perform poorly and heighten their anxiety if they do well. Multiple-choice test scores have a finality and an importance far beyond their validity. Low-achieving students believe that they are less capable of pursuing a rewarding career, when in effect the tests are only measuring in a limited way how well the students will do in jumping through hoops presented by college professors. Unfortunately these students are not aware that these educational goals are themselves not directed at helping students succeed in most careers. High-achieving students become more individualistic and more competitive, since the scores are normed and they know their connection to reality is attenuated.

The overall impact of higher educational institutions on K–12 education has been devastating. With the help of aggressive and competitive parents in a foolishly free society, K–12 schooling alienates students not just from educational institutions but from all institutions in our society. It creates an artificial demand for college by promoting the myth that the only way to economic success for all is through college. Teachers and guidance counselors, who know better, are afraid to tell Johnny's parents that Johnny should pursue a career in auto mechanics because the parents have been sold a bill of goods about college. It does not help that our school administrators keep using "percentage of graduates going to college" as the primary measure of success to gain political support.

A Failed Promise

Institutions of higher education ask us to contribute huge sums of money from both private and public sources, and they have helped to create a K–12 system that convinces virtually all graduates that college is good for their future careers. In making and generating such demands on our society, they promise to help people reach fulfillment as individuals, workers, and citizens, and to improve society. Unfortunately, the promise is only partially kept.

To some extent, the goods are delivered with respect to economic and career development. Higher educational institutions promote economic development through basic research and an environment for the wildest imaginable experimentation. College graduates make more money than high school graduates, and those with graduate or professional degrees make more money than those without them.

However, economic development and career goods are only partially delivered and at an unnecessarily high monetary and emotional cost. Few companies have use for university-based research, and almost all complain bitterly about the poor preparation of college graduates as future workers. Colleges and universities lure students into their seats by promising career preparation. They then pull a bait-and-switch tactic by providing too much education that is at best recreational and at worst not even fun, and too little development of the skills and attitudes necessary to succeed in the workplace. The degree to which the career interests of students are met varies from program to program but is much less than it should be.

The reason institutions of higher education only partially deliver the economic goods to their students is that the goals of the liberal arts faculty, for the most part, have to do more with professional interests in narrowly defined areas of expertise than with what the students want and think they are about to learn. Too many faculty members love their subjects and their artifacts more than their students, and in doing so, are the primary source of the devastation higher education brings to our society.

Undergraduates, and even many graduate students, frequently are faced with a curriculum and a faculty that have only marginal relevance to the students' career development. This is particularly true for liberal arts students and for elementary and secondary division students in undergraduate professional school programs who are forced to fill their freshman and sophomore years with liberal arts requirements. Colleges require freshman and sophomore course work that rarely connects to future careers and creates a set of hurdles that appear to most students, many faculty members, and other observers to lack credibility. The effect is to alienate students at the outset of their college careers who, for reasons of sanity, come to the conclusion that the only thing that makes sense is to get high grades and, as Mark Twain said, not to let schooling get in the way of their learning.

Faculty members insist on bringing the insights of their disciplines to introductory courses rather than teaching what may be useful to nonspecialists. They spend more course time introducing their students to the specialized jargon of their disciplines than in making application to the students' experiences. When professors define themselves in an introductory public issues course as professors and not citizens, or when a course in medieval religion is justified as part of the freshman core, we know we have a very big problem.

Professors provide these overspecialized courses not because they are irrational or incompetent, but because their educational goal is to mold the students into copies of themselves. They seek to convert them into little sociologists, physicists, education professors, organizational theorists, scholars of antiquity, or game theory devotees. Since 99.5 percent of their students will never be professional scholars, the primary educational goal of too many college faculty members is inappropriate. The justification may be that the search for a future Nobel prize scientist or president of the American Economic Association requires a competitive process in which the vast majority fail, and that life is unfair. However, the real motivation could be to ultimately have the pleasure that one's student made it "big time."

Undergraduate programs become, for the majority of students, a series of credits to be amassed as efficiently as possible. Because the faculty emphasizes theory and specialized bodies of writings and then grades using multiple-choice tests or occasional essay tests, students do not become engaged in the educational process. Evidence of this disengagement is demonstrated by low class attendance, the pervasive search for the easiest of courses, frequent instances of plagiarism, and a college dropout rate of 50 percent. Whether students stay the course or drop out, the consequence of this disengagement is to convince them that the only thing that counts is one's self-interest.

The problem is not just that the students' primary goals are out of sync with the goals of their instructors but also that their instructors are acting in a way that is contrary to what was promised. Attempts to justify this specialized education on the grounds that "students are learning how to think" is a smoke screen that most students do not buy. Coerced to work through the large number of specialized courses, students go into automatic pilot by maximizing their grades while minimizing their effort.

Our institutions of higher education are teaching their students to pursue their own self-interest at the expense of the public good. The lack of fit between what is promised by institutions of higher education and what is delivered drives home the lesson students have already brought with them— that college, like high school, is a place for getting credentials as efficiently as possible, not a place for relevant learning. By failing to deliver on a promise that costs students and their parents dearly, students are learning the lesson that looking out for number one is the only rational course.

Students learn the same lesson by observing the self-serving behavior of faculty. To provide one pervasive example, most universities and colleges have distribution requirements for elementary and secondary division students. Students are required to take an uncoordinated smattering of the physical sciences, the social sciences, and the humanities in their initial years. The official reason for these requirements is that students need to have a well-rounded education—to be a little bit like a Renaissance person. However, the information explosion makes that goal out of reach even for the most learned students. In fact, most professors will admit that they do not really know very much about their own entire disciplines, let alone the range of subjects covered in most liberal arts cores. It could be argued that the real reason for the distribution requirement is that faculty members want to have enough enrollment to keep their departments afloat. If this is the case, then while the requirements are justified on broad educational grounds, they are shaped by the narrow self-interest of faculty. Core requirements can thus provide an immediate and powerful lesson to undergraduates of how the self-interest of the faculty betrays them and the public good.

If the collective behavior of faculty members in establishing curriculum requirements sends the message that they are more concerned with market share than with student learning, and therefore serves as a role model for the foolishly free, the individual behavior of some does so even more. Faculty members who do not keep office hours, who teach whatever they feel like teaching, who can't wait to get to their computers or their labs, who would prefer to talk with the few colleagues they can stand rather than with students, who complain about being overworked and brag about meetings in Vienna, and who have almost nothing of use to say about the careers of their students, teach by example of what it is to sacrifice the public good for their own self-interest. This negative model is reinforced when those faculty members who spend time with students, who teach what students need to know for their careers or their own interest, and who work in the community are denied tenure for not publishing enough.

College faculty members are failing many of their students by providing an education inappropriate to their students' needs and by pursuing their own self-interest at a cost to their students, to their institutions, and to society. The failed promise not only provides bad services at outrageous costs; it also sets an example of how to use the veneer of the public good to gain individually at great expense to society.

Institutions of higher education make the claim that they are supporting the good and the beautiful in society through the generation of knowledge, the education of students, and the service rendered to the community. However, the reality the students see is much different, and the gap between the reality and the promise leads to a cynicism that breeds a greedy and apathetic citizenry.

Why Higher Education Is Against the Public Good

How can our institutions of higher education play a more positive role in developing citizens who care for the public good? The movement to incorporate more community-based learning in the college experience is one answer. The idea behind community-based learning is that students will be able to work in the community to ground their classroom education and at the same time build positive attitudes toward working for the public good. However, the heralding of such a movement as a major breakthrough illustrates the existence of the problem in the first place. Moreover, the movement is supported more by administrators and marginal faculty than by the bulk of liberal arts faculty, who behind closed doors dismiss the movement as a fad and, in any case, peripheral to academic requirements. These answers and others, like courses focused on citizenship, do not address the core source of the problem—the attitudes of faculty.

The key to developing a group of future citizens who temper their self-interest by a concern for society is in changing the faculty. College faculty members set the standards that determine what students learn from kindergarten through graduate school. They are the key to finding a solution because they are a primary source of the problem.

Leaders of the American Association of Higher Education (AAHE) recognized the centrality of the faculty on the question of the public good when they called a conference in 1994 to discuss why there is a lack of "professorial civic virtue." This phrasing is an elegant way of saying that professors are as self-serving as the most narrow-minded and selfish individuals in our society. The AAHE organizers were primarily motivated by the need to encourage professors to be better citizens for their home institutions, but they also recognized the need for professors to be better citizens to their local communities, their country, the world, and their students.

Faculty members behave in a self-serving way because the process through which they became faculty made them that way. First, they are the winners in an education system that values competition for grades rather than learning and caring. Second, they were recruited by people looking for copies of themselves. Third, as if the process leading up to their entering graduate school were not enough, getting a Ph.D. degree is all too frequently a nightmarish exercise in petty academic politics among warring faculty that creates a cynical perspective. Fourth, the Ph.D. program attracts and trains people who are so enamored of abstraction and specialization that they cannot (or will not) help students make a connection to the real world. Ph.D. training values research far above all else and appeals to those who find the search for truth and beauty addictive. The obstacle course itself tests candidates to see if they cherish the value of discovery and creativity no matter what the costs to society and even their home institutions.

The socialization process against the public good does not end after graduate school. It continues throughout the professional life of the faculty as they search for self-validation and bigger salaries. To publish in a scholarly journal, one needs other scholars to say that the manuscript is worth publishing. With the search for psychic stability tied to collegial approval, and both tied into cash and job guarantees, faculty members see little point in working for the good of society or even of the institution that pays their bills.

The process also creates an "abstract-bound" faculty, a condition analogous to muscle-bound. Although the people in those muscle-bound bodies look strong, they might not be. Body builders seek muscles, and professors seek abstraction because the successful quest is inherently valuable. In many areas of the academy, not just in the physical sciences, but even in home economics, the drive for general explanatory theory and elegant but parsimonious concepts is done for its own sake as a path to self-validation and job promotion.

The emphasis on abstraction may have a serious selection effect because it rewards those good in abstraction, who may not be so good in taking care of their community. With their eyes on the big picture and the high end, they may fail to focus on the next step to take and what seems to them to be the mundane. They are good at rushing to the top of the ladder, regardless of who is, or should be, in front of them. They are an impatient lot, wanting to be efficient not only in their theories but also in their solutions. Consequently, they may have a special predisposition toward foolish freedom and away from the public good.

The hypothesis presented in the preceding paragraphs is pure conjecture. I know of no empirical studies showing the link between the nature of our undergraduate education and the emergence of an elite that cares too much about itself and not enough about the public good. But we do know we have such an elite today, and most of them are college graduates. The hypothesis may even be worthy of research and perhaps even National Science Foundation funding, but hopefully not of a new journal, interdisciplinary or otherwise.

Making Higher Education Serve the Public Good

In any case, my thesis is that for higher education to change its direction, we need to change faculty members so that they take their share of responsibility for what American society has become. I have listed several strategic steps, all with the single purpose of giving a wake-up call to faculty.

First, we need to stop referring to college and university education as "higher" education. Let me ask the question, higher than what? The term *higher* has an unfortunate connotation implying that faculty members engage in an educational activity that is better than other educational activities. As long as colleges and universities send the message that what they do is more godlike than say, trade schools, professors will have a tough time seeing themselves as servants to students or society and realizing that scholarship without purpose other than peer praise is scholasticism.

The term *higher education* also fails to make clear that professors are in a service industry. Faculty members rail against the idea of students as clients, although they have no difficulty using the market metaphor when arguing for a raise. They rarely introduce themselves as teachers or see themselves as public servants. As long as they deny the reality that they are in the business of preparing students at the undergraduate level to succeed in their careers and as citizens, they will be forced to live with a dissonance that estranges them from their students. Until faculty members accept the reality that they are serving others, civic virtue will be limited to serving their own special academic subdisciplines. They will delude themselves into thinking they are serving the public good by pursuing their own collective specialized scholarship. They may think there is some "invisible hand" piecing together all the fragments of scholarship into something of use to society. They would know better if they themselves were not so enamored of the beauty of the abstraction or, in this case, of a metaphor that has done as much harm as good in the evolution of society.

Second, we need to change the influence and orientation of liberal arts faculty. Faculty members in liberal arts colleges control the curriculum of higher education far beyond their numbers and relevance. Although they seem to have somehow cornered the symbolic market on citizenship, they are less likely than faculty from most professional schools to exercise the civic virtue that they supposedly learned from their classical education. They are more likely to have bad attitudes about colleagues in other schools and to treat students like a group of potential protégés who will mostly fail to achieve their standards of academic excellence. Their attitude toward curriculum is shaped by protecting their market share rather than by the needs of their students.

Liberal arts faculty members need to take seriously their own belief that liberal arts develop the ability of students to think and discuss a variety of subjects intelligently, as well as to care about society. They need to stop pretending to do so by offering students specialized training in their disciplines and justifying it on the grounds that they are teaching how to think. If they could do that, they would help students develop a broad perspective and a wide range of skills applicable to the real world. They could teach most of their undergraduate courses as concerned citizens helping to bring their scholarly perspectives to real-world problems rather than as professional scholars trying to procreate. To the extent that they refuse to step out of the role of professional scholar in their undergraduate classrooms, they are relinquishing their claim to the true meaning of liberal arts. If they persist in the primary undergraduate teaching goal of creating scholars in their own image, they need to be replaced by faculty who want to help their students understand the world around them. Finally, they need to recognize that much of true liberal arts teaching is going on in courses in the professional schools, and by giving liberal arts core credit to selected professional courses. For example, at Syracuse University, the Newhouse School of Public Communication's introductory course in communications deals with major social conditions and ethical issues, and could easily be justified as part of a general undergraduate education for all students.

Third, we need to replace the Ph.D. degree as the union card of choice for much of the teaching in college. As discussed, Ph.D. programs train their students to value research far above all else. Ph.D. training selects and is selected by those who find the search for truth and beauty addictive. The course of study itself tests candidates beyond civil endurance to see if they cherish the value of discovery and creativity above all else. Unfortunately, it does not test or value the skills of communication, teaching, or citizenship. Ph.D. programs train their candidates to eschew application and to ignore simultaneously the problems of society and the students who pay their salaries.

To remedy the situation, we need to hire faculty who demonstrate a willingness and capability to help prepare undergraduates for successful careers, fulfilling lives, and the responsibilities of citizenship. Chairs and faculty members have to see themselves as creating a learning environment for this purpose, managing a mix of instruction provided by practitioners, community-based learning, and authentic learning options. Our colleges and universities should be staffed with people with knowledge and skill regardless of whether they have completed formal Ph.D. training.

Fourth, we need to replace the term *research* as describing what college faculty do other than teach and provide service with the term *creative development*. Research is considered the most important task of higher education. Unfortunately, the term has been captured by the physical scientists. For reasons having to do with history and triumph of technology, the scientific model of theory building and peer evaluation became the norm for research in almost all fields. The prestige of scientific research led to the academic peer review system, which has created excesses such as people teaching journalism who have no experience as journalists, and Ph.D.s in business who only know about linear and nonlinear programming. Because research is evaluated by the number of publications in peer review journals, generations of scholars have been created who can only be understood by their closest intellectual buddies.

A recent development to redefine the meaning of scholarship shows the widespread understanding that something needs to be done to get professors to see beyond this narrow definition of research. In *Scholarship Reconsidered: Priorities of the Professoriate* (1991) Ernest Boyer argued that scholarship has become too narrowly defined as meaning research or, as he called it, the scholarship of discovery. He called for two other kinds of scholarship: integration, which is finding relationships among disciplines, and teaching, which is self-explanatory. The strange use of the phrase "scholarship of teaching" can only be understood as an attempt to boost the prestige of teaching among the professors who think traditional research is of the highest value. The attempt is clumsy, but given the power of the almighty "s" word, it could have some impact.

However, the semantic trick is too indirect to produce the kind of revolution we need if faculty are to serve the public good. We need to use a term like *creative development,* which has the benefit of including faculty outside of the liberal arts, many of whom produce things and do things other than publish research. Painting a beautiful picture should help someone in visual arts get a raise, just as developing a new manufacturing process that is actually used in the real world ought to help an industrial engineer get tenure. We don't want to reward all real-world activity, but we do want to reward those activities that improve society.

We also need to weigh more traditional research publications differently. Instead of relying on peer review academic procedures, we need to explicitly include considerations of the size and nature of the readership. For example, an article in *Foreign Affairs,* a journal read by foreign policy elites as well as academics, should be weighted much more than an article in the flagship journal of the American Political Science Association, *American Political Science Review*. Readers of the former are more numerous and more powerful than readers of the latter. If college faculty outside the physical sciences and other highly technical fields stopped writing only for their small coteries of former professors and graduate students, they would be writing more interesting and useful articles, and at the same time finding themselves able to communicate more easily with their students about their own research.

Fifth, we need to encourage the community-based learning movement at the college level. Courses that include fieldwork will help to reengage students in the educational process, in part because faculty will need to constrain their drive for abstraction in order to engage in the messiness of the real world. Most colleges and universities already encourage students to volunteer in their local communities and to take courses that require community experience. Institutions like the University of Pennsylvania and Brown as well as my own, Syracuse University, are working to increase the scope and depth of these activities. Campus Compact is a nationwide organization of more than five hundred colleges and universities that was started in 1985 by the presidents of Brown, Georgetown, and Stanford universities to encourage service learning. Although only a very small proportion of faculty supports these efforts, the movement is growing in importance among the students themselves. However, learning outside the classroom has to become more central to all college programs if the movement is to have the desired effect of enhancing the willingness of students to serve the public good.

Sixth, we need to support the use of standards and measures in the college admissions process that values things in addition to academic performance. A careful study of each applicant's goals and attitudes with respect to the public good needs to be used in admissions decisions and the change in standards needs to be publicized. The admissions offices also need to have more influence on the behavior of the faculty. With more competition for students in all but the very prestigious designer-label schools, admissions could have some leverage, just as marketing has on production in any business organization.

Admissions officers are ready to use different criteria to admit students if they thought the faculty would buy the practice. In an informal telephone survey conducted under my direction by a freshman honors class, twelve admissions officers in public and private colleges were asked to comment on the value of high school educational programs that required portfolio assessment and research projects for community agencies. Most of the twelve respondents said that this type of work would not be highly valued in admissions decisions because it would not provide a good predictor of success in college, but they offered the opinion that it would be good job preparation for the students. They stated in their open-ended comments that such educational experiences would be more highly valued if college faculty were doing what they should be doing.

These far-reaching suggestions point the way to some midcourse changes that could have beneficial impact on changing the current, de facto role of colleges and universities in creating generations of those not willing to limit their freedom for the good of society. Fortunately, considerable discussion within academia on these issues is now under way. The high cost of college education, the demand by parents and students for more value, an enrollment downturn, and a string of highly critical books and newspaper articles, such as Charles Sykes' *Profscam* (1988) and Richard M. Huber's *How Professors Play the Cat Guarding the Cream* (1992) sent a major wake-up call. These muckraking books are supported in a less strident way by the writings of prominent college presidents like Derek Bok (1986). My institution, Syracuse University, has received several awards for outstanding development in bringing undergraduate education closer to the needs of our students and society, and there is change everywhere.

However, these changes are fragile because most faculty members have yet to buy into them. Some think the pressures will go away, while others lament that the good old days of the "gentleman scholar" will never return. We have reason to have some optimism because we are headed in the right direction, but the odds against a thorough and enduring transformation are imposing.

For the Public Good

This chapter has argued that institutions of higher education have done a great deal of damage to the public good. They have reinforced the competitiveness and lack of compassion associated with the individualism that defines this country. They have reinforced foolish freedom rather than helped support attitudes and behaviors that harness the power of each individual to support the public good. Their faculty have acted, much like our politicians and our citizens, to serve themselves too much and the public good too little. They need to appreciate that the privilege of having a job at a college or university carries a major responsibility to serve society. Faculty have become an increasingly important secular priesthood whose influence stretches from kindergarten to the halls of Congress, and they need to lead their flocks in the direction of the public good, not foolish freedom.

Note

I would like to thank Evans Clinchy for encouraging me to write this chapter; Stephanie Pasquale for her time-consuming work and her insight in helping me develop my arguments; Joanna Grossman and Natalie Nodecker for editorial assistance; Margaret H. Hill, of the Institute for Higher Education Policy, and Christopher Walsh for advice on college costs; Rosaria Champaigne, Cindy Decorse, Jane Miller, and Melissa Thibedeau for their thoughtful comments on earlier drafts; and Janet Brieaddy for copyediting, proofreading, and preparing the final manuscript.

References

Bok, D. 1986. *Higher Learning*. Cambridge, Mass.: Harvard University Press.

Boyer, E. L. 1991. *Scholarship Reconsidered: Priorities of the Professoriate*. Princeton, N.J.: Carnegie Foundation for the Advancement of Teaching.

Clinchy, E. 1994. "Higher Education: The Albatross Around the Neck of Our Public Schools." *Phi Delta Kappan* 75, no. 1D(June): 745–51.

Comer, J. 1980. *School Power: Implications of an Intervention Project*. New York: Free Press.

Hoyt, K. B. 1996. Career Counseling in the Knowledge Age: Implications for Counselor Change. Unpublished paper, Kansas State University, Manhattan, Kansas.

Huber, R. M. 1992. *How Professors Play the Cat Guarding the Cream: Why We're Paying More and Getting Less in Higher Education*. Fairfax, Va.: George Mason University Press.

Mansnerus, L. 1994. "New Pressures on Vocational Education." *New York Times*, August 7, p. 4.

Sykes, C. 1988. *Profscam: Professors and the Demise of Higher Education*. Washington, D.C.: Regnery Gateway.

TERI. 1995. *College Debt and the American Family*. Boston: The Education Resources Institute; Washington: The Institute for Higher Education Policy.

———. 1996. *Graduating into Debt: The Burdens of Borrowing for Graduate and Professional Students*. Boston: The Education Resources Institute; Washington: The Institute for Higher Education Policy.

United States Bureau of the Census. 1997. *The American Almanac 1996–97: Statistical Abstract of the United States*. Austin, Texas: Hoover Business Press.

6

The Loss of Context and Connection

EVANS CLINCHY

Throughout the entire two-million-year-history of the human genus, and in particular during the last six thousand or so years of the history of the Western world, the education of the vast majority of the human population has *not* been conducted in anything that might be called a school.

Although a few institutions we would call private elementary and secondary schools existed in the earliest civilizations of the Near East, in classical Greece, and Rome, these institutions and, of course, *all* institutions of higher education were reserved for a carefully selected and limited but all-powerful and, with few exceptions, entirely male elite.

This elite was, according to Merlin Donald (1991), "a relatively small percentage of the population of the ancient world, but they wrote all the books, kept all the records, ran the schools, academies and universities, controlled religious observances, wrote the history of the period, interpreted the past, determined fiscal and political policies, regulated trade, produced most of the art and all of the literature and increasingly dominated the social order as a class" (346).

In short, this small group of men ran the show and did just about everything there was to do—except for one thing. They did very little of the actual hard, day-to-day work of the world. They did not produce any goods nor provide any of the workaday services that kept people (including themselves) alive. They did not grow or harvest food, tend the herds, bake the bread, ferment the wine, cook the food, sew the clothing, bear or nurture the young, or maintain the households, and they rarely invented, used, or improved upon the technologies that made their so-called civilized life possible.

71

All of these mundane tasks were performed by the great mass of common folk, the unschooled non-elite, which included virtually all women and both female and male slaves. The nonformal, "unschooled" education of this great bulk of the Western population was limited to and completely conducted *in the context* of the performance of all of those everyday endeavors and everyday social life. It was an educational process based upon and conducted within the great contextual university of the mentorship/apprenticeship system.

That part of the formal, noncontextual educational system we think of today as the world of higher education—our colleges and universities—was solidified by Plato in the civilization of classical Greece. It was Plato who established his Academy, the original Groves of Academe and the precursor of all our later Western academic institutions. He located it not in downtown Athens as an integral part of the business and political life of the agora or marketplace, but out in the pastoral surroundings of the countryside. This was perhaps the first real campus, that piece of land set off by itself and devoted to the cultivation of the mind and the education of a carefully selected, elite group of the male young, relatively free of the distractions of the workaday world. It was also Plato who located reality in the distant and changeless realm of ideas and the ideal rather than in the mundane sphere of actual people and objects, which he considered to be mere shadows on the wall of the world's cave and therefore of far lesser rank and essentially of no value at all.

As the philospher Edward S. Reed puts it,

> The Western philosophical tradition about which we hear so much these days in arguments over so-called "cultural literacy" has been an intellectual force for undermining everyday experience from its beginnings. The great Athenian thinkers promulgated a dichotomy between reality and appearance in order to denigrate everyday experience as mere appearance, and to emphasize that one's experience is never so real as one's thoughts, as even a casual reading of Plato reveals. (1997, 1)

As Gideon Sjoberg sums up this attitude,

> Among the ancient Greeks, as with other traditional urbanized peoples, the scholarly activities of learned men were, with rare exceptions, divorced from everyday, mundane existence. While some individuals in Athens and other cities made observations of the world around them that added to the store of data in astronomy, biology, physics, and other fields, their general attitude toward life was in many cases a positive aversion against increasing knowledge by experiment. In the ordinary affairs of life, they esteemed mental activity far more highly than physical, which they thought unworthy of free-men and fit only for slaves. (1960, 311)

While Plato's Academy itself and many subsequent institutions of higher education have been located out in the country, still others in ancient, medieval, and modern times have been housed in the heart of some of the Western world's largest cities. But even these urban institutions are almost always found within a physical enclave or a series of enclaves isolated from their surrounding urban environment—Oxford, Cambridge, the Sorbonne come to mind here, as do many of our most prestigious American universities such as Harvard, Yale, MIT, Columbia, the Universities of Chicago, Pennsylvania, California at Berkeley, and so on.

Following the model thus established by our institutions of higher education, this same physical disconnection has existed in the past and still exists now for virtually every elementary or secondary school in the United States, urban, suburban, or rural. Each of these schools sits on its own plot of land surrounded, if possible, by playgrounds or playing fields and thus physically cut off from its immediate, everyday surroundings.

The result of this standardized practice at both the elementary and secondary and the higher educational levels has been the conscious and deliberate creation of *educational ghettos,* secluded enclosures inhabited solely by teachers and particular age groups of students with the rest of the world carefully excluded.

But this fact that our educational institutions in the West have traditionally been physically isolated from their surrounding communities is only one manifestation of the even more important fact that they have also traditionally been *intellectually and educationally isolated* from the everyday lives of their students and the larger society.

Indeed, what we see at the beginning in the classic Greek and Roman civilizations and then in Western medieval educational institutions is the separation, *the disconnection,* in the Western world between the life of the mind and the ordinary, everyday life of the larger, nonacademic society. That disconnection from first-hand experience in the real world was in both the ancient world and the Middle Ages embodied first in the fact that admittance to the universities and monasteries was limited to those very few, carefully selected elite male individuals. The vast majority of the populace and the everyday world they lived in were relentlessly shunned.

This elitist disconnection was then further enhanced by the medieval higher education curriculum, which consisted, according to Donald (1991, 311), first of the Trivium, the intensive study of grammar, rhetoric, and logic (the oppositional, confrontational, and highly competitive dialectic). If a student aspired to an advanced degree of master of arts, he advanced to the Quadrivium, comprising the study, again in Latin, of arithmetic, geometry, astronomy, and music.

Coming from and living within these ancient traditions of the Trivium and the Quadrivium, the academically learned elite found themselves most often dealing not with everyday reality but with dryly abstruse topics, many of them having to do with language itself and with recondite theological issues on the order of whether a monotheistic God could logically be embodied in the Christian Trinity.

In the study of what we now think of as the academic disciplines, those medieval scholars of the Trivium and Quadrivium were engaged almost entirely in passing on and reinforcing the established orthodoxies of the past. The scholars determined what the ancients had decided was true; they then organized the lessons and lectures and rendered the verdicts on what the young should learn.

In such fields as medicine and science, the primary activity of the learned scholars appears to our supercilious modern eyes to have been the codifying and dissemination of vast amounts of total misinformation and very dangerous ignorance. In the field of medicine, for instance, the body of medieval "knowledge" upon which the presumed curing of the sick was based did not come from any detailed empirical study of the workings of the human body but from the writings of the ancients, who had not themselves studied an actual human body. The horrors imposed on an unsuspecting populace by medieval "doctors" and "barber-surgeons" unable to free themselves from the pronouncements of Aristotle, Galen, and other ancients—the bleedings, the leeches, the barbaric chopping off of limbs, the innocent unleashing of pestilence and plague—are almost too sickening to contemplate.

This disconnection from the everyday world was sealed and made irrevocable by the fact that during and well beyond the medieval period all university- and monastery-based learning and education were conducted in— and all books were written in—Latin, a language that the common folk of the day could not understand and to which they had no access.

Thus throughout the European continent the populace spoke not Latin but the vernacular, which meant the local native languages. At the same time the learned were engaged in an enterprise characterized by what the historian Daniel J. Boorstin (1983) has called "a narrow farsightedness. They thought over the heads of their marketplace contemporaries to a special language and literature of far away and long ago" (489).

As Jean Gimpel, a historian of the Middle Ages, describes this situation,

The scorn of men of letters for engineers throughout history has kept them, all too often, oblivious to the technology created by those engineers, who were of lower social status and worked to earn their living. They had no idea that in this other world there was an uninterrupted tradition of technological writing. Leonardo da Vinci is a case in point. As an engineer, he was despised by the literati of his time, and they, like the majority of Western intellectuals today, were ignorant of the fact that Leonardo had borrowed a great many of his inventions from technological treatises by engineers of previous generations. (1976, x)

Indeed, says Gimpel,

Leonardo's greatest problems were caused by the contempt in which he was held by the humanists. Having lacked the opportunity of attending a university to study the liberal arts, he had learned no Greek and little Latin. This was to prove a stumbling block in his life. The Renaissance humanists, who were his contemporaries, glorified the great culture of classical antiquity, but to him that culture was largely a closed book. He was probably never accepted in a humanist milieu, where discussions would often be carried on in Latin. . . . Thus time and time again in his writings Leonardo returns to the scorn of the humanists: "Because I am not a literary man, some presumptuous persons will think that they may reasonably blame me by alleging that I am an unlettered man. Foolish men! . . . They will say that because I have no letters I cannot express well what I want to treat of." He questions the right of these literati to judge him. "They go about puffed up and pompous, dressed and decorated with the fruits not of their own labours but those of others, And they will not allow me my own. And if they despise me, an inventor, how much more could they—who are not inventors but trumpeters and declaimers of the works of others—be blamed." (1976, 142–143)

Antonina Valentin in her *Leonardo da Vinci, The Tragic Pursuit of Perfection* (1952) points out, however, that Leonardo perhaps could have received a "better," i.e., a more conventional classical education than he did had he not skipped most of his early schooling classes and spent his time exploring and sketching out in the fields and mountains of the countryside. Nevertheless, she does describe that classical education as one in which

the educated class shut itself off with pitiless arrogance from any contact with the life of the mass of the people. Humanism was a tyrannical intellectual discipline, monopolizing a man's thoughts; it called for a concentration on classical studies from his earliest youth, confining his interests to a single field; and it presupposed his possession of a means of existence during the period of his studies. A handful of largely poor clergy, who owed their success to immense industry backed by the favor of a patron, had a monopoly of knowledge; it was imparted under less than rigorous conditions only to the patrician children, the sons and daughters of the rich. As

Alberti said: "A nobleman by birth who is without education is reputed no more than a peasant." (16)

Meanwhile, that great unlearned populace, although held in almost total intellectual and political thrall by the iron authoritarian rule of their religious, academic, and feudal "betters," continued to keep the earth turning, and gradually and against great odds changed the world they lived in. They were able to do this because those carefully selected members of the higher humanistic intellectual worlds of church, university, monastery, and court studiously did not concern themselves with such mundane topics as mere technology (with the single exception of the Cistercian monastic order, whose members were quite interested in technology and practiced it well). In general, the intellectual elite chose not to control and perhaps rarely understood the powerful threat represented by tool making and the invention of improved methods of producing goods, providing services, and growing food, or what Donald refers to as "pragmatic or opportunistic science and engineering"—the hands-on, empirical knowledge of how the crops were grown and harvested, how the ships were built and sailed, how bridges and buildings were built, how accounting records were kept, and so on.

Had a Dutch spectacle maker named Hans Lippershey not invented the telescope in the early 1600s, for instance, Galileo would not have been able to see the great mass of stars in the Milky Way, the pitted surface of the moon, and the four moons of Jupiter, and thus finally have the evidence to begin the dismantling of the Aristotelian/Ptolemaic universe. Similarly, if Zacharias Jansen had not invented the microscope, Robert Boyle would not have had the information necessary to revolutionize our notions of biological reality. It was homespun inventions such as these that led to and made possible the gradual and perhaps inevitable evolution of the everyday world's "pragmatic or opportunistic science and engineering" into the Scientific Revolution: the scientific and nonmystical universe of Copernicus, Galileo, Kepler, and Newton and the modern science of Lavoisier, Cuvier, Darwin, Wallace, Einstein, and the present investigators of quantum physics, molecular biology, and genetic engineering.

Even so, Edward Reed is not happy with the creators of that Scientific Revolution:

Although Greek philosophy and its offshoots tended to downgrade ordinary experience in the hunt for ideal essences, it took the great scientific revolutionaries of the 1600s to make the destruction of experience a basic tenet of philosophical thinking. First, Galileo insisted that the book of nature was written in the language of mathematics—and therefore that ordinary human experience could not decipher the world's meanings. . . . According to the scientific revolutionaries, all appearances derive from ideas, which in turn derive from the mind's reaction to physical stimulation coming into the nerves. Some thinkers, such as Newton, considered ideas to be little images in the brain. . . . For an ordinary observer to find out about the real world, according to this standard philosophical view, the observer must follow just those special "rules of method" that the new philosophers had put forth. Many of these texts on method are quite dismissive of the problems of daily life. (1997, 3)

It would, however, be quite wrong to assume that the great masses of common folk in medieval and Renaissance times were not being educated because they were unable to take part in the Latin and mathematics of the formal schools and universities. There was, first, that quite elaborate, all-encompassing contextual university set up and run by the medieval craft guilds—the apprenticeship system that became the standard in every walk of common life. But there was also the experiential university of everyday agricultural and commercial life and its nonformal educational system, beginning with what Gimpel calls the first Industrial Revolution in the Middle Ages, from which the great and transforming inventions began to come—the mechanical and social inventions that eventually led to the modern world. These seemingly simple innovations, including the first mechanical clocks and the first elaborate industrial factory systems based on the taming of water and wind power, produced the medieval first Industrial Revolution. But there was also a medieval agricultural revolution, based on such innovations as the introduction of the horse to replace the ox, the shoulder-based horse collar and the horseshoe, the three-field crop-rotation agricultural system, and the heavy, wheeled, iron-tipped plow.

A most important innovation—once again, brought about by humble artisans and craftsmen—was the fifteenth-century invention of movable type, cheap paper, and permanent inks, and thus a higher-speed, less expensive printing process, that ushered in the Renaissance. The dramatic result was the almost immediate translation into the vernacular, and the printing and distribution, of documents that had long been secreted in the libraries of universities, monasteries, and churches.

This last event greatly disturbed the monastic, academic, and ecclesiastical keepers of Western society's closely guarded cultural and religious secrets, for now almost anyone could, at least in theory, have access to the contents of those sacred libraries. Elizabeth Eisenstein describes the effect of the printing revolution on the scholarly medieval world in this fashion:

The closed world of the ancients was opened; vast expanses of space (and later of time) previously associated with divine mysteries became subject to human calculation and exploration. The same cumulative cognitive advance which excited cosmological speculations also led to new concepts of knowledge. The notion of a closed sphere or single corpus, passed down from generation to generation, was replaced by a new idea of an open-ended investigatory process pressing against ever-advancing frontiers. (1993, 259)

She goes on to say,

The communications shift altered the way Western Christians viewed their sacred book and the natural world. It made the words of God appear more multiform and his handiwork more uniform. The printing press laid the basis for both literal fundamentalism and for modern science. It remains indispensable for humanistic scholarship. It is still responsible for our museum without walls. (1993, 275)

As Eisenstein points out, the great example of "pernicious" use—pernicious at least in the eyes of the Roman Catholic Church—of both the new technology of printing and the resulting access to documents previously held in relative secrecy was the vernacular rendering, and the printing and wide distribution, of the Bible. As Martin Luther suggested, if an individual could now know the Word of God directly by reading it in his (and undoubtedly His) native tongue, there was less need for a (corrupt) Church.

Indeed, a close examination of Western historical change from the medieval first Industrial Revolution through the second and third Industrial Revolutions and our most recent history makes it clear that it was *technological innovation* and its economic and social consequences that brought about the great cultural transformations in Western society. Until the advent of World War II and the scientific/military/political alliance that produced our present fourth Industrial Revolution based upon the digital computer and modern communications technology, those crucial inventions that have changed our lives in general emerged *not* from the disconnected scholarly world but rather from the everyday life of the workaday world.

The men and women who created the second Industrial Revolution, based upon the introduction of steam power and the use of coal as a fuel— the financiers and entrepreneurs who created modern capitalism, the artisans and craftspeople who invented the machines—were not for the most part university-educated scholars. The products of the third Industrial Revolution based upon the internal combustion engine and electric power fueled by oil—Nikolas Otto's engine, Henry Ford's mass production automobile, the Wright Brothers' airplane, Edison's incandescent bulb, the movie camera and the phonograph, Tesla's alternating current electric power system, the radio of Marconi, DeForest, and Armstrong—were invented by extraordinary tinkerers rather than by learned university savants.

The Disconnection Continues

Given this long history of scholarly disconnection from the world of everyday work and technology, we should then perhaps not be surprised if our present colleges and universities still exhibit these same patterns of physical and intellectual insularity. As Ira Harkavy and John Puckett (1990) point out, some of the most prestigious U.S. institutions of higher education are located in distressed inner cities but maintain themselves as "islands of affluence in a sea of despair" (1). And others are located on bucolic campuses far from the workaday world.

One Great Missed Opportunity

This overpoweringly self-centered continuing reluctance of our practitioners of higher education to connect with the larger society was painfully brought home to me through a sad but highly instructive experience that came my way in the early 1970s when I was asked to assist the Board of Regents of the University of Massachusetts to determine where in the Boston area the university's then embryonic urban branch should be located. This brand-new institution was intended to be a full-fledged component of the university, the complete urban equivalent of the school's main rural residential campus in Amherst. UMass-Boston was to be a nonresidential university, drawing its student body of young people and working adults from all over Greater Boston, people who would commute to school via the eastern Massachusetts (and Boston) public transportation system. This urban component was already underway when I came on board and was housed in a former gas company building in the downtown heart of the city, just a block or two from the Boston Common and the Boston Public Garden.

The question that faced the administration of the new university branch, its faculty, and the planners was superficially simple: Where should this new high-powered, distinctly and deliberately *urban* public institution of higher education be physically located? But, of course, it was a far from simple question, since it involved not only decisions about how and where millions of dollars of state money were to be spent but, most fundamentally, what the form and function of an urban public university should be.

Just about everyone involved, including the professional planners like me, agreed that there were only two feasible philosophical/educational directions in which the new university could move. One was to follow the normal pattern of creating a self-contained, Platonic campus in or near Boston. The other was to abandon the Groves of Academe model and to adopt and carry to its intellectual and educational conclusion the premise that an urban university should be deeply and intimately involved in the life and fortunes of the city and the society of which it is a part.

If we were to follow the first path of creating a self-contained campus for the new university, there was only one piece of vacant land in the Boston area that was large enough to house such a campus and that happened to be relatively uninhabited and therefore available. This was a peninsula called Columbia Point, a piece of land jutting out into Boston harbor and almost completely cut off from the rest of Boston by the harbor waters, by acres of unattractive industrial land, and by major local and interstate highways. In addition to being physically cut off from access by foot or car, the proposed site was nowhere near a stop on the mass transit system (though it is now somewhat improved). Thus, a journey from anywhere in or around Boston to the outer reaches of Columbia Point would be extremely difficult and inconvenient.

But access was not the only problem. The Columbia Point peninsula had been in Boston's early days the site of the city's chief dump, a huge landfill that even to this day has not fully compacted and still has ancient fires smoldering in its depths. Consequently, the surface level of the land is sinking at a rate of several inches every decade.

But Columbia Point was not completely uninhabited at the time of the UMass location debate. In the early days of the nation's disastrous post–World War II public housing ventures, the city and the state had built on the inner part of Columbia Point a public housing project, which over the years had became a typical public housing ghetto of low-income, welfare, and largely African-American and other minority people. It was an area of high crime, drugs, and personal despair for its inhabitants. One of the reasons advanced for locating the university there was the possibility of its serving as a catalyst for upgrading and improving the life of the Point's inhabitants.

The second possible direction for locating the university was precisely the reverse of the first—that the entire design of the new institution, not only its bricks and mortar but its entire educational program, would be based upon the idea of reciprocal, collaborative arrangements between the university and all of the political, cultural, artistic, economic, and social institutions and life of metropolitan Boston. This would be manifested by the university's physical facilities being planned and built as an integral part of the general redevelopment of downtown Boston, which was progressing at full speed in those days. All or most of the university facilities would be "joint occupancies," that is, they would be collaboratively built and their use shared with their appropriate counterparts in the public and private sectors of Greater Boston.

For us advocates, the plan embodied not the idea of the medieval European university but that expressed by Benjamin Franklin in his founding of the University of Pennsylvania, that the purpose of any American university should be "the development and application of knowledge to improve human welfare." This aim, said Franklin, should be accomplished through an integrated threefold educational program of research, teaching, *and community service.* Our contribution to this original purpose was simply adding the reciprocal arrangement that this could be an enterprise in which the nonuniversity world joined with the university in the development and application of such knowledge.

What this meant in terms of the physical planning of the university was that the performing arts facilities would be built as an integral part of the revival of the city's theater district; the business and economic sections of the university would jointly construct and operate buildings with the business and economic sectors (banks, the financial sector, the Federal Reserve Bank); the historical and cultural parts of the university would be jointly planned and operated with the city's and the state's rich historical and cultural institutions; the sciences would share space and programs with the emerging high tech industry and with the city and state efforts at environmental control (the massive task of cleaning up Boston harbor, for instance); and so on.

One of the most important parts of this reciprocal "community service" arrangement was to be a very close working relationship with the Boston public schools. I had just finished four years of serving as the school system's chief of research, development, and experimental schools, so I was determined that the new university and the public school system would at all times work closely together. This would be a joint task: creating a wide variety of different kinds of public schools; crafting a systemwide school desegregation and school improvement plan; collaboratively educating future school teachers and college faculty; participating jointly in research in human cognition and human development; and so on.

All of these joint arrangements, not just in the field of education but in all other fields, would be truly collaborative. Courses would be designed and taught by university and nonuniversity people to undergraduates, graduate students, and working adults in both the private and public sectors. These formal educational experiences and all other educational activities could take place either in the university's spaces or in the contextual nonuniversity world, or preferably both. We foresaw, for instance, that university faculty, graduate students, and undergraduates in the university's school of education would spend a large part of their time working and studying in the real world of the public school system, and that the working stiffs out in the school system would be serving as part-time university faculty.

We advocates of a downtown university thus envisioned a campus spread throughout the central city, with the public transportation system serving as the network to link the pieces of the university together. For its renewal and revitalization, the city would gain a major partner that brought not only the brainpower and energy of the academic community but the millions of dollars (and thousands of jobs) the state was planning to invest in the physical facilities and the expanded personnel of the university.

The heated discussions about where to locate the new university raged back and forth for well over a year among the faculty, the Board of Regents, and the city as a whole. The action very soon devolved into a clash between two distinct camps—downtown Boston versus Columbia Point. The downtown faction, led by the chancellor of UMass-Boston, had many vigorous faculty proponents as well as the support of us planners and of the Boston Redevelopment Authority, Mayor Kevin White, and much of the downtown business and cultural communities.

This seemingly radical notion of a dispersed downtown campus, however, caused great concern on the part of many members of the university's faculty and some members of the university's board of trustees. They simply had great difficulty envisioning how such a proposal could work and feared that the collegial scholarly atmosphere and the lines of communication available on a unitary, self-contained campus would be destroyed. We tried to quiet these apprehensions by developing a map superimposing the proposed Boston campus on the university's huge existing campus at Amherst, showing that the distances between facilities were much greater at the rural Amherst campus than they would be if dispersed throughout downtown Boston.

All in all, it seemed to us downtown advocates that our plan had a great deal going for it. But in the end, we could not persuade the majority of the university's faculty, the Board of Regents, and the university's central administration in Amherst that it would work. So the board voted to put UMass-Boston into a single megastructure campus on Columbia Point. Before construction of the huge building could begin, the largest and costliest pile-driving operation in the nation's history had to be accomplished to support the building so that it would not eventually sink out of sight into the landfill below it. As it is, the ground is now gradually sinking away from the university's building at the rate of two to three inches per decade.

So, once again, a major, supposedly urban institution of higher education is operating within its disconnected academic ghetto, cut off from the life of the urban community it was supposed to serve.

It would be quite wrong, however, to say that UMass-Boston has had *no* effects on the life of the urban area it calls home. The university's presence on Columbia Point *has* been the catalyst for transforming the old Columbia Point housing project into an attractive mixed-income community. And the university's College of Public and Community Service has a long record of admitting low-income and minority students not on the basis of their academic records but by giving academic credit for life experiences. It also conducts community-based research. Indeed, it was this college and its faculty who fought hardest for the university to be built downtown and to stay in the gas company building. But eventually it, too, had to move to Columbia Point. Further, the university houses the New England Resource Center for Higher Education, headed by sociologist Zelda Gamson, which has become one of the nation's leaders in advocating many of the reforms of higher education set forth in this book.

These, then, have been the university's primary contributions to the life of its home city. But in general, the university and its school of education have over the past twenty-five years had little impact on the city of Boston itself or on the city's public schools, even including the two Boston public schools that are located on Columbia Point.

One Triumph for Higher Education

If our institutions of higher education have in all these ways and all too often divorced themselves from the world around them, there is one area in which the learned academics of the college and university world have since medieval times continued to exert their pervasive control—the highly academic, disconnected system of elementary and secondary education we in the West developed for and imposed upon our children and young people.

Both the detached intellectual content of the formal academic curriculum and the authoritarian, disconnected information transmission pedagogical process we instituted in our elementary and secondary schools were conceived by the academic, disciplinary elites of the world of higher education.

Early in this century, this strictly academic curriculum and its medieval practice of scholarly information transmission were wedded to the equally disconnected and thoroughly mechanical practices of the "scientific" industrial management engineers, thus yielding the Great American Academic and Social Sorting Factory School System we still labor under and are now spasmodically and haltingly trying to change.

This detached, academically determined, and unremittingly authoritarian instructional approach to the education of the young is a mental model of education that, like the medieval academic war games of the dialectic, is very much based upon the idea of competition. For our modern students, such competition begins in kindergarten and culminates for those who make it through high school in the final academic cleansing on the killing fields of the SATs and the College Boards. But those are, of course, simply the end game of a scholastic sorting and elimination process that seeks to determine every child's place in later life and requires that the bulk of the population be excluded from the Groves of Higher Academe.

This intellectually autocratic, thoroughly undemocratic situation will continue as long as our institutions of higher education insist upon using as the primary admissions tool a student's success or failure on standardized, strictly academic, paper-and-pencil SAT and College Board tests and such numerical fabrications as grade point averages and rank in class. As long as they determine access to higher education and its social and financial rewards in this detached, authoritarian fashion, our colleges and universities will be able to keep all of our elementary and secondary schools in thrall to their disconnected, decontextualized educational mission.

The questionable effects of this continuing control of the higher academy over our system of elementary and secondary schooling can perhaps best be illustrated by the results of comparative studies of the in-school and out-of-school lives of children and young people that have been conducted by many prominent developmental psychologists and anthropologists.

According to the developmental psychologist Howard Gardner (1982), these researchers have discovered that children's education outside of school walls (and particularly in those societies that do not have formal schooling) occurs almost exclusively in the context in which the training will be used: "Children acquire skills through observation and participation in the natural context in which the skills are used. First they watch adults weave or hunt; later they participate as helpers; and eventually they assume the key role themselves. There is little talk, little formal teaching: learning comes from doing" (448).

And, as many researchers have noted, children in our own society up to the age of five also learn contextually and informally through their own direct, first-hand experiences, simply by living in a family and learning from whatever adults and older children happen to be around. This includes the rapid acquisition of spoken language, the minimal rules of acceptable and unacceptable behavior, how to dress themselves, and so on.

They do all this, for the most part, with little formal instruction on the part of adults. No unhandicapped child ever goes to a school to be given formal lessons or to take a course on how to speak his or her native tongue. They learn these things in an easy and natural manner simply because they intrinsically *want* to learn them. Indeed, it appears that they are in some mysterious way genetically *impelled* to learn them. They want to—or have to—become as competent, as grown-up, and as effective as the older children and adults they see around them.

Indeed, it has often been argued that children and young people learn most of what they will find useful in later life not in school but in their out-of-school lives. This greatly useful knowledge includes not only such things as the rapid acquisition of language but the basic skills of getting along with other people, the fundamental economic rules of supply and demand as practiced in the home and the neighborhood, and at least the rudiments of the great social principle of reciprocity, the fact that the survival of any human society depends upon the cooperation and collaboration of the individuals making up that society. The local stickball game out in the streets or the sand-lot baseball game in these instances can be the very best kind of "school."

Upon entering the typical public school and the sphere of formal school learning, children face a totally different situation. Children who have been learning contextually are suddenly confronted with a world in which they are asked to learn little from their own direct, first-hand experience in a natural context. Instead of pursuing their own innate curiosities and following their natural bents, they are now required to learn what *other people* (teachers and the school) tell them they should learn whether the children see any clear and natural reason for doing so or not.

And they are asked to learn all these things out of context, in that artificial invention called a classroom and through the mediating second- and third-hand instructional experience of words and symbols in books, or words and symbols conveyed by teachers, rather than through their own direct, first-hand experience.

Gardner (1982) describes this world of formal schooling in the following fashion: "For better or worse, the standard classroom is entirely different [from learning outside of school]. There is scarce opportunity for active participation. The teacher talks, often presenting material in abstract, symbolic forms or relying on inanimate sources such as books and diagrams to convey information" (448).

In two columns in the *New York Times* (Shanker 1988), the late Albert Shanker, then president of the American Federation of Teachers, reported on work done by Lauren Resnick of the Learning Research and Development Center at the University of Pittsburgh and Sue E. Berryman, then the director of the National Center on Education and the Economy at Teachers College, Columbia University.

Resnick, says Shanker, identified four ways in which out-of-context school learning differs from the kind of thinking and learning that occurs in and is required by what we are here calling the real world, that is, the larger society that the 98 percent of our students who will not become academic scholars will be living and working in when they finish school.

First, Resnick says, school learning is mostly done on the student's own, whereas most nonschool learning is shared with others. While there are *some* group activities in school, students are ultimately judged on what they can do by themselves—on individual tests, homework, in-class exercises, and the like.

On the job, in the family, and at play, Resnick points out, we are expected to ask those close to us to show us, explain, and help. The important thing is to get something done right, and usually that means doing it together with others. In school, asking others for help is often called cheating.

A second major difference, according to Resnick, is that school learning consists mostly of "pure thought" activities—what individuals can do without the external support of books, notes, calculators, or other complex instruments. But in most jobs and other situations outside of school, thinking is done with the use of such tools. People more often get the job done with tools than without. "The problem," comments Shanker, "is that schools continue to downgrade the very skills that are most valuable on the work site."

Resnick's third difference is that school knowledge consists of manipulating purely abstract symbols while thinking outside school is always in a specific context. We all know of people who didn't do well in math at school but who can do math quite easily out in the worlds of banking or investment or at the local bowling alley.

Resnick's final point is that school learning is generalized, but the knowledge needed outside of school is specific to given situations. Resnick points to specific differences between school knowledge and the skills learned on the job in a number of fields. For example, she cites a study showing that expert radiologists interpret X-ray images using mental processes different from those taught in medical courses, textbooks, and even hospital teaching rounds. There is mounting evidence, she concludes, that very little can be transported directly from school to out-of-school use.

Shanker goes on to suggest that "the *way* we make students learn in school may undercut their chances of functioning and learning on the job or in social settings—or even in school itself."

He quotes from a speech by Dr. Berryman in which she says that we have in our schools a large number of youngsters—and not just our so-called at-risk young people—"who do not perform well in traditional schools or in training programs arranged like traditional schools."

"We need," says Shanker, "to consider the possibility that . . . many youngsters don't see the point in playing the game of mastering material or skills that are so radically different from what people are doing in the outside world." As Berryman puts it, students who are failing may not be willing "to tolerate or make some sense out of a school-based experience that is relatively isolated from nonschool experiences. . . . From this perspective, traditional schools may be creating their own problems . . . mainly because children see clearly that our schools offer a system of learning so completely at odds with the way people function in the outside world."

Gardner reinforces this point:

> All cognitive abilities exist in all human beings, needing only the proper circumstances or motivation to be elicited. . . . And yet, inflamed in part by the superior rewards given to those who have been to school, a pervasive antagonism often develops between the school's logical, out-of-context knowledge system and that practical participation in daily activities fostered informally by the culture. If this antagonism is to be lessened, schools . . . must be designed and viewed as comfortable and significant environments, rather than *hostile providers of useless knowledge* [emphasis added]. This means that schools must contain everyday life within their walls and must make clear the relation between the skills they teach and the problems children find significant. (1982, 452)

It is this disconnection, this antagonism between what goes on in school and what children and young people know goes on in the world outside school that may well cause so many of our students to find their education in our public schools to be so "boring" and "irrelevant." Indeed, when we put thirty students in an isolated classroom with a teacher who verbally instructs them in the content of an academic discipline, we have managed to divorce education from life. We are essentially asking students, indeed we are teaching them, to be what the educational philosopher Jane Roland Martin terms spectators of life rather than active livers of life, active agents in and of the larger world. This may be one important reason that so many of our students, failing to see how the abstracted, decontextualized activities in school would possibly be of use to them out in that larger world, drop out of school or drop out in school.

The Latest Juggernaut of "Reform"

To underscore the continuing dominance and power of the world of higher education in our public schools, we need only remind ourselves of the U.S. Department of Education's 1983 report *A Nation at Risk* and the Clinton administration's version of that autocratic national education agenda, Goals 2000, the Educate America act, with its eight national educational goals, an agenda now written into national legislation by Congress. Unfortunately, as desirable as at least six of those goals may be, attaining any of them (such as the goal of making sure that all children are "ready to learn" when they enter school) will require spending enormous sums of federal, state, and local money if the physical, social, and intellectual needs of our children—and especially the needs of the one-quarter of our children living in poverty—are even to be minimally met. The clear fact that no political body at any level in this era of outright war against the poor would be willing to invest those large sums in our children renders all those goals essentially pointless and largely irrelevant.

The two goals, however, that involve the setting of "world-class" academic standards in the traditional scholarly disciplines of English, mathematics, history, geography, science, and the arts and foreign languages are alive and well.

The leading scholarly organizations in all of these academic fields, assisted by their colleagues in the elementary and secondary schools, have in good medieval fashion set forth an incomprehensible raft of elaborate and complex "standards" in every curricular subject, passing on and reinforcing all of the established orthodoxies of the past and present. They determine what past and present scholarship has decided is true and then lay out "what *all* students should know and be able to do" in each academic subject grade by grade from kindergarten until every student has graduated from high school.

Thus those traditional academic subject matter compartments and the "high" academic standards accompanying them (even if labeled voluntary) are now in the process of becoming the de facto official national curriculum that all schools will have to institute and follow. These new academic content standards are, of course, accompanied by the creation of a national system of standardized, pencil-and-paper, strictly academic achievement tests to make sure every child and young person measures up to the new "world-class" standards. It would thus appear that our scholarly disciplinarians still believe that *all* students in our public schools are academically inclined in the same fashion as those docile, dutiful, and more or less academically inclined students they select to admit to their sacred groves. This suggests that these scholars are still living in some never-never land of far away and long ago.

Nel Noddings (1992) states the problem most eloquently in her tripartite argument against the current dangerous version of liberal education's "relentless and hapless drive for academic adequacy": "the ideology of control that forces all students to study a particular, narrowly prescribed curriculum devoid of content they might really care about; the need for a greater respect for the wonderful range of human capacities now largely ignored in schools; and the persistent undervaluing of skills, attitudes, and capacities traditionally associated with women" (xii).

It is precisely this "ideology of control" that has over the years kept the principals and teachers in our public schools from becoming truly professional educators. How can they exercise their own intelligence, their own creativity and ingenuity, and their own sense of what the students entrusted to their care need to know and might respond to if they are told at every turn precisely what they must teach and thus precisely what their students are going to be tested on by the scholarly authorities?

And how can our students begin to develop their curiosity and their own intellectual initiative, how can they begin to assume responsibility for their own learning and development, how can they learn to use their minds and especially their critical faculties if at every turn some group of scholarly "experts" is ordering them to study this, remember that, then this, then that, and then take the test on all of it. How, for instance, can we expect them to become active, caring citizens in a fully functioning democratic society if they never experience democracy in the sixteen years of their education?

As Mihaly Csikszentmihalyi, Kevin Rathunde, and Samuel Whalen put it,

The problem with our technologically inspired views of education is that we have come to expect learning to be a function of the rationality of the information provided. In other words, we assume that if the material is well organized and logically presented, students will learn it. Nothing is further from the fact. Students will learn only if they are motivated. The motivation could be extrinsic—the desire to get a well-paying job after graduation—but learning essential to a person's self must be intrinsically rewarding. Unless a person enjoys the pursuit of knowledge, learning will remain a tool to be set aside as soon as it is no longer needed. Therefore we cannot expect our children to become truly educated until we ensure that teachers know not only how to provide information but how to spark the joy of learning. (1993, 195)

Theodore Sizer, the creator of the Essential Schools movement, puts his finger on the precise pressure point here when he worries about the "mindlessness of the world of . . . schooling":

The fact is that there is virtually no federal-level talk about intellectual coherence for [a student]. The curricular suggestions and mandates leave the traditional "subjects" in virtually total isolation, and both the old and most of the new assessment systems blindly continue to tolerate a profound separation of subject matters, accepting them as conventionally defined. Coordination of subjects, much less fundamental reform, appears only at the margins. The mathematics sequences, for example, may make sense to the mathematics teachers who teach them. However [the student] does not address mathematics this way. He must attend simultaneously to science and history and music and more as well as mathematics. The crucial, culminating task for [the student] of *making sense of it all*, at some rigorous standard, is left entirely to him alone. (1992, 2)

Sizer continues,

Why is this so? . . . Federal education policy is shaped powerfully by . . . professional and scholarly associations, organizations whose very design depends on the status quo. They and the university specialties they represent reinforce the fractionalization of the school curriculum and its stuffing with ever more obligations and content. Further, these organizations are usually led by their mandarins, worthy folks but who within their disciplines are the least likely to break with the conventionalities. (3)

One More Era of Massive Nonreform

In all of these senses, then, we have not in our educational practices in the West moved all that far from the educational practices of the medieval world. We may have attempted to extend the process of elementary and secondary vernacular learning to practically everyone, and we may have broadened the content of the academic curriculum beyond what the Trivium and Quadrivium had to offer. We have also replaced the nonformal apprenticeship system with a formal, in-school, and therefore decontextualized "vocational" education system, giving those among us who will remain relatively unlearned a greatly watered-down version of the standard academic curriculum along with some lessons on how to conduct outdated versions of hewing wood and drawing water.

But we have retained the basic intellectual and pedagogical structure of that ancient system. We still assume that the education of the young must be conducted by "those who know" (the scholars in our colleges and universities assisted by a handful of other members of adult society), who decide what is worth learning and therefore what should and must be learned by "all those who don't know" (children, young people, and anyone else who can be labeled as culturally illiterate or just plain ignorant). And, of course, the best and often the only way to do this is by the paternalistic, authoritarian, thoroughly undemocratic (and patently less than successful) "instructional" pedagogies we cannot imagine ourselves *not* using.

All of the criticisms of higher education listed so far, however, pale alongside the questions raised by Alejandro Sanz de Santamaria and William Coplin in previous chapters in this book. These questions deal with the fundamental nature of the scholarly enterprise itself. These are problems that connect with and actually underlie the problems our colleges and universities have functioning as simply *educational* institutions whose structure and pedagogical practices have been and still are being imposed with devastating effects upon the children and young people in our elementary and secondary schools.

Indeed, it is the clear need for the radical reform of our colleges and universities that explains why so many people inhabiting the world of public elementary and secondary education resent so mightily what appears to be the appalling and unmitigated gall of those people in our institutions of higher education who declare themselves to be educational "experts." These are the people who then presume to tell educators in our elementary and high schools and the public at large how badly the public schools are doing in educating our children and who then discourse at great length on how those school people should run the elementary and secondary educational enterprise.

This arrogance is particularly appalling to school people in the case of our colleges and schools of education. The medieval, disconnected structure of these institutions simply will not, cannot, does not allow for any ongoing, healthy interaction with real schools and school systems. The time and energy of the people in those institutions are almost completely used up instructing their own students and conducting their own scholarly research, with no time left for directly working with, learning from, and helping the public schools. Many of the faculty members of these places haven't been in a real school in years. Indeed, in order to make it possible for many of these institutions to have some relevance to and some connection with the real world of the schools, they have to create independently funded nonprofit thinking and technical assistance subsidiaries, such as Sizer's Coalition of Essential Schools and the Institute for Responsive Education, with which I work.

To make matters worse, our colleges and schools of education are the institutions charged with educating the teachers we need in those real schools. Yet, except for a few months of "practice teaching," all too often in suburban schools, those future teachers are taught *about* teaching in precisely the way they were taught *about* everything else in elementary and high school—in classrooms with the teacher up front lecturing or in "discussions" conducted in those disconnected classrooms.

If our teachers are to be adequately educated so that they have some real understanding of what goes on in our public education systems, then they should be educated for the profession not in some disconnected, decontextualized school of education but out in those real schools by veteran teachers, with the assistance, *out in the schools* as and when necessary and useful, of scholars and other faculty from the colleges and universities.

These same qualities of disconnection and decontextualization are also the reason that we need to rethink and replace the incestuous practice of tying state certification for advancement in the teaching and administrative ranks and increases in teacher salaries in most of our school systems to the taking of additional graduate-level courses and getting advanced degrees at our institutions of higher education.

The fact that most teachers and administrators only occasionally find such courses anything but a waste of time and money does not seem to have any effect on this neat little bit of interprofessional logrolling. While this practice does manage to keep the faculty at the colleges and schools of education employed, it unfortunately also serves to protect our school systems from having to develop sensible and relevant ways of assessing professional performance out in the schools for purposes of promotion and salary increases.

And this same problem of disconnection from the real world of the schools applies as well to virtually the entire field of scholarly educational research (see Chapters 4, 5, and 10).

Unless and until we begin to move in the direction of *recontextualizing* the education of our children and young people, we will not even begin to see how our system of public education might make a large and substantial contribution to a reshaping of American society into that more benevolent and humane culture we so desperately need.

References

Boorstin, D. J. 1983. *The Discoverers.* New York: Random House.

Csikszentmihalyi, M., K. Rathunde, and S. Whalen. 1993. *Talented Teenagers: The Roots of Success and Failure.* New York: Cambridge University Press.

Donald, M. 1991. *Origins of the Modern Mind.* Cambridge, Mass.: Harvard University Press.

Eisenstein, E. 1993. *The Printing Revolution in Early Modern Europe.* New York: Cambridge University Press.

Gardner, H. 1982. *Developmental Psychology.* Boston: Little, Brown.

Gimpel, J. 1976. *The Medieval Machine.* New York: Penguin Books.

Harkavy, I., and J. L. Puckett. 1990. "Toward Effective University–Public School Partnerships: An Analysis of Two Contemporary Models." University of Pennsylvania, Center for School Partnerships.

Noddings, N. 1992. *The Challenge to Care in the Schools.* New York: Teachers College Press.

Reed, E. S. 1997. "Defending Experience: A Philosophy for the Postmodern World." *The Genetic Epistemologist* 25 (3): 1–3.

Shanker, A. 1988. "School Learning and Job Learning: Exploring the Missing Connection." *New York Times,* June 19, Sec. 4, p. 2. "Rethinking Failure and Success: The School/Student Connection." *New York Times,* June 26, Sec. 4, p. 3.

Sizer, T. 1992. "School Reform By the Feds: The Perspective from Sam." Paper delivered April 21, AERA Panel.

Sjoberg, G. 1960. *The Preindustrial City.* New York: Free Press.

Valentin, A. 1952. *Leonardo da Vinci: The Tragic Pursuit of Perfection.* New York: Viking Press.

7

Daydreams Believer

PATRICK SHANNON

In the *Phi Delta Kappan* special editorial section on higher education, authors were asked to dream about new relationships for schooling and society, starting from their definition of "from the bottom up."

Let's assume that everyone's dream comes true. Why not? It's a postmodern world. This would mean schools based on developmentally appropriate curricula for preschool through college, and perhaps even graduate school, will be organized locally under voluntary national content and assessment standards and mandatory state procedural standards for evaluation and access to the next levels of schooling. Teachers in these schools will make professional decisions at building and even classroom levels that will help specific groups of students to determine why, what, and how they want to study less or in more depth. Without tracking, treating everyone the same, or closing doors to students' later decisions, schools will help students understand themselves, others, and the world today while they work their way toward access to employment in the market, government, civic society, or some combination of the three. Such schooling will require cooperation in equal amounts from all current institutional levels of schooling.

Students who attend the new schools will find the developmentally appropriate curricula welcoming and challenging. The integration of academic knowledge will continue students' natural learning patterns through inquiry projects concerning everyday life experiences and the real problems we face in natural and social environments. Opportunities to apprentice within one or more sectors of work will help students make valuable decisions about what to do with their lives. In order to open doors of opportunity, students will find appropriate ways to represent themselves as learners to whomever is interested. The real prospects of their futures will have little impact on their motivation and abilities to learn.

Don't you just love it when plans come together? Although they are not always valued in our pragmatic society, dreams can be very useful.

> Dreams come in the day as well as at night. And both kinds of dreaming are motivated by the wishes they seek to fulfill. But daydreams differ from night dreams; for the daydreaming "I" persists throughout, consciously, privately, envisaging the circumstances and images of a desired, better life. The content of the daydream is not, like that of the night dream, a journey back into repressed experiences and their associations. It is concerned with, as far as possible, an unrestricted journey forward, so that which is not yet can be fantasized in life and into the world. (Block 1970)

Like Block's image of "that which is not yet," education always presupposes a vision of the future. Regardless of who defines the what, why, and how of education, it is someone's plan for how we will live together. What we see separately in the chapters of this book and combined in my amalgam of authors' thoughts are their daydreams—expressions of hope for a better tomorrow through teaching and learning. And while I have my doubts about the ease with which these dreams might come true, for the most part I am a daydreams believer. Yet, we dream in a specific time and place.

When Evans Clinchy sent the original articles to me with an invitation to participate in this book, he enclosed two additional articles that be suggested represented "two prophesies of the shape of things to come." The first was a commentary from *Education Week* in which Jeremy Rifkin offered his views on how schools might adapt to a world without work. The second was an editorial from the *Wall Street Journal* by Michael C. Jensen and Perry Fagan, which proclaimed that "Capitalism Isn't Broken." I understood these two additional pieces to be a call for me to place the arguments offered in the special issue within some sort of economic frame.

Very briefly, these two opinion pieces offered polar opposite frames for those arguments. Jensen and Fagan, a professor and research associate from the Harvard Business School, argue that current economic realities of job loss, increased income gap, and centralization and internationalization of capital are natural cycles in the triumph of capitalism over communism. While they acknowledge these temporary hardships, they see them as necessary adjustments in the general growth of prosperity for all. Moreover, they forecast the upswing for jobs and greater income parity for the early part of the twenty-second century. They argue if it ain't broke, don't fix it. Any adjustments will simply prolong the hardships, not ameliorate them. Rifkin, president of the

Foundation on Economic Trends, does not foresee this expected upswing. Rather, he explains the current realities as natural consequences of capitalism in which technology has been and is being used to conquer labor in production, government, and now service industries. Jensen and Fagan's Third Industrial Revolution, Rifkin argues, will treat social classes more harshly and differently than the last one and its treatments will not end without political and social adjustments.

According to Rifkin, some few will amass enormous wealth while many will lose their well-paying jobs or not find employment sufficient to keep a family above the poverty line. Many, or most, workers will be forced into a third sector of the economy, the civic sector, which is composed of more than 1.4 million nonprofit organizations from schools to youth organizations, hospitals, theaters, art galleries, and so on. This sector has combined assets of more than $500 billion, contributes 6 percent of the gross national product, and employs more than 10 percent of Americans. According to Rifkin (1996), "The opportunity now exists to create millions of new jobs in the third sector. Freeing up the labor and talent of men and women no longer needed in the market and government sectors to create 'social capital' in neighborhoods and communities will cost money" (33).

Rifkin says that those who have jobs and the multinational and national corporations for which they work will pay increased taxes to fund tax breaks for employed "volunteer" workers in the civic economy and guaranteed incomes for all unemployed "volunteer" workers creating social capital. Because human capital arguments will not be abandoned in these harsh economic times, citizens—actually the minority with taxable incomes—will be willing to part with sizable chunks of their earnings in order to create the expanded civic sector. Somehow they will recognize that it is in their best interests to do so.

Rifkin's ideas for the construction of this recognition involves a new type of schooling. For Rifkin, schools should be redesigned to expand the conception of paid vocations—to acknowledge the possibilities of the civic sector and to engage students in the production of social capital in their communities. "Service learning is an essential antidote to the increasingly isolated world of simulation and virtual reality children experience in the classroom and at home in front of the television and at their computer workstations" (33). Those engagements will require a two-tier teaching system of curriculum teachers who handle classroom learning and clinical teachers responsible for education within the community. According to Rifkin, open public dialogues will help the public reach consensus on these matters.

In what follows I attempt to make explicit two bridges that may help us to traverse the gap between our lives around current schools and some of the dreams expressed in these two articles. I begin by accepting Rifkin's forecast for our economy and the challenges it sets for schooling—What does it mean for schooling if work can no longer serve as its primary rationale for being? Second, I look closely at the people who are being and will be inconvenienced in that economy and what schools might do with and about them.

Schooling Without Work Waiting

For at least the last fifteen years, the federal policy toward schooling has been based on an assumption that the performance of schooling directly affects the economy. According to this logic, better schooling means a better economy. Or at least, more schooling means more effectiveness, versatility, and earning power for individuals personally and for a community and country collectively. Accordingly, school improvement has become a national economic imperative (Tyack and Cuban 1995). During the 1980s and 1990s, federal and state governments, corporations, and philanthropic organizations have been applying steady pressure on public schools through sponsored research, content standards, and accountability schemes to improve their outcomes. Ray Marshall, former Secretary of Labor in the Reagan administration and current trustee for the Carnegie Foundation, and Marc Tucker, president of the Center for the Economy and Education, present a history of this human capital rationale for U.S. schools.

In the first part of this century, we adopted the principle of mass-producing low-quality education to create a low-skilled workforce for mass production industry. Building on this principle, our education and business systems became very tightly linked, evolving into a single system that brilliantly capitalized on our advantages and enabled us to create the most powerful economy and the largest middle class in the world. The education system, modeled on industrial organization, was crafted to supply the workforce that the industrial economy needed. The U.S. systems of school organization and industrial organization were beautifully matched, each highly dependent on the other for its success, each the envy of the world. But most of the competitive advantages enjoyed at the beginning of the century had faded away by midcentury, and advances in technology during and after World War II slowly altered the structure of the domestic and world economy in ways that turned these principles of American business and school organization into liabilities rather than assets (Marshall and Tucker 1992, 17).

Even in critiques of current schooling, the continued strong ties between schooling and work are assumed. Yet according to Rifkin and others, this remedy for the future presupposes precisely what needs to be explored: "For if the job culture proves to have been a historically situated way of measuring value, then the ethical basis of contemporary life requires reexamination and, with it, the goals and purpose of schools" (Aronowitz 1994, 141). Few educators have taken this ethical question seriously, and even fewer have moved away from the rationale of schooling as preparation for work. Even Rifkin's suggestion that educators include social education about the third sector in their curricula is simply an alternative proposal of schooling for work. Although workless factories and virtual companies may force Americans to rethink the ethics of work as the primary marker of our social and self worth, I don't think it will be easy for us to extract paid work from our identities.

Paid work is the root of capitalism; it's sanctioned in Protestantism as the material benefit of doing good; and it's a central protagonist in the story of how the United States was built. Working for pay has contributed as much as any other factor to Americans' construction of our identities, and certainly it is a primary means by which we are judged by others. For example, after losing his job as an operations manager of a manufacturing plant in California, James Sharlow asked *New York Times* reporter Rick Bragg (1996), "How could my family not think less of me now?" Beyond our personal and social identities, the very structure of our modern lives is defined by paid employment. "In the absence of regular employment, life, including family life, becomes less coherent . . . and hinders rational planning of daily life" (Wilson 1996, 30).

Under these circumstances, long-term unemployment or "different employment" does not seem to be a badge that many Americans are ready to wear with any sense of honor, no matter how much civic volunteering they do. Today, the civic involvement spurred by the free time available after an eight-hour workday has already begun to abate. According to Uchitille and Klienfeld (1996), civic involvement has tumbled at PTAs, Rotary Clubs, town meetings, even bowling clubs since downsizing became a common business practice of the 1990s. Apparently, without a steady, sustaining paycheck, individuals cannot find the time or the will to help others or to participate in civic life.

As Marshall and Tucker (1992) report, public schooling and U.S. business enjoyed a dialectical relationship of mutual development, and schooling has played an important role in our learning to put our complete faith in paid work as this personal and social ruler. The virtues of work extolled in the McGuffey Readers were repeated in the lives of Dick and Jane in the reading textbooks of the twentieth century, and they are resurfacing in the stories William Bennett is telling through school materials. The structure of the school day is designed to prepare children for work—timed classes, academic tracking, and continuous monitoring all have as much to do with internalizing the practices of paid labor as they do with learning. Even the physical surroundings—the single desks, stark walls, and lighting—are work-oriented.

Discrepancies in funding for districts and schools within states and across the nation—even the fetish for "good" universities—are related to gaining advantage over others in obtaining or maintaining better jobs. And school personnel from preschool to college have relied on the fact that students and their parents have almost unquestioned faith in the connection between schooling and work to continue many questionable practices. Because the connection has not been questioned, many of the proposed changes for schools—business partnerships, national standards and examinations for students and teachers, and uniforms—increase the ties between schooling and paid work.

My point is that regardless of the social circumstances and institutional change, the personal and social meanings of paid labor will retain a prominent place in our social knowledge for a long time to come. Although we are currently in the midst of what Rifkin calls the "end of work," we face generations of struggling through its psychic and social consequences. And just as John Dewey (1888) proposed at the turn of the last century, schools could play an important role in helping people come to grips with their lives, their communities, and the world. However, the loss of work as the rationale for schooling creates a series of tensions and opportunities for educators. Without the promise of a good paid job waiting, students may not be as patient with current or even proposed school content and procedures that do not appear to serve their interests. We can already see this growing impatience in rural areas, towns, and cities in which factories, mines, and businesses have closed and are closing, and employment and perhaps life prospects seem dim. In these circumstances, students, even young ones, seem less willing to put up with the "crap" of going to school. Higher standards, tougher admissions policies, uniforms, or many of the other recently suggested remedies will not calm student anxieties for long. Moreover, the decline in the need for an educated population to fill jobs may reduce the public's willingness to support public schooling at its current levels. This logic has not been lost on political conservatives (e.g., Chubb and Moe 1990; Hanushek 1994; Herrnstein and Murray 1994), who can think of many reasons to save money on schools that do not contribute, even indirectly, to corporate profits.

In order to discuss what schools might do to help people in a jobless society, we must first look closely at the people who are currently and in the future the likely victims of this economic "cycle." As did the first three industrial revolutions, the fourth will serve Americans according to their race, class, and gender. For example, currently one-third of all African and Hispanic Americans live below the poverty line; the lowest paid, 60 percent of Americans, receive only 30 percent of total U.S. income; and nearly 50 percent of single female heads of households live below the poverty line. Perhaps the failure of the U.S. economy to overcome these facts during the last two hundred years proves that the market isn't all that free. The last to be hired after the third revolution have been and will continue to be the first to be fired during the fourth.

Yet as we have already experienced during the 1990s, these firings reach across these traditional employment boundaries to grab white working-class and middle-class males. Even before this recent rash of "inconveniences," working- and middle-class Americans experienced not just the fear, but the reality, of falling wages.

The prototypical middle-class American worked for the better part of two decades, during which he or she saw communism collapse, four presidents occupy the White House, and five San Francisco 49er teams win Super Bowl rings. He or she collected eight hundred and thirty-two weekly paychecks, the last one for an amount twenty-three dollars less than the first one (Cassidy 1995, 114).

Poor and working-class wages have dropped even further—0.78 and 0.33 percent annually, respectively. The current economy—the instability of employment, the growing income gap, and declining real wages—places between 60 and 80 percent of the U.S. population into the category of already or likely to be "inconvenienced."

This fact suggests a two-class structure in the U.S. economy. Twenty percent of Americans—a minority—will continue to enjoy the psychological, social, political, and economic benefits of relative job security and rising wages (particularly if capital gains taxes are repealed), and 60 to 80 percent must brace themselves for lives without economic security. Rifkin hopes that the minority will provide for the majority by financing the civic sector of the economy. That is, employed Americans and corporations will pay sufficient taxes to allow tax deductions for tax-paying volunteers and a guaranteed income for the unemployed willing to work as volunteers according to some formula.

I doubt that the minority and corporations are suddenly going to develop generous habits of the heart. At this point, neither is acting as if it is prepared to fund an expanded third sector or even to continue the modest safety net already in place in the U.S. (Gordon 1996). In fact, most of the social welfare laws for all citizens have been neglected, reduced, or eliminated during the last two decades. Even funding for Social Security and public schooling, two previously sacred cows, is subject to economic scrutiny as personal savings and voucher plans are seriously proposed by senior members of both major political parties. Of course, the minority will be able to make full use of these options because they do not actually need such support for themselves and they will enjoy the personal and corporate tax savings that will follow, but the majority strapped for income in an insecure economy will face life and death decisions that pit their futures against their presents. These attempts to give citizens more "choice" with "their" money serve the minority and transfer more public funds into private hands as corporate and upper-class welfare continue to grow.

However, the minority doesn't always win. At the turn of the last century, and in the 1930s and 1960s, large public displays helped the minorities of those times recognize that it was in their best interests to aid segments of the majority. These displays—strikes, marches, boycotts, and so on—let the minority see what would come of further neglect of majority rights, needs, and dreams. As a result, the U.S. majority enjoys antimonopoly legislation (Kolko 1963), labor reforms (Zinn 1995), civil rights laws (Bell 1992), and gender rights (Shreve 1989). Today, we lack public demonstrations to force the present minority to acknowledge and act on their moral obligation to fund the third sector. In fact, recently the majority seemed unable or unwilling to muster a sufficient display to save over a million children from being forced below the official poverty line. Even Senator Daniel Moynihan, no friend of the majority, remarked that few attempted to dissuade the president, the House, or the Senate from passing welfare reform. "Why do we not see the endless parade of petitioners, the lobbyists, the pretend citizen groups, the real citizen groups? None are here!" (Clymer 1996, 14)

What is it that schools could do to help the majority of Americans at the economic bottom? I agree with many of the points other authors in this book make about starting reform from the sensibilities of kindergartens and not the narrower mission of universities. Moreover, I believe in the dreams of the caring curricula that Meier and Nodding present, the urgency of today in Ohanian's position, and Rifkin's civic apprenticeships. Yet I fear that these dreams will not be sufficient to help the majority to gain greater control over their lives, particularly in times when they will be in even greater economic jeopardy than they are today. Educators and students caring for one another, emphasizing being over becoming, and moving beyond the classroom should aim at democratic control for the majority. Toward that end, I think school curricula should be negotiated around developing solidarity among the majority in order that they can participate actively in the civic life of their communities today.

Solidarity Among the Majority

Although job security and income provide the basis for my definitions of the majority and minority classes, they cannot define entirely the identities of the individuals and groups. The 60 to 80 percent majority of Americans are a diverse lot—women and men, old, young, and middle-aged, many races, cultures, ethnicities, and religions (Sklar 1995). There is even a range of incomes, from destitute to insecure, but with reasonable comfort (Roper 1994). On the other hand, the 20 percent minority is secure and relatively homogeneous in terms of race, gender, and age (Schiller 1995). In the past, the diversity of the majority has worked against the development of feelings of solidarity in pursuing majority interests. At times, the minority has used this diversity to divide and conquer the majority. Crime can serve as a familiar current example of this strategy.

> What bothered me most about the hysterical, bloodthirsty TV ads during the last election was the absolute certainty of the candidates that the prison cells they promised to construct, the draconian prison terms, and the prison conditions they would impose, if elected, would never confine them or those who voted for them. . . . the ones they were promising to lock up and punish, by design, would never be their people. (Widemann 1995, 504)

Widemann suggests that 1994 candidates for Congress and local offices used crime as a marker for race in order to drive a wedge between diverse groups within the majority and to symbolize the need for whites to be fearful of those of color. The growing prison system and the annual "get tough on crime" bills keep the majority apart and divert their attention from their common interests.

However, the minority is not solely responsible for the lack of feelings of solidarity among the majority. Struggles for recognition of differences among the majority are fast becoming the primary form of progressive political action in the United States. Demands for recognition fuel the struggle of groups mobilized under the banners of nationality, ethnicity, race, gender, and sexuality. Group identity has supplanted class interest as the chief medium of building subgroup solidarity, and cultural domination has replaced exploitation as the fundamental injustice. Although these struggles address the cultural blindness of the materialist positions among the American Left during the last one hundred and fifty years, cultural groups spin off in different directions with varying social agendas. However, as Nancy Fraser writes,

> Neither of those two stances is adequate. Both are too wholesale and unnuanced. Instead of simply endorsing or rejecting all of identity politics, we should see ourselves as presented with a new intellectual and practical task: that of developing a critical theory of recognition, one which identifies and defends only those versions of the cultural politics of difference that can be coherently combined with the social politics of equality. . . . For only by articulating recognition and redistribution can we arrive at a critical theoretical framework that is adequate to the demands of our age. (1995, 69)

Fraser sets a remarkable challenge before schools: How can they organize around redistribution and recognition when each thrust appears to pull us in opposite directions? Clearly, mainstream pedagogies of multiculturalism cannot lead educators forward because they redress disrespect by revaluing unjustly marginalized group identities while generally leaving intact both the content of those identities and the group differentiations that underlie them. Marginalized groups and others learn new respect for certain cultures, but the causes and consequences are often left unexamined by anyone. In this way, mainstream multicultural pedagogies work against majority interests because they neglect the underlying generative frameworks and cultural valuational structures. Individuals and groups of people may feel better about themselves, and this is of certain value, but nothing changes fundamentally, either personally or socially. However, by destabilizing existing group identities and generative frameworks through closer examination of ways in which they are symbolically encoded in everyday language and life, new pedagogies could not only raise the self-esteem of members of currently disrespected groups but could change everyone's sense of belonging, affiliation, and self, thus making new alliances possible.

For example, a colleague of mine begins her college developmental literacy courses with the expectation that her students will not only acquire appropriate literacy skills to continue their academic studies but will also develop a critical understanding of how text works for and against them in their lives. My particular favorite of her curriculum stories involves her sponsoring a semester's work on students coming to locate themselves, their families, and others with respect to government support. She embarked on this curriculum in response to a particularly nasty statement by one student during a general discussion of how students ended up in a non–credit-bearing course. This student remarked that some students shouldn't be bothered by a lack of credit because they were fully funded by the government and their tuition was free. In this particular situation, my colleague reported, the remark had decidedly racist undertones, implying that African-American students received the bulk of the social and economic benefits from government.

Instead of challenging the speaker for what might be considered a politically incorrect statement on many campuses, she accepted his remark as a question worthy of investigation and a semester's worth of reading and writing. The students read and wrote in a variety of genres on a variety of subjects, including tax law, public assistance history, census data, personal narratives from social service workers and recipients, identity construction and mobilization of bias, and many political cartoons and editorials from varying perspectives. During the semester they improved their analytical skills and ability to detect authors' intentions and to identify how symbols are used (often as facts) to convey those intentions. The students learned that government support comes in many forms, most of which are not discussed in the popular media, and that government support is not distributed equally among classes or social groups. In fact, their findings demonstrated that the majority of the support went to corporations and the wealthy. Moreover, they entertained the possibility that their thoughts were not independently developed, as they had previously thought, and that their actions based on those thoughts could work against their better interests.

I consider this a good example of pedagogy designed to develop feelings of solidarity among the majority. It challenged learners' comfortable acceptance of "facts" about our lives, and it invited new coalitions across previously impenetrable boundaries. Although I'm certain that students did not sort out issues of race and class once and for all during this course, they did have an ethical opportunity to see themselves differently in relation to other groups. In that opportunity, many found that while they were all different in important ways, there were also profound similarities in their circumstances and dreams. During the course, the students learned ways to examine symbols that divide the majority and a language to question both the textual representations of their lives and the real consequences of government support. And in the end, most members of the class came together to produce a document to explain government support to their peers in other sections of the developmental literacy courses and anyone else who might be interested.

Acting Democratically

But, solidarity is not enough. Although the majority must search to find its interests and must act to make its interests the rules by which we live, diversity within the majority reduces the possibility of permanent consensus on all issues. Destabilizing relational boundaries among groups in order to foster feelings of solidarity will, at best, bring fluid coalitions among the majority around specific issues in particular circumstances. Marginalized cultural groups need not worry that issues of recognition will again be consumed by issues of redistribution in progressive politics. Yet our diminishing prospects for well-paying jobs require majority action in order to ensure, at least, the financing of the civic sector in Rifkin's or others' schemes to provide guaranteed livelihoods for all Americans.

Based on the last two decades of legislative retreat from this responsibility, the corporate influences on government will preclude an easy transition to a tax policy that protects the majority. According to Ralph Nader (1996), Americans grow up corporate rather than civic because the pedagogical forms of present-day society—the media, popular culture, and social institutions—

emphasize symbolic knowledge and sets of factual information only to support the status quo. Therefore, schools designed to serve the majority must couple the solidarity developed through the critique of symbols that divide the majority with the belief among the majority that change is possible and that it is their responsibility.

> [We] need to develop a discourse that unites the language of critique with a language of possibility, so that [we] recognize that we can make change. In doing so, we must speak out against economic, political, and social injustice, both within and outside schools. At the same time, we must work to create the conditions that give students the opportunity to become citizens who have knowledge and courage to struggle in order to make despair unconvincing and hope practical. As difficult as this may seem, it is a struggle worth waging. (Giroux 1988, 128)

I believe that the creation of these conditions is part of what Rifkin and Meier have in mind when they call for student inquiry into the civic sector of the economy and the pursuit to understand the complexities of everyday life. The imperative for students to discover their interests and to act upon them provides further direction to these suggestions. Obviously, we cannot dismiss the importance of giving youth a sense of how to make it within the existing realities, but if schools are going to serve the majority then, "teaching and learning must be linked to the goal of educating students to take risks, to struggle with ongoing relations of power, to critically appropriate forms of knowledge that exist outside of their immediate experience, and to envisage versions of a world which is 'not yet'—in order to be able to alter the grounds upon which life is lived" (Simon 1992, 144).

For example, a grade-school reading specialist in my local area works according to the premise that reading the word and the world also involves naming the word and the world. In each classroom of the school in which she teaches, she sponsors the writing of newspapers that provide opportunities for students to interpret their worlds and to represent themselves as learners in and citizens of the school. While five- and six-year-olds stick close to their classrooms, they do represent school life as they see it. As students grow older and become more sophisticated in their thoughts, they venture beyond the classroom into the community. These adventures afford them opportunities to bring the community into their classroom and to represent it for themselves, their peers, and the larger audience to which their newspaper circulates.

Early in the 1995–1996 school year, a fifth-grade student sought to describe the immediate surroundings of her school for all those readers (students' relatives, primarily) who could not see it or who hadn't given it much consideration previously. In her report, she mentioned, in passing detail, the

fact that students pass daily an alternative-to-bail counseling center for of-
fenders who are freed from jail while they await trial. As part of her research
for the article, she had interviewed the director of the center, but she decided
that the whole interview was "too boring" to include in her finished piece. As
the article passed through regular editorial channels, the head of the school
decided that the reference to the bail-alternative program should be deleted
from the article or that the article should not be printed. His rationale was that
knowledge of the center might be upsetting to the school community.

The author, her fellow students, the reading teacher, and the classroom
teacher balked at this suggestion. In fact, they refused to publish until they
had had a meeting with the head of the school to hear his explanation for the
censorship. During the discussion, students offered a knee-jerk response based
on the First Amendment and the public's right to know. But in their objec-
tions to censorship, they developed an understanding about how editorial
policies must shape the information in other newspapers. They asked, What
has someone else decided is inappropriate for us to know? In the end, the head
admitted that the problem arose only from his previous lack of candor with
the school community about the alternative-to-bail center, and the article was
published as written.

I understand this to be a good example of curriculum for the majority on
several counts. First, the opportunity to name what's important and to represent the world to others counteracts the din of media and institutional practice
that tells students that what others think is more important than what they
think, know, and do. Additionally, the fact that this reading teacher believes
that five- and six-year-olds can make such decisions on their own and write
about them unsettles "developmentally appropriate" theories that keep young
children from all the good stuff of project work in schools. And these young
children do name their experiences in ways that contradict what the teacher
believes is happening and is important in the classroom. Second, the risks of
naming and representing seem to lead to the risks of taking action in a democratic challenge to relations of power. Because of their action, decisions did
change and the ground on which they lived was altered. Third, the immediate
lessons learned were associated with societal lessons that will serve the majority better. Just what is allowed in those "news holes" between the adver-
tisements in newspapers? These are civic, not corporate, voices in the making.

I selected my examples from university and elementary school settings
in order to display my belief that the pedagogical and curricular possibilities
of these two levels of schooling are more similar than different. In order to
serve the majority by fostering solidarity and democratic action, each must
break from scholarly disciplinary structures that artificially separate the social
from the scientific, the emotional from the rational, and the practical from the

theoretical. Rather, each must harness all these ways of knowing into inter-disciplinary forces that will enable us to overcome the problems that seem to engulf us, and see through the rhetoric that clouds our vision of majority in-terests. This does not deny the value of academic expertise, although it does challenge the currently privileged status of university educators vis-à-vis pub-lic school teachers in a way that makes all educators public servants. Can we imagine outreach programs to the majority that involve historians, literature professors, kindergarten teachers, and anthropologists as well as engineers, li-brarians, mathematicians, and artists?

Perhaps the dreams captured in this book offer the greatest challenges to university educators, who have enjoyed increased enrollments and funding through the schooling-for-work equation. As it becomes more apparent that this equation no longer works for the majority, the role of universities in society must change drastically. To a degree, universities will remain gate-keepers to high paying jobs, but they already grant more bachelor's, master's, doctoral degrees, and professional diplomas than there are jobs waiting for graduates in their chosen fields of employment. Some university administra-tors and faculty may take the cynical, perhaps undemocratic, approach and continue to serve only the minority. But most will be forced to change their relationships with society to become less focused on degree programs and admissions and disciplinary requirements, and more interested in helping the majority address their problems and to build a different, more fair, social contract.

Believers

If schools are to serve society in what has been called a jobless future, they must be redefined and reorganized from kindergarten through graduate school. Along with Meier's dreams of developmentally appropriate pedagogy, Nodding's caring curriculum that counts, and Ohanian's teaching focused on today, I offer dreams of solidarity and democratic action for the 60 to 80 per-cent majority of Americans. These dreams add direction to our trek away from schooling set for paid work toward a commitment to freedom, equality, and social justice expressed not in moral platitudes but in concrete struggles of everyday life in and out of classrooms. Such redefinition and reorganiza-tion requires new texts, new sponsored experiences, new mindsets for educa-tors and the public. And this takes leadership.

Current forms of leadership in education are focused on narrow instru-mentalism—standardized culture, knowledge, and morals. This leadership bends "all areas of life to the rule of the market and all democratic and inter-mediate institutions to the rule of the executive" (Mouffe 1991, 29). Yet the type of leadership that favors "business-like" solutions—national standards, vouchers, and high-stakes testing—has served schools and the public poorly. First, it continues to cite paid work as a rationale for public schools, when clearly that is no longer tenable. Second, it retreats from the connection between schooling and the public good and democratic living, when clearly public and democratic discourses are in need of revitalization.

As Meier and Ohanian imply, the needed leadership becomes most effective at a local level from principals and teachers, and not from central executives, bureaucrats, and legislators. Local leadership is demonstrated personally within specific contexts as educators and others bring schools and communities together by broadening the curricula to include issues of work, health care, living conditions, and recreation within the tensions of diversity and solidarity. In their own communities, leaders can demonstrate a new value for schooling without the increasingly doubtful goal of work waiting, and they can help individuals and communities develop new dreams about the present and future and new ways to believe and to act on those dreams.

References

Aronowitz, S. 1994. "A Different Perspective on Educational Inequality." *Review of Education/Pedagogy/Cultural Studies* 16: 135–152.

Bell, D. 1992. *Faces at the Bottom of the Well.* New York: Simon and Schuster.

Block, E. 1970. *A Philosophy of the Future.* New York: Herder and Herder.

Bragg, R. 1996. "Where Dignity Used to Be." In *The New York Times Special Report on the Downsizing of America.* New York: Times Books.

Cassidy, J. 1995. "Who Killed the Middle Class?" *New Yorker* 68 (October 16): 113–124.

Chubb, J., and T. Moe. 1990. *Politics, Markets, and America's Schools.* Washington, D.C.: Brookings Institution.

Clymer, A. 1996. "Class Warfare? The Rich Win by Default." *New York Times,* August 11.

Dewey, J. 1888. *The Ethics of Democracy.* Ann Arbor, Mich.: Anderson & Co.

Fraser, N. 1995. "From Redistribution to Recognition? Dilemmas of Justice in a 'Post-Socialist' Age." *New Left Review* 212: 68–93.

Giroux, H. 1988. *Schooling and the Struggle for Public Life: Critical Pedagogy in the Modern Age.* Minneapolis: University of Minnesota Press.

Gordon, D. 1996. *Fat and Mean: The Corporate Squeeze of American Workers.* New York: Free Press.

Hanushek, E. 1994. *Making Schools Work: Improving Performance and Controlling Costs.* Washington, D.C.: Brookings Institution.

Herrnstein, R., and C. Murray. 1994. *The Bell Curve.* New York: Free Press.

Jensen, M. C., and P. Fagan. 1996. "Capitalism Isn't Broken." Editorial. *Wall Street Journal,* March 29, p. E11.

Kolko, G. 1963. *The Triumph of Conservatism: A Reinterpretation of American History.* New York: Free Press.

Marshall, R., and M. Tucker. 1992. *Thinking for a Living: Education and the Wealth of Nations.* New York: Basic Books.

Mouffe, C. 1991. "Democratic Politics Today." In *Dimensions of Radical Democracy,* ed. C. Mouffe. New York: Verso Editions.

Nader, R. 1996. "Growing Up Corporate/Growing Up Civic." Speech presented at Haverford College, Haverford, Pennsylvania, April 24.

Rifkin, J. 1996. "Rethinking the Mission of American Education." *Education Week,* January 31, pp. 31–34, 44.

Roper, R. 1994. "Income Survey." *The American Enterprise* 4: 9–10.

Schiller, B. 1995. *The Economics of Poverty and Discrimination.* Englewood Cliffs, N.J.: Prentice Hall.

Shreve, A. 1989. *Women Together, Women Alone.* New York: Fawcett.

Simon, R. 1992. "Empowerment as a Pedagogy of Possibility." In *Becoming Political,* ed. P. Shannon. Portsmouth, N.H.: Heinemann.

Sklar, H. 1995. *Chaos or Community: Seeking Solutions, Not Scapegoats for Bad Economics.* Boston: South End.

Tyack, D., and L. Cuban. 1995. *Tinkering with Utopia: A Century of Public School Reform.* Cambridge, Mass.: Harvard University Press.

Uchitille, L., and N. R. Klienfeld. 1996. "The Price of Jobs Lost." In *The New York Times Special Report on the Downsizing of America.* New York: Times Books.

Widemann, T. 1995. "Doing Time, Marking Race." *Nation* 261 (October 30): 503–505.

Wilson, W. J. 1996. "When Work Disappears." *New York Times Magazine,* August 18, pp. 26–31, 40, 48, 52–54.

Zinn, H. 1995. *People's History of the United States.* New York: New Press.

PART III

THE PROSPECTS FOR THE REFORM
OF AMERICAN EDUCATION FROM
KINDERGARTEN THROUGH
GRADUATE SCHOOL

Introduction

Is Reform Possible?

Having attempted so far to describe at least some of the problems of our current educational system, from the "bottom" of pre-school and kindergarten through the "top" of graduate school, we now face the question of whether any of these problems can actually be solved, whether change on such a massive scale is even possible, or whether reform is simply one of Pat Shannon's wonderful daydreams.

From the analyses presented in Parts I and II, one thing seems reasonably clear: there will be little or no significant reform of our elementary and secondary schools unless there are simultaneous changes of equal magnitude in our colleges and universities. This does not mean that nothing can be done in the meantime in our elementary and secondary schools. All sorts of interesting and potentially important things are going on in these schools, such as the charter school movement, the creation of new, small schools within our public systems, and such innovations as the microsociety schooling at Lowell's City Magnet School and the integrated-day type of developmental schooling at such schools as Central Park East Elementary. But, as Meier, Ohanian, and Nathan point out, the archaic and arid hand of college admissions requirements all too often descends on middle and high schools, suppressing continued innovative reform and forcing them back into the orthodox academic mold. In the case of City Magnet's microsociety curriculum, for instance, there is no such program available at Lowell High School, much less at the collegiate level, a fact that causes considerable distress to the City School's graduates and their parents. In the Central Park East example, Meier has already described the compromises she had to make in order to get her students into institutions of higher education, and her experience is, of necessity, being repeated in many of those new, small charter and pilot schools springing up all around the country.

To begin the lengthy process of instituting the developmental mode of education into the kindergarten though graduate school system of American schooling, it probably makes sense to begin by continuing to question some of the fundamental assumptions underlying our system of higher education and to explore ways in which those institutions might begin to operate more in the kindergarten tradition while simultaneously fulfilling Franklin's dictum of research, teaching, and community service.

Nel Noddings begins this process in Chapter 8 by arguing for a much broader definition of what a postsecondary education should be. Nona Lyons then describes what a revised, developmentally based system of teacher education might look like. In Chapter 10, I examine in greater detail some of the dangers inherent in our existing system of educational research (and social science research in general). Chapter 10 is based on Sanz de Santamaria's explication of this problem and describes the very positive example of the collaborative research process undertaken by higher education people at the Institute for Education in Transformation at the Claremont Graduate School and the people of four California public schools. Ira Harkavy and John Puckett then describe in Chapter 11 the innovative practices being conducted at the University of Pennsylvania in working with its surrounding West Philadelphia neighborhood and its public schools.

And finally, in Chapter 12, I attempt to sum up all that has been said here about reforming the U.S. system of education from the bottom to the top. We then offer a truly immodest proposal for moving toward that elusive goal.

8

Rethinking the Benefits
of the College-Bound Curriculum

NEL NODDINGS

Deborah Meier and Susan Ohanian ask us to think about how secondary schools and colleges might approach education if they were modeled on the early elementary grades and the needs of students instead of on the images and demands of the elite colleges and universities. The claim is that such education might be characterized by greater freedom, sustained activity, playfulness, sense of purpose, and a healthy skepticism born of genuine curiosity. The elite colleges and universities do in fact exercise more control than they should over a vast number of students who will never enter their doors. Can anything be done to change this? I will argue that we should rethink two sets of beliefs that support the current top-down model: one, a set of faulty notions about equal opportunity, sameness, and the inherent worth of the college-bound curriculum; two, an equally faulty set of beliefs about the dangers of specialization and the benefits of breadth. Rethinking these matters may weaken the rationale for our current mode of operation.

Faulty Notions About Equality and Sameness

Advocates of the standard precollege curriculum usually offer one or both of two arguments for requiring students to take college preparatory mathematics, science, English, history, and foreign language. One argument seeks to persuade us that all children should have the opportunity to qualify for an elite education. The second argues that a curriculum designed as preparation for Harvard or Stanford is, inherently, the best education for everyone. It

113

seems to me that both of these arguments are wrong and, in some forms, actually harmful.

Let's consider the first argument—that all children should be given an opportunity to qualify for the best colleges. The first thing to notice is that opportunities might be provided without coercion. Too often those who insist on equal opportunity want to force students into the curriculum that will "give" them the desired opportunity. On this account, high school students are simply not mature enough to make important curriculum choices; for their own good, the school must make these choices for them.

Mortimer Adler (1982), for example, has insisted that, left to their own choices, some students will "downgrade" their own educations and therefore adults should control these crucial choices so that such downgrading does not occur. But there are two powerful responses to Adler's concerns. First, it should not be possible for students to downgrade their educations no matter what choices they make. Why should responsible educators allow schools to offer a set of good courses and a set of bad courses? As John Dewey pointed out years ago, a course in cooking, well planned and executed, can induce critical thinking, increase cultural literacy, and provide valuable skills; it can be a good course. In contrast, a course in algebra may discourage critical thinking, add nothing to cultural literacy, and lead students to despair of acquiring useful skills; it can be a bad course. Thus, before we abandon the variety of courses typical of the "shopping mall" high school, we should ask genuine and penetrating questions about the value of these courses. I've already offered three criteria for judging them. I'd also ask: Are they interesting? Are they challenging? Do the teachers treat the students with respect? Are the students likely to grow as whole persons—that is, is it reasonable to predict that the students will grow socially, morally, and intellectually? When I say that these questions should be asked genuinely, I mean that we should not decide a priori that the conventional academic subjects are superior to others. We should investigate. We should ask teachers to justify what they do in light of the criteria we establish, and we should continually ask penetrating questions about the criteria themselves.

The second response to Adler's worry is equally important. When some of us object strongly to the coercion inherent in a standardized curriculum, defenders often suppose that we are recommending a permissive, hands-off freedom for students. In fact, what we are recommending is something much more demanding and realistic. We are recommending a system of teacher counseling and guidance that approximates parental interest in students. We reject the simple (and highly deceptive) notion that students are given equal opportunity by force. The very notion is antithetical to democratic education.

We need to live with our children, assess their gifts and interests both realistically and generously, talk with them, listen to them, and help them to make well-informed decisions.

But, sincere advocates of standardization protest, despite commendable guidance (and it won't always be available), some students will land in the wrong slots. They will not be prepared if they change their minds and want college after all. This complaint underscores the criticisms raised by Meier and Ohanian. Why *should* the colleges be allowed to continue their stranglehold on the school curriculum? Why should rigorous, alternative courses not be acceptable for college admission? And why shouldn't our educational system be flexible enough to accommodate the changes of mind that increasingly characterize a postmodern society? The crucial educational point here is that students may learn better how to learn and may have greater confidence in their capacity to learn if they are encouraged to make well-informed decisions about their own education. Changing their minds should lead to new challenges, not to helpless despair.

Before leaving the discussion of the "equal opportunity" argument, I want to say something about political aspects of the argument. Politicians often argue that education is, or should be, the way out of poverty. Teachers are urged to have the same expectations for poor children as for rich children; all should meet the rigorous standards that are now being recommended. This recommendation may be well-intentioned, but its logic is muddled. We know that, by and large, children from stable, economically secure homes do fairly well with standard schooling (I am *not* arguing that they are, therefore, well educated, just that they do well on standard measures.) In contrast, children from poor homes often have a difficult time with the usual pattern of schooling. How will this be changed by simply declaring that poor kids *will* now do as well as richer ones? It would be more logical to launch a massive social program against poverty on the assumption that the formerly poor would now do better in schools.

Many of us worry that the current emphasis on high achievement for all is a monumental distraction from the social problems that should command our attention. Consider what would happen if we succeeded in bringing all students to whatever standards we establish. Our society would still need people to grow and harvest our food, to pack and deliver it, to sell it in supermarkets; we would still need waiters, cooks, and people to clean up; we would still need people to drive our trucks, buses, and taxis; we would still need hotel maids, street cleaners, repair persons, retail clerks, and servers of fast food. What excuse would we then have for letting many of these people live in poverty? Would we argue that, although they met the standard, they did less well than others? What excuse do we have now? It is clear that poverty is a social problem—a moral problem—not an educational one. *No person who works at a legitimate job should live in poverty* [emphasis added by editor].

As we wake up and acknowledge our interdependence and the obvious worth of so many jobs that are now devalued, we should begin to look at our students with greater appreciation. What a wonderful range of talents and interests they bring to their first years in school! Howard Gardner (1983) has identified seven intelligences, only two of which are recognized and developed in schools. Whether or not further research confirms seven (or forty-nine) intelligences, anyone who has taught knows that children have different gifts. To expect all children to do well in a course of study designed for a few seems very unfair. Moreover, such a system is wasteful; it demands higher and harsher methods of coercion, loses more students through discouragement, and wears teachers out. Ultimately, it is disrespectful, denying the very talents and interests on which the society depends.

When we face the fact that the schoolchildren before us will do all kinds of work as adults, we have to ask why they should all have the same education. I have already argued that the equal opportunity rationale is faulty; supposing that a child who is interested and talented in a subject has the same opportunity as one whose interests and talents lie elsewhere is heartless. But there remains the possibility that the standard curriculum is inherently valuable, that it is important for all children no matter what occupations they enter.

This is an argument made popular early in this century by Robert Maynard Hutchins (1936). Hutchins argued, "Education implies teaching. Teaching implies knowledge. Knowledge is truth. The truth is everywhere the same. Hence, education should be everywhere the same" (66). In today's atmosphere of recognized pluralism, Hutchins' syllogism sounds both arrogant and ludicrous, but the standard curriculum reflects an underlying acceptance of similar notions. Many believe that the truth is somehow discoverable (or has already been discovered) and that it should somehow be made into a standard curriculum. I am not suggesting, of course, that our curricula should be liberally sprinkled with falsehoods. I am simply pointing out that notions of universal truth are, in reality, too parochial and too limited to serve as the foundation of education. Further, much education is properly aimed at skills, attitudes, and forms of thinking that cannot be characterized as "truths," although they may serve in the continuing inquiry that leads in the direction of a form of truth.

However, there is an important point to consider in Hutchins' argument. To the degree that people are alike and share a common human condition, they need some common education. Deborah Meier emphasizes citizenship, and surely future citizens need some knowledge and skills associated with that status. But it is unlikely that they need the chronological history demanded by some policy makers or that they need a great deal of specific information about the holders of various offices, the number of congressional representatives, or the dates on which various laws were enacted. Much that is regarded as necessary for citizenship is probably not essential, and yet the concept itself is impoverished. Too often we concentrate on cramming students' heads with easily testable facts and ignore the discourse of responsibility, interdependent sociality, community, and commitment. Further, we often fail to provide our students with the practice they need to participate effectively in democratic citizenship.

Moreover, as human beings, we have more in common than citizenship. The emphasis on citizenship as contrasted with private life is, at least in part, a product of masculine domination of the curriculum. Where are all the matters traditionally assigned to women? Our children need to know something about the commitment required for intimate relationships, what it means to be a parent, what it means to make a home. They should become good neighbors, responsible pet owners, concerned guardians of the natural world, and honest colleagues in whatever activities they engage. They should know something about the stages of life, the various approaches to spirituality, suffering and compassion, violence and peace. These are the common learnings teachers should include in their courses; these are the topics that arise in common human experience.

It is perhaps understandable that successful people educated in the traditional way might mourn the demise of the curriculum they studied. To some it is deplorable that English teachers no longer find Shakespeare essential. But many English teachers are working with kids who carry weapons to school, who may be assaulted or killed, who will produce babies while they are themselves still children. To insist on the traditional curriculum in such circumstances is irresponsible.

Advocates of traditional curriculum might grant my point but insist that something must be done to prepare students for the standard curriculum. They might argue that resources should be made available so that kids will be ready for a "real" education. In a sense, these advocates want the curriculum to be made safe for Shakespeare. In opposition, I would argue that *all* children need a new sort of common studies as outlined here and that Shakespeare, like so many other staples of the traditional curriculum, should become a treasured option, not a requirement. Today, we cannot think in terms of one ideal model of the educated person. There obviously are many such models living and working all around us. Some well-educated and successful people cannot recognize the music of Beethoven, some cannot tell a Monet from a Manet, many have no concept of mathematical functions, most cannot name the parts of an insect or any of the great geologic ages. Unavoidably, as knowledge continues to expand, we will become more ignorant as well as more knowledgeable. What is truly deplorable, however, and must be avoided is raising generations of violent, irresponsible, uncaring, and unhealthy adults.

Faulty Notions About Specialization

This part of my argument is tied very closely to the first part. On the one hand, many Americans fear early specialization and argue for a breadth in precollege (and sometimes even in college) education that will "keep the doors open"; they want a broad education that will not commit their children to any specific form of work or field of study. One the other hand, many of the same people have accepted an array of narrow specializations as an adequate representation of breadth. This is the kind of anomaly that arises when we fail to think deeply enough on an issue.

One wonders whether the parents and educators who argue against early specialization really want something called breadth or whether what we are hearing is just another variant of the "change of mind" argument. If it is the latter, we can reiterate and deepen our earlier response. The *system* must be transformed to make such changes of mind easier and to keep the pursuit of learning vital and meaningful.

But suppose people really want breadth; suppose, that is, that the argument is for broad cultural knowledge—knowledge that spans the space of human disciplines. I have already argued that advocates of the standard curriculum cannot have in mind the full range of human *concerns* or they would not leave out of the curriculum most of the matters traditionally assigned to women and associated with private life. Hence the concern must be with the recognized disciplines—history, literature, philosophy, mathematics, and so on. Is the aim of breadth accomplished by requiring students to take a wide array of courses in these disciplines?

Here I will argue that the present system accomplishes nothing of the kind. Consider one powerful piece of evidence. In high school, students aiming for college must take such an array of courses. They study four, five, or six disciplines, but their teachers know only one. Their teachers have, for the most part, been subjected to the same required breadth and over several more years, and yet the end result is an educated adult who knows only one discipline and rarely has any breadth even in that. How often can a student get help on an algebra problem from her English teacher? And try asking the math teacher for help in interpreting *Heart of Darkness* or *Moby Dick*.

As the disciplines are taught now, the breadth argument is a sham. The true concern has little to do with knowledge; its focus is credentialing. We are not so concerned that students *know* some mathematics, for example; we are far more instrumentally concerned that their records should show that they have *taken* mathematics. Then, if they decide to apply to college, they are "prepared." I am not condemning this argument. Indeed, it is the most powerful and convincing one that can be given for going along with the required curriculum. But we ought not to deceive ourselves and suppose that there is a sound educational rationale for the present structure.

If we really want breadth in the disciplines, we would begin to broaden each discipline from within. We would reconsider our views on specialization. As it is now, we reject specialization when it means that a child will be allowed to concentrate on an area of his own special interest. But we accept presentations of the disciplines that are overly narrow and often specialized to the point where few generalists can find anything to whet their interest. The development of narrower and narrower specialties is, of course, one of the manifestations of the Weberian bureaucratic system in which we now live. Its signs are all around us. We regularly ask questions about exactly who should do what, scarcely questioning the supposition that every agency and role should have well-stated functions and that these functions should not overlap. Thus we ask, who should provide moral guidance for our children? And argue over whether the parents or school should do this. It rarely occurs to us that, in some matters—surely in education—the organization should be more holistic. In holistic enterprises, the answer to questions about who should perform certain tasks is "everyone concerned." In such domains we refuse to chop everything into small pieces, each one handled by a particular expert, technician, or assembly-line worker. "Prescriptive technologies" have their place, of course. They are enormously powerful in fields of material production. The physicist Ursula Franklin (1992) remarks, "Today, the temptation to design more or less everything according to prescriptive and broken-up technologies is so strong that it is even applied to those tasks that should be conducted in a holistic way. Any tasks that require caring, whether for people or nature, any tasks that require immediate feedback and adjustment, are best done holistically" (24).

Franklin explicitly names education as a quintessential holistic enterprise. By dividing the disciplines in a narrow and exclusive way, we have in fact fragmented the mental life of schooling and, perhaps even worse, we have made it impossible for students to catch a glimpse of their teachers as whole persons, as models of educated persons.

It is possible to teach the individual disciplines in a way that does not sacrifice the special quality that attracts a few to each and yet connects each discipline to the wider intellectual and social world. Wayne Booth (1988) has described the influence on his own life of a high school chemistry teacher who, in his chemistry class, taught the liberal arts. Booth does not mean by this that his chemistry teacher literally taught bits of disjointed mathematics, literature, or history. Rather, he means that the teacher skillfully shared with his students great ideas and how they arose, something of the aesthetics and epistemology of his subject, pieces of biographical and historical information when those were relevant or potentially interesting; that he could move about freely in the various domains we declare to be important and draw out stories and concepts that enriched both his chemistry instruction and the cultural literacy of his students.

I have myself argued in several places that mathematics teachers should be prepared to teach in this way (Noddings 1992, 1993, 1994). Every subject should retain the special identity and encourage the special talent that draws students to it, but it should also increase students' moral and aesthetic sensibilities, increase their cultural literacy, and reveal the teacher as an educated person. Mathematics teachers should have a wide repertoire of stories connecting mathematics (or mathematicians) to theology, logic, and science but also to classism, sexism, mysticism, militarism, and a host of other topics of general interest. They should be prepared to discuss what it means to live in a mathematicized world and how to cope with that world. The mathematics teacher, like every other teacher, should feel an obligation to discuss the great existential questions: What is the meaning of life? What are its origins? its destination? How should I live? Why is there suffering and what is my obligation in relieving it? Have mathematicians thought about these questions? Of course! But one would never guess it from what appears in most high school classes.

We would not have to worry seriously about early specialization if everything taught in schools were approached this way. Students could pursue their own interests with the enthusiasm of children and experts, and still expand their horizons. They would gain specialized skills and, at the same time, get a sense of how their subject, talent, or special interest fits within the larger culture.

Can Higher Education Change?

By way of concluding remarks, I want to explore the feasibility of changes in higher education. Susan Ohanian says that she has "no quarrel with the entrance requirements of Harvard," but that she refuses to accept a system of precollege education designed to prepare all students for Harvard. The problem here, of course, is that some parents want their children prepared for Harvard. They are quite right in assuming that, even if their kids are not accepted at Harvard, some other "good enough" school will be impressed by the preparation. It will take courage and imagination for other colleges to break away and establish their own criteria. A very few have done so already.

Many people in higher education admit that the traditional admission criteria are faulty. But the criteria are well established and widely accepted by a huge public. Even though several features of the system have been attacked as unfair, it is thought to be more fair than a system that might be more responsive to individual talents and more specialized preparation. Any change in a system so widespread and so deeply entrenched would have to be gradual. Two separate standards of preparation—for scientific and nonscientific fields—might be a start.

I think it is more feasible to work toward broadening the disciplines from within and toward the establishment of a solid variety of precollege courses of study. The latter must grow out of a genuine commitment on the part of parents and educators to provide an excellent education for the work-bound as well as the college-bound. It is a project in which industry could be a valuable partner.

However, higher education could take the lead in broadening the disciplines from within, in restoring the liberality to liberal education. The most obviously pressing need in this project is to educate teachers adequately. To do what I suggest, however, requires the courage to insist that teachers need a highly specialized form of education, that is, one designed especially for teachers. As undergraduates preparing to teach, their majors should reflect the breadth described earlier. Excellent teachers possess more than narrow subject matter knowledge plus some tricks of the trade. They have both broad general knowledge and an impressive breadth of knowledge in their own discipline.

The course of study I've outlined could in no way be considered "watered down." Indeed, its richness and rigor might well be the envy of others majoring in the same subject. Oddly enough, even here we encounter the "change of mind" argument. People have actually said to me, "But what if a student majors in math-for-teaching and then decides to do something else?" My first answer is that he or she will probably have a better mathematics education than most other mathematics majors, one characterized by deeper understanding of basic concepts and a fuller appreciation of mathematics in the wider culture. But my second answer is, "Would you ask a question like this of preparation for, say, engineering?" If people decide to be social workers or ministers after preparing for engineering, then they must acquire the requisite preparation for their newly chosen field. Why should we suppose that preparation for nothing-in-particular is sound preparation for teaching?

Ohanian and Meier are basically right. Education modeled from the bottom up would be characterized by greater freedom, more energetic pursuit of continuing interests, and greater sense of purpose. But to bring it off will require greater trust in both our students and teachers. Will students make wise choices? Will teachers guide them well? And will teachers prepare themselves so well that every course they offer is rich in a wide range of human concerns?

References

Adler, M. 1982. *The Paideia Proposal.* New York: Macmillan.

Booth, W. C. 1988. *The Vocation of a Teacher.* Chicago: University of Chicago Press.

Franklin, U. 1992. *The Real World of Technology.* Concord, Ontario: Anansi Press.

Gardner, H. 1983. *Frames of Mind.* New York: Basic Books.

Hutchins, R. M. 1936. *The Higher Learning in America.* New Haven, Conn.: Yale University Press.

Noddings, N. 1992. *The Challenge to Care in Schools.* New York: Teachers College Press.

———. 1993. *Educating for Intelligent Belief or Unbelief.* New York: Teachers College Press.

———. 1994. "Does Everybody Count?" *Journal of Mathematical Behavior* 13: 89–104.

9

Reimagining Teacher Education

Through a Kindergarten Looking Glass

NONA LYONS

The editor had put the question to me, a teacher educator: Could the idea of kindergarten practice be a useful concept to hasten the reform of teacher education? In contrast to reform rooted in teacher testing or in standards, knowledge, or technique, could "kindergarten," that is, the practice of a good kindergarten teacher, become a transforming metaphor for reimagining how teachers should be educated for today's complex classrooms?

Contemplating the question, my mind veers towards particulars. Images of kindergarten classrooms come into view. Vibrant with color, these classes showcase children's work: It is everywhere—on walls, hanging from ceilings, along hallways and in corridors. Bright with children's imaginings, rooms appear nearly alive—no matter what the setting, whether a now-shabby public school building or a magnificent, new "children's center." But mostly when I think of kindergartens, I see children with each other and at play. They are at easels with paint streaming down papers before them, at water tables, experimenting with containers of all shapes and sizes, in doll corners at play in some family drama, by a set of blocks constructing great towers, sitting on the floor listening to a story, or standing as storytellers, eager eyes riveted upon them. I am aware of the intensity, the animated engagement of the children with each other and with things, their teachers at work quietly but competently among them, figures who appear as coaches, eager to join their students at play. But could kindergarten indeed serve as a transforming idea for rethinking teacher education at a time of intense urgency about reform? to take to teacher interns learning to teach? or experienced teachers? to the sometimes stark, difficult school and home situations of today's rural and urban students?

123

Suddenly one thing becomes clear: Any serious consideration of this idea has to come not from some verbal recommendation or pronouncement but from being in a kindergarten classroom, from seeing a kindergarten teacher at work. But who could mentor such a process, allow entry into her classroom? One person stands as a possibility, Vivian Paley, the writer and teacher who has chronicled her own kindergarten experiences through a set of award-winning books—an acknowledged good kindergarten practitioner. While there are many good kindergarten teachers with differing beliefs about kindergarten whose experience could be relevant here, Vivian Paley's writings provide the rare combination of being both vivid descriptions of classroom life and a teacher's reflections on them. But what could teacher interns learn from apprenticing themselves to a Vivian Paley in her classroom? And what good might that be for reforming teacher education?

This chapter takes up that speculation. It draws primarily on the experiences of one kindergarten teacher to consider just how good kindergarten practice might refocus a conversation about what teachers today need to know and be able to demonstrate, and how they might be educated to do that. I first present a vignette of Vivian Paley at work, retelling a classroom story from her own writing, noting themes that emerge as the story unfolds. Then I take up what we learn from her experience as we examine how she comes to know what she knows and how she learns. Finally, I suggest what it is that we might take to teacher education from a kindergarten experience and what use that might be to teacher education reform.

Vignette: The Kindergarten Teacher in Her Classroom

In her classroom, Vivian Paley is deemed a master. For some thirty years she successfully taught preschool and kindergarten children at the University of Chicago Laboratory Schools. From time to time, she paused to write up what she had learned about teaching and her students. She gathered these ideas into books: *Wally's Stories; White Teacher; Boys and Girls: Superheroes in the Doll Corner; The Boy Who Would Be a Helicopter; Kawanzaa and Me; You Can't Say You Can't Play;* and most recently, *The Girl with the Brown Crayon.* Typically, each book is a story of some puzzle the teacher encountered and her efforts to understand it, her students, and herself. The titles of the books reveal these themes. *You Can't Say You Can't Play,* for example, recounts Paley's experiment instituting that new rule in her kindergarten. *Kawanzaa and Me* is an examination of integration, self-segregation, and racism. But each of Paley's narratives is also a story of her own development in knowing children. To explore one example, I turn to the book, *The Boy Who Would Be a Helicopter* (1990).

In it, Paley seeks to understand a child, Jason, who seemed determined to remain an outsider. Paley tells us that while there are labels that might be attached to Jason, "we'll neither define nor categorize him," but see him in his school setting (xii).

The Story of Jason

To Paley, the child Jason seemed the quintessential outsider. He spoke only of helicopters and their broken blades. He appeared not to see other children in the kindergarten classroom. As he crouched behind the arrangement of blocks he called an airport, the children listened to his monologue:

> This blade is turning around now you're going faster now you're going faster now you're going to crash now you're going off the ground now you're going up, up, up, up now you're going pshshsh loud br-r-r-rooooom now you're going to land . . . okay all safely. (29)

Curious about the boy and his helicopter fantasy even though he will not play with them or let them touch his helicopter, the children keep track of Jason. The teacher, however, worries about the boy, who mostly plays alone, tells stories to himself, and can respond only about his broken helicopter. The teacher realizes, "Some intuition tells Jason he must oppose our purposes and protect himself from our intrusions. He wails in fright if his helicopter is touched, and he breaks up our talk with earsplitting noises. Appearing to push us away, he achieves the opposite: We cannot take our eyes off him" (29).

For the teacher, the questions are compelling: What happens to those children who remain on the outside? Although they can shed the strongest light upon the classroom, illuminate one's teaching, they present the greatest challenge: How can the teacher mark this child's growth? or foster it?

In the past, Paley tells us, she would have used a list of the words and phrases Jason learned to borrow from the children who pushed their way into his private world. Yet she is surprised that this discovery—one of her own with other children—should work, would work with this child. She tells herself,

> I have said as much before. But apparently have not entirely understood or believed in the process until Jason came along. As I learn to listen to what he tells us about his helicopter fantasy, I begin to see in new ways that only by reaching into the endemic imagery of each child can we proceed together in any mutual enterprise. All else is superficial; we will not have touched one another. (11–12)

Thus Paley enters into a profound inquiry: to uncover Jason's story, observing and looking for ways of connecting with him through the children of her classroom, as they through their imaginations join their play fantasies with Jason's. It will be a school year's journey. How will she reach the boy who seems trapped in a private fantasy? Can he be brought into the life of play that surrounds him?

For years Vivian Paley has tape-recorded her students and thoughtfully listened each night to them as she puzzled to understand exactly how play functioned in their lives. Through her rich and careful observations, she allows us to see these children and her own developing ways of thinking as she joins in their fantasies. Her story of Jason is a teacher's diary. It tells the dramatic story of the boy Jason and his ultimate triumph and return into the society of his classmates. As we follow Jason's struggle, we see the classroom as Paley does: as the crucible of children's storytelling through which they learn to exert control over their own fantasies. For Paley, play with its core of storytelling is all:

> "Pretend" often confuses the adult, but it is the child's real and serious world, the stage upon which any identity is possible and secret thoughts can be safely revealed. . . . Children newly arrived in school, drift and worry until someone shares a fantasy and there are roles to play. Then there comes a sense of place and person, and the words flow with purpose and pleasure. (6–7)

Thus Paley understands,

> [Children] do not pretend to be storytellers; they are storytellers. It is their intuitive approach to all occasions. It is the way they think. . . . We were taught to say that play is the work of children. But, watching and listening to them, I saw that play was nothing less than Truth and Life. (17)

The Teacher As Inquirer, a Student of Her Students

Through the story of Jason, Vivian Paley offers an important idea, the image of the teacher as a questioner, an inquirer, the teacher as a researcher of her own practice, one who uses narrative as a mode of inquiry to further her own understanding. In this role, Paley is the seasoned practitioner who never takes her understanding of her practice for granted. The work that she has done recording the play of her students, listening and relistening to the tapes of their conversations repays us as readers as well as it has her. By following her line of experimentation over time with Jason, we see revealed her practice, her attentiveness, her reformulations of ideas and theory through her own hard-earned discoveries.

Early in the school year, Paley begins her work with Jason with an invention. She tells us of a special day in her kindergarten:

> One day when Jason is not in school, I tell a story to the small group that sits at his snack table.
> "There once was a boy who would not say hello to anyone, not even to the teacher."
> "Is it a true story?" [the child] Lilly asks.
> "I'll tell you some more and you can decide [says the teacher continuing the story]. Instead of hello he said 'Br-r-room!' Every day he roared as he walked past the teacher on his way to the blocks."
> "'Good morning!' the teacher would call out. 'You brought your red helicopter today!'"
> The children smile in recognition. "Is it Jason?"
> "I'll tell more. The boy did not answer the teacher. He was busy carrying big blocks to a corner by the window."
> "It's Jason, I know," Alex beams. "You're just pretending a story, right?"
> "Yeah, yeah," they all tell me. "It's just pretend. That's really Jason."
> The children are pleased with my story; they see nothing wrong with someone saying, "Br-r-room!" instead of hello.
> "Is the story finished?" Lilly asks.
> "One more part. Then the boy landed his helicopter in the airport. And when it landed something happened."
> "The blades got broken!" everyone yells happily. "And he fixed them!"
> "That's the end." My story is done, and I've found out what I need to know. Jason's story makes sense to the children. It is up to me to discover why.
> "Tell it again," Joseph says.
> "I will when Jason is here. Do you think he'll like to hear it?"
> "Of course he will," Lilly assures me. "It's about his helicopter." (30)

But when Jason is in school, he resists the children's attempts to bring him into their play. When Joseph has an idea that Jason's helicopter could be a rescue helicopter in one of Joseph's own stories, Jason refuses. Joseph tries to persist and glares at the silent boy bent over a helicopter.

Paley muses,

> His best logic will not work, and he is puzzled. So am I. The function of classroom fantasy, as both Joseph and I see it, is to communicate ideas and influence group culture. But Jason's play seems to have a different goal. He wants us to know his helicopter story, yet we are not to enter its sphere. (31)

Rethinking the Meaning of Play and Fantasy in Children's Lives

This acknowledgment brings for Paley a questioning, particularly of her belief that fantasy theories on which she is basing her work with students can serve to bring all children out of isolation and into social groups. But if it does not work for Jason, the teacher will change her stance: from theory maker to storyteller, a storyteller who likes suspense, not knowing fully about characters, nor plot outcomes, but watching for the unexpected. Thus, Paley goes on following and recounting Jason's story. She recounts as well her own changing understandings of play, how she has moved from a "glib acceptance of play to a serious analysis of its content."

She says,

> I have studied the subject through teaching and writing, and I cannot do one without the other. For me, the tape recorder is a necessity. I transcribe each day's play and stories and conversations and then make up my own stories about what is happening. The next morning my reality will be measured alongside of the children's. . . . I continually expand my definitions of what we are doing in the classroom. (18)

Once Paley believed it was her task to help students solve their problems. After several years she realized she needed to study children's play to sort out *how* play helped children solve their own problems. But, Paley observes,

> Today I would add: Put your play into formal narratives, and I will help you and your classmates listen to one another. In this way you will build a literature of images and themes, of beginnings and endings, of references and allusions. You must invent your own literature if you are to connect your ideas to the ideas of others. (18)

Children, Paley discovered, through their own and others' fantasies "played out solutions to their immediate problems and distant fears" (19). Once Paley began to view the children as storytellers and playwrights, the potential of fantasy for her as a learning tool overwhelmed her conventional expectations of the classroom. Thus, life in the classroom constantly reinterprets and refines theory.

It seems important to note that Paley does not seek to name causes, to find a causality in a child's behavior. She deals with finding the logic of a child's thinking within the life of the classroom. That is why play becomes so important.

Thus Paley is alert to the moment when Jason one day interrupts his helicopter fantasy. On that day Jason's classmate Simon is telling his story on the square in the center of the story room rug, a sacrosanct place. The class rule is that children other than the storyteller cannot come on stage unless they are players in the story. But this day Jason refuses to abide by the rule and enters the story. He revs up his helicopter motors. Over the din of Jason's helicopter, Paley says to Simon,

> "Is there a helicopter in this story?"
> "No," Simon replies.
> "Then you mustn't come on the stage, Jason." (37)

Jason has heard this reasoning before. You may not enter a story unless the author gives you a role to perform. Commentary is welcome anytime, but permission is required to insert a new character into someone's story.

Paley continues,

> I resume Simon's story and again Jason forges loudly onto the stage.
> "Simon, is there a helicopter in your story? Do squirrels see a helicopter?" Simon can barely hear me over Jason's tumult.
> "No . . . uh, yeah, they do. They heered it flying over there. Then it lands on this spot. Right here."
> Jason winds down and stops on the designated place. "Br-ur-rumpt! I turned off the motor," he says. Jason has deliberately furthered another child's story. Why does he respond now, not earlier . . . ? In any case, today for the first time Jason has listened. (37–38)

Thus through a long experience of play, Jason attends to his classmates. Why now? The next day, Jason says, "Yes," when the teacher asks if he wants to tell a story. Jason begins, "And a helicopter. A turbo prop. It's flying." Paley comments, "How could his first story be anything else?" As Jason zooms around as his story comes to an end, Paley asks,

> "I wonder if the helicopter sees another plane."
> "Someone," he [Jason] answers.
> "Which someone?"
> "The squirrel someone."
> Simon stands up, "He means me! I'm the plane, right?" Jason nods, and Simon imitates the helicopter roar we have come to know so well. Chins forward, arms in motion, the boys fly together in formation. (38–39)

Why now? Paley wonders. Why now? Extending her ideas about the role of play and fantasy, she sees an answer in a child's need to have a friend and be part of a dramatic structure:

> Children see themselves, always inside a story. Indeed, friendship itself is defined in terms of fantasy roles. You are a friend if you take part in someone's

play, and you are most likely to listen to those with whom you are acting out a series of events. . . . Friendship and fantasy form the natural path that leads children into a new world of other voices, other views, and other ways of expressing ideas and feelings they recognize as similar to their own.

If friendship and fantasy provide links to individual children, there is yet a third condition that completes the frame within which school makes sense: the need to become part of a larger group. It is the group that most influences the development of the storyteller. (33–34)

Through Paley's research, Jason, his classmates, and their interactions become available to us. We see Jason with his playmates as they construct their own understandings. But peering into their lives, we are fortunate to be able to see Paley's as well.

Lessons from a Kindergarten Experience

Stepping back from these experiences, what have we learned from being in a kindergarten classroom? What do we find compelling from listening to children's stories and their teacher's narrative? What could we take from this to teacher education? I want to revisit some of the examples we have been examining to elaborate several points, some ways to think about being a teacher.

The Teacher As a Curious Seeker of Children's Meanings

It is clear that Vivian Paley has an enormous curiosity. She does not stand as an authority in her classroom nor as an observer. Rather she presents herself as energetically and imaginatively engaged with her students, curious about a child, his or her classmates, her own ways of understanding, and most clearly about how children learn. She expects to be surprised. "We want to talk about what we don't understand and ask what has not worked according to expectations" (47). Because of this curiosity, Paley pays attention to the most minute details of what kids do and say. And she finds ways to do that, tape-recording children's interactions, transcribing them each night, reading and rereading them, and then erasing them to use her single tape another day. She does not seek first to impose an interpretation of what a child may be up to. Rather through her reflections she seeks instead the child's meaning in the context of the small, social world of the classroom. She lets that be her guide to action. She empowers children by her stance. They know she listens. She cares passionately about them. But she reveals how much we as teachers may not know about our students and need to discover. Paley shows us how, portraying the role of teacher as inquirer.

But can this role be learned? How? Paley acknowledges that "I was neither a good listener nor an able storyteller when my name became teacher" (15). In her *Harvard Educational Review* article, "On Listening to What Children Say" (1986), Paley describes how she learned to be an inquirer, curious in the classroom. Once she witnessed a visitor to her classroom who held a different stance in interacting with her students, attentive to what the kindergarten children were doing, open and curious to uncovering the sense children made of their experience, delighted at discovering children's own ideas. Paley describes the shock of recognition she faced when she, observing this visitor, realized that in contrast "she listened more to herself than to any of the children in the classroom" (123). That awareness made her truly curious about her own role. When she simultaneously discovered the tape recorder and began taping children's interactions with her and with one another, she realized, "I could become my own best witness":

> The tape recorder, with its unrelenting fidelity, captured the unheard or unfinished murmur, the misunderstood and mystifying context, the disembodied voices asking for clarification and comfort. It also captured the impatience in my voice as children struggled for attention, approval, and justice. The tape recordings created for me an overwhelming need to know more about the process of teaching and learning and about my own classroom as a unique society to be studied. (1986, 123–124)

Paley discovered how she could be a reflective practitioner, becoming vulnerable to learning from her own misunderstandings.

Connecting Practice to Children's Lives, Interests, and Meanings

It is clear that Vivian Paley has her eyes on children, on their ways of making sense and meaning. By paying attention to, searching out the meaning children give to their experience and to the experiences of their classmates, the teacher redirects her actions with her students. Meaning becomes her starting point for the lessons she will encourage, for thinking about what she knows and understands, and for revising it. Paley drives home the necessity for the teacher to be an ongoing learner, revising understandings, rethinking her practice. She makes clear why there are no simple pedagogies to be mastered once and for all, why every class is new and teaching itself a lifelong act of learning. "The act of teaching became a daily search for the child's point of view accompanied by the sometimes unwelcome disclosure of my hidden attitude" (1986, 124).

Refining, Revising, and Constructing Theory in the Crucible of the Narratives of One's Own Classroom

Vivian Paley not only knows theory about play and fantasy in the lives of children, she creates it. Her knowledge is actively reviewed and refined through her daily reflections on the interactions of her students with each other and with her. She knows what she knows but she constantly puts it to a serious test. Clearly, Paley does not disdain theory. Rather she is attentive to it and puts it in her service. In doing so in her classroom, she extends and refines it. Her documentation of her understanding of play in the life of children and the role of fantasy in it is a stunning example. Fantasy, she believes, is a real and present way for children to enter each other's lives, to extend and know another. Her knowledge of this has been constructed because she pays attention to how children are and what they consider meaning to be. Through her daily reflections on a classroom's happenings, on the things that don't make sense, and on the logic of children, she refines and revises her understandings.

The Usefulness of Story to the Teacher as Well as to Students

It is important to note the role of storytelling here. Storytelling is a mode of knowing for teachers as well as for children. Events in a classroom mostly can be read like the scripts of plays. They are temporal, things happen in time, with key players, key actors. There is action and intention (Bruner 1985). But things can and do go awry, creating new puzzles. Storying experiences may be the most productive mode for capturing and trying to understand them. Thus teacher narratives can be important sources of a teacher's own knowledge of practice and of understanding how students learn. Constructing narratives of classroom practice, telling stories of practice, keeping journals, doing one's own research are exemplary forms of reflection for teachers (Carter 1993; Connelly and Clandinin 1990; Lyons 1998; Witherell and Noddings 1991). In the example presented here, Vivian Paley through her own narrative constructs new knowledge, something she did not know before. Teachers can remain students of their own practice. They can do so through story making.

Taking Kindergarten to the Reform of Teacher Education

It seems clear that being in Vivian Paley's classroom is a powerful and compelling experience. Through it we find an effective way of seeing and acting with children, of being a teacher. We could usefully take that image to the reform of teacher education. But before we do so, the history of educational reform urges a word of caution.

Recently David Tyack and Larry Cuban have argued that when thinking about school reform, it is as important to consider how schools change reform as it is to consider how reform changes schools. And although policymakers might "lament that their plans become transformed in practice," Tyack and Cuban offer another equally plausible view, a pragmatic yet creative one:

> Goals and plans might be construed as hypotheses; alterations of policies in practice might then be expected as institutional facts of life. If policymakers anticipate and encourage adaptations of their plans, they can design reforms to produce hybrids that are blends of the new and the old, the cosmopolitan and the local. (1995, 60)

To make their argument for this interactive view of how schools change reforms and are changed by them, Tyack and Cuban use two case studies, one about the introduction of the junior high school and the other the story of the kindergarten. It seems useful to review here, however briefly, this history of kindergarten as one school reform effort.

When kindergarten was introduced into the United States in the nineteenth century, it immediately became the hope of pioneers of the movement who were critical of the existing, traditional school curriculum. One advocate of kindergarten, Elizabeth Peabody of Boston, referred to it as "the children's garden." As reported by Tyack and Cuban (1995, 64–65), Peabody believed that the then-graded public schools treated children as "automata, learning machines, rather than as spontaneous, curious, active, impressionable children." She urged that kindergarten teachers treat their pupils as "children in society . . . a commonwealth or republic of children" in contrast to the absolute monarchy she found in public schools. Reformers of the day hoped that kindergarten would be a cure for urban social ills as well as a model of education for young children. Although founded largely as independent institutions, kindergartens become so popular a concept that they soon became a regular part of public school systems, growing from only about 7 percent in 1900 to about 20 percent by 1920 to 60 percent by 1970. But as Tyack and Cuban document, as kindergarten became institutionalized it became not the instrument of reform for elementary schools, but rather was modified by them. The kindergarten story did not go undiluted:

> In many ways . . . in both theory and in practice, public school kindergartens became assimilated to the primary grades, a departure from the earlier praise of the kindergarten as an antidote to the traditional school. When the kindergarten became institutionalized, the original claim of

reformers . . . was diluted if not forgotten. A much more modest bureaucratic rationale became central: that the kindergarten would prepare five-year-olds for first grade in a scientifically determined developmental way. Some of the features that had made the kindergarten exotic were slowly trimmed away or changed to fit the institutional character of the elementary school. (1995, 69)

While the advocates of kindergarten did not transform the system as they had hoped, they did "focus attention on serious problems and experimented with practices that rippled through corners of the traditional pattern of schooling" (75–76). Thus in a kind of interaction kindergarten was modified by the elementary school and in turn modified it.

Reflection: Reimagining Teacher Education

If we take seriously the thoughtful advice of Tyack and Cuban and expect school reform efforts to be seen in interaction with existing practices and adaptations of them, then I believe the idea of good kindergarten practice can be a useful and important idea and ideal to take to teacher education and its reform. That is, we would expect adaptations but be guided by Paley. Learning from Paley, new and experienced teachers would (1) deliberately foster a curiosity about one's students and their ways of making meaning; (2) find ways to study the puzzles encountered in a classroom around how children learn; (3) seek to understand how to link lessons to students' interests; and (4) interrogate theory to enhance one's observations and learning. I would also add, make use of narrative, of stories of teaching experiences, telling these stories as stories to others and oneself as a critical, reflective activity for shaping one's knowledge of practice (Lyons 1998). These practices would in fact help to realize the student-centered practice and a constructionist view that reformers today hope to achieve. Keeping in mind how a kindergarten teacher is in the classroom surely would encourage attending to children, apprenticing oneself to them in learning, becoming in fact a particular kind of reflective practitioner. Gazing at a kindergarten looking glass could provide a potentially powerful perspective to reimagine teaching in any classroom today.

References

Bruner, J. 1985. "Narrative and Paradigmatic Modes of Thought." In *Learning and Teaching the Ways of Knowing*, ed. E. Eisner, 97–117. Chicago: National Society for the Study of Education.

Carter, K. 1993. "The Place of Story in Research on Teaching and Teacher Education." *Educational Researcher* 22 (1): 5–18.

Connelly, M., and D. J. Clandinin. 1990. "Stories of Experience and Narrative Inquiry." *Educational Researcher* 19 (5): 2–14.

Lyons, N. 1998. "Constructing Narratives for Understanding: Using Portfolio Interviews to Scaffold Teacher Reflection." In *With Portfolio in Hand: Validating the New Teacher Professionalism,* ed. N. Lyons. New York: Teachers College Press.

Paley, V. 1979. *White Teacher.* Cambridge, Mass.: Harvard University Press.

————. 1981. *Wally's Stories.* Cambridge, Mass.: Harvard University Press.

————. 1984. *Boys and Girls: Superheroes in the Doll Corner.* Chicago: University of Chicago Press.

————. 1986. "On Listening to What Children Say." *Harvard Educational Review* 56 (2): 122–131.

————. 1990. *The Boy Who Would Be a Helicopter.* Cambridge, Mass.: Harvard University Press.

————. 1992. *You Can't Say You Can't Play.* Cambridge, Mass.: Harvard University Press.

————. 1995. *Kawanzaa and Me: A Teacher's Story.* Cambridge, Mass.: Harvard University Press.

————. 1997. *The Girl with the Brown Crayon.* Cambridge, Mass.: Harvard University Press.

Tyack, D., and L. Cuban. 1995. *Tinkering Towards Utopia: A Century of School Reform.* Cambridge, Mass.: Harvard University Press.

Witherell, C., and N. Noddings. 1991. *Stories Lives Tell: Narrative and Dialogue in Education.* New York: Teachers College Press.

10

The Problems and Possibilities
of Contextualized Educational Research
in the Democratic Tradition

EVANS CLINCHY

As Alejandro Sanz de Santamaria suggests in Chapter 4, describing his economics research in Garcia Rovira, higher education's disconnection from the real world—in his case, the real world of the peasant community he was researching—applies to large portions of the scholarly educational research that is conducted in contemporary American society. Such research is all too often conducted not *by* or *with* actual practitioners out in the schools but *at* and *upon* them by college and university social scientists, primarily psychologists and sociologists but also university-trained social science researchers in the private consulting sector. The first allegiance of such researchers is not to education or to the public schools but to their scholarly disciplines and to the disengaged, purely "objective" research practices of the social sciences. It is only through such "scientifically respectable," abstracted, impersonal, and almost always decontextualized and mathematically reductive disciplinary research and publication—and through teaching students in those disconnected college and university classrooms—that college and university researchers get college or university jobs, receive tenure, advance to full professorships, and attain eminence in their scholarly fields.

This does not mean that all educational or social science research is useless and irrelevant. We can point to the examples of useful research in human cognition and human development by Gardner, Resnick, and others cited in this book and to the work of such people as Piaget, Vygotsky, Bruner, Eleanor Duckworth, Michael Cole, Margaret Donaldson, Jane Roland Martin, Nel Noddings, Linda Darling Hammond, and the four authors of *Women's Ways of Knowing*. There is also the growing field of qualitative, participatory action research that is beginning to have a transformative effect on the scholarly world.

136

Still, the great bulk of everyday educational research conducted in and by institutions of higher education, and in particular by schools of education, is all too often irrelevant to the needs of people out in the schools and is thus ignored by practitioners in those schools.

As in the case of Sanz de Santamaria's economics research, this does not mean that such educational research is harmless. Quite the opposite. It does a great deal of harm.

As Sanz de Santamaria describes the personal results of his academic research in Garcia Rovira (and substituting *educational* for *economic*),

> It has revealed to me the totalitarian nature of the exercise of social power that is ingrained in the conventional forms of producing and using [educational] knowledge. This pattern in the exercising of social power is embedded in the radical separation between, on the one hand, the few individuals who participate in the production and use of [educational] knowledge and, on the other, the [people in the schools] who, in spite of being the most deeply affected by these processes, are maintained as nonparticipants in the production and use of this knowledge.

He goes on to say (and now substituting *educational researcher* for *economist*),

> As for the role of the academic [educational researcher], this experience has taught me that it cannot be any more than that of an "external" agent in charge of the limited and comfortable task of producing knowledge to justify recommendations. Such a role leads only to undesirable scenarios: the production and circulation of useless knowledge and recommendations that nobody takes seriously; or the use of knowledge and recommendations as weapons to exert subtle but violent forms of social power through science.

But, in the case of much contemporary educational research, his first scenario is not quite applicable. Although a great deal of the knowledge generated by educational researchers may be useless and have little to do with the realities of life in our schools, it is often the case that it *is* taken seriously, not by the people in the schools who know that it is useless and irrelevant, but by many of the people who influence or actually make the decisions about what will happen in our public schools. This includes policy makers in state and federal bureaucracies, state and federal legislators, citizens elected to local school boards, administrators in school system central offices, and people in the print and visual media who report the findings of such "objective," "scientific" research as the simple truth and thus badly mislead both the decision makers and the public at large.

In short, much of this research-generated "knowledge" is taken as literal fact and reality by the nonschool people who set our national, state, and local political and social priorities, who make the decisions about how much money will be invested in our schools, and who invent the "goals" and "standards" and authoritarian mandates that are laid upon school people. The latter are thus "maintained as nonparticipants in the production and use of this knowledge."

It is precisely because powerful decision makers *do* pay attention to this educational research, useless and irrelevant though it may be, that Sanz de Santamaria's second scenario comes into play. It is through the use of this "knowledge," operating under the cloak of objective, disinterested science, that our schools and the students and adult staffs in them are coerced into organizational structures, educational practices, and human relationships that many of them know in their heads and hearts to be educationally unsound. And many members of adult staffs are fully aware that these practices are actually harmful to the young people in their charge.

Although many examples could be cited here, one major one will perhaps suffice: the case of the current *A Nation at Risk*/Goals 2000 educational reform agenda.[1]

In this instance, a National Commission on Excellence in Education was formed in 1981 by the then U.S. Secretary of Education Terrell Bell. The commission consisted of eighteen people: four college or university presidents, two university professors, two business executives, one former state commissioner of education, one past president of the National School Boards Association, one immediate past president of a big city school board, one member of a state board of education, one former governor, one superintendent of schools, one educational consultant, two principals, and *one teacher*.

The commission's charge from Secretary Bell did not begin with the mission of dispassionately exploring the question of the excellence or nonexcellence of our educational system, beginning with a discussion and explanation of methods for defining and then recognizing excellence. Nor did Bell assign the commission members the task of spending many hours, days, and weeks in the daily routines of real schools inhabited by real students and real school people, listening carefully to what they had to say, living the lives they live, and finding out at first hand what those people believe the real problems of public education in this country to be. Rather, Bell asked them to begin with his own premise (he called it "the widespread public perception") that "something is seriously amiss in our educational system."

He instructed the commission to pursue several tasks: "assessing the quality of teaching and learning in our public and private schools, colleges, and universities"; "comparing American schools and colleges with those of other advanced nations"; "studying the relationship between college admissions requirements and student achievement in high school"; "identifying educational programs which result in notable success in college"; "assessing the degree in which major social and educational changes in the last quarter century have affected student achievement"; and "defining problems which must be faced and overcome if we are successfully to pursue the course of excellence in education." In actual fact, the commission decided that the problems of higher education were being handled by someone else and that the private schools were not the real problem, so the focus came down to the vast array of problems created by what was "seriously amiss" in the public elementary and secondary schools of the country.

Given the fact that the commission and its staff did not base their investigation on a direct, first-hand immersion in the schools, they were forced to rely on five main indirect, "radically separate" sources of information: (1) a series of fifty-three papers to be produced by academic research experts in colleges, universities, policy research centers (Sanz de Santamaria's "external agents"); (2) the staff's analysis of already existing academic research on "problems in education" (more "external agents"); (3) testimony gathered from "administrators, teachers, students, representatives of professional and public groups, parents, business leaders, public officials, and scholars, who testified at eight meetings of the full commission, six public hearings, two panel discussions, a symposium, and a series of meetings organized by the Department of Education's regional offices"; (4) "letters from concerned citizens, teachers, and administrators who volunteered extensive comments on the problems and possibilities in American education"; and (5) "descriptions of notable programs and promising approaches in education."

After roughly eighteen months of study and report writing, the commission and its staff issued *A Nation at Risk* in April 1983. It outlined fourteen "dimensions of the risk before us" that "have been amply documented by the testimony received by the commission" and inadvertently spelled out the commission's definition of "educational excellence" and the measures for judging it:

> International comparisons of student achievement, completed a decade ago, reveal that on nineteen academic tests American students were never first or second and, in comparisons with other industrialized nations, were last seven times.
>
> Some 23 million American adults are functionally illiterate by the simplest tests of reading, writing, and comprehension.
>
> About 13 percent of all 17 year olds in the United States can be considered functionally illiterate. Functional illiteracy among minority youth may run as high as 40 percent.

Average achievement of high school students on most standardized tests is now lower than years ago when Sputnik was launched.

The College Board's Scholastic Assessment Tests (SAT) demonstrate a virtually unbroken decline from 1963 to 1980. Average verbal scores fell over 50 points and average math scores dropped nearly 40 points.

College Board achievement tests also reveal consistent declines in recent years in such subjects as physics and English. Both the number and proportion of students demonstrating superior achievement on the SAT's (i.e., those with scores of 650 of higher) have also dramatically declined.

Many 17 year olds do not possess the "higher order" intellectual skills we should expect of them. Nearly 40 percent cannot draw inferences from written material; only one fifth can write a persuasive essay; and only one-third can solve a mathematics problem involving several steps.

There was a steady decline in science achievement scores of U.S. 17 year olds as measured by national assessments of science in 1969, 1973, and 1977.

Between 1975 and 1980, remedial mathematics courses in public 4 year colleges increased by 72 percent and now constitute one-quarter of all mathematics courses taught in those institutions.

Average tested achievement of students graduating from college is also lower.

Business and military leaders complain that they are required to spend millions of dollars on costly remedial education and training programs in such basic skills as reading, writing, spelling, and computation.

The Great Danger

Although *A Nation at Risk* is only one example, it illustrates the great danger of the almost universal use to which this brand of educational research is put throughout the educational establishment itself and, through the popular press and other media, the general American public. And that danger is that such "research data" are used *as virtually the only method of defining and then rendering judgment upon the quality of the education offered in this country's public schools.*

Whenever the question of educational quality—or in the case of *A Nation at Risk,* educational excellence—is raised, we do not find ourselves talking about the overall growth and development of students as thinking, feeling, caring human beings, as thoughtful and responsible future citizens of a possibly more just and humane democratic society. Rather, we find ourselves defining the question and rendering judgment *solely in terms of academic achievement scores on those standardized tests.* It is those tests, the result of almost one hundred years of the application of social science methods of research in the field of education, that have now become virtually the sole arbiter of whether our schools are doing the job they should be doing. By their very nature, these tests and the research based upon them, purporting to describe the gains or losses in academic achievement of our students, are "objective," abstracted, decontextualized, dehumanized sets of mathematical figures, charts, and graphs. Students and teachers disappear as flesh-and-blood livers of lives.

In the case of *A Nation at Risk,* there is a great deal of rhetoric about students' fulfilling their individual potential and having the necessary skills to become productive members of society and good workers in the global economy. But when we come to the recommendations for improving the schools, we get the following main prescriptions:

> That all students seeking a high school diploma be required to take the New Basics: four years of English, three years of mathematics, three years of science, three years of social studies, and one half year of computer science, along with other less basic things such as a foreign language, fine and performing arts, and vocational education. . . .
>
> That schools, colleges, and universities adopt more rigorous and measurable standards, and higher expectations for academic performance and student conduct, and that four-year colleges and universities raise their requirements for admission. . . .
>
> That significantly more time be devoted to learning the New Basics. This will require more effective use of the existing school day, a longer school day, or a lengthened school year. . . .

The overpowering thrust of these recommendations is clear: the answer to what ails us educationally is not more money or a greater share of national resources put into the public educational system or a radical devolution of power down to people actually working in the schools. It is once again Sanz de Santamaria's "totalitarian . . . exercise of social power that is ingrained in the conventional forms of producing and using [educational] knowledge . . . embedded in the radical separation between, on the one hand, the few individuals who participate in the production and use of [educational] knowledge" from "the [people in the schools] who . . . are maintained as nonparticipants."

What *A Nation at Risk* recommends, and what has subsequently become the nation's education agenda through the Goals 2000 program, is simply a tightening of control over public schools by the federal, state, and local authorities who control the educational policies and the educational purse strings. The people in the schools are left essentially powerless and unassisted. The message to everyone in the schools is simple and unambiguous: the only important thing that needs to be accomplished in the "reform" of public schools is to increase the academic achievement scores on standardized tests. The school people are told, "Pull up your socks! Work harder, keep your nose to the grindstone, do more teacher and student homework, and don't expect much if any additional funding, more and better materials, or decent facilities. Above all, don't expect to be given more autonomy, more authority to do what *you* think is best for your students. Do, instead, what we say you should do. Meet the standards we determine you should meet, whether you agree with them or not." Hardly a welcome prescription for radical change and improvement.

The Questionable Basis for Research-Based Policy Making

Few if any school people would dispute the idea that there is great room for improvement in the public schools, and no one believes there is any excuse for situations in which children are not taught the fundamental skills of reading, writing, and computation. But the fact remains that there is great educational and social danger in the attempt to define and judge our educational system through the use of social science research and solely on the results of standardized, pencil-and-paper academic tests.

To no small degree, this danger stems from the fact that there is simply no agreement within the social science community itself as to whether this research and the tests themselves are reliable measures of educational quality.

An instance of this is the fact that in the years since the publication of *A Nation at Risk,* not a single one of the research findings upon which that report was based has gone unchallenged. Indeed, the research and the data in this and most subsequent cases have been either refuted or at the very least substantially challenged, not simply by the people in the schools but by other social science researchers.

The work of Gerald Bracey, one of the country's most respected educational researchers, is a perfect example here. Bracey once a year for the past five years has published in the education profession's foremost journal, *Phi Delta Kappan,* an article entitled "The Bracey Report on the Condition of Public Education." (He also writes a monthly column on educational research for the journal.) Every year for those five years Bracey has reviewed the educational research field and assessed not only the quality of the research conducted over the past year but also the quality of the public rhetoric about education and of the policy decisions and recommendations that may or may not be based upon the research as well as upon the ideological rhetoric.

In his report in the journal's November 1995 issue, Bracey attempted to sum up the American public's still prevailing ideological attitude towards its public school system. He quoted from a *Business Week* cover story article entitled "Will Our Schools Ever Get Better?" published in the magazine's April 17, 1995, issue:

> Americans are fed up with their public schools. Businesses complain that too many job applicants can't read, write, or do simple arithmetic. Parents fear that the schools have become violent cesspools where gangs run amok and that teachers are more concerned with their pensions than their class-rooms. Economists fret that a weak school system is hurting the ability of the U.S. to compete in the global economy. And despite modest improve-ments in test scores, U.S. students still rank far behind most of their inter-national peers in science and math.

"Not one statement in this litany," Bracey claims, "is true, of course, but all are widely held as gospel." While mercifully refraining from pointing out that the national media are in no small measure responsible for these wide-spread misconceptions, he went on to cite compelling counterstatistics sug-gesting that test scores are actually at an all-time high (including the SATs and the College Boards when one takes into account the vastly larger number of students taking the tests) and that very few schools are cesspools of gang vio-lence—and most of those are inner-city schools suffering from what Jona-tha;º Kozol has called "savage inequalities." Further, he said that U.S. studen*ts actually rank high on international tests of math and science, that there is no evidence of any link between the educational performance of American stu-dents and the health of the economy, and that indeed American economic productivity leads all other nations.

In attempting to dispel some of the rampant misconceptions about the low state of academic achievement of American students, Bracey cited a 1992 international study entitled "How in the World Do Children Read?" that found in a comparison of thirty-one nations in the industrial world that only Finnish nine-year-olds outscored American nine-year-olds in reading achievement scores, and a follow-up study by the National Center for Educa-tion Statistics that found that only fourteen-year-old Finnish children scored better than American fourteen-year-olds.

Bracey and many others have clearly spelled out the dangers inherent in relying on such social science research, including their own. But the public at large, misled by the research community and the media, believed that the scores our students make on decontextualized, paper-and-pencil, multiple-choice, standardized academic achievement tests are an acceptable—indeed, the ultimate—way of judging whether those students will become successful, productive members of American society and therefore whether the schools are doing the job we have asked them to do. To the thoroughly unwarranted extent to which our public schools and the people in them are then supported, encouraged, and rewarded on the basis of these public perceptions, this is the *real* national educational scandal that truly puts this nation "at risk."

Does all this mean that we should abandon the use of all standardized tests in our schools? Not necessarily. Some such testing, even the use of standardized achievement tests, can be useful and productive as long as it is purely for diagnostic purposes to determine what reading and writing skills individual students need to learn (although most teachers are already well aware of what their students need to learn). Indeed, historically, these tests, including the IQ tests, have served to rescue many students who have been discriminated against and mislabeled as uneducable.

One possible useful way in which such tests can be used—particularly in those cases where the educational authorities have decreed that they *must* be used—is to employ them in what has come to be called a value-added fashion. That is, the tests are given to all children but are never used to determine whether those children are at that mysterious thing called grade level. Rather, the tests are given at the beginning of a school year to determine where each individual child is in terms of learning how to read, write, and compute. The tests are then given again at the end of the year. If that individual child has advanced roughly one year as measured by the tests, then the child is succeeding—and so is the school itself.

Used in this fashion, the tests then can serve some useful purpose, but only if they are used by teachers and administrators who understand their limitations, who do not use them to make gross and unwarranted comparisons and rankings between students, between schools, and between school systems. The tests can be useful if people do not use them as a primary means of selecting students for advanced or gifted classes and academically selective high schools, and do not assume that scores on such tests can be used to determine whether students are capable of going to college or succeeding out in the real world.

What School People Need

What the people in the schools need from our colleges, universities, schools of education, and the social science profession in general, and from the media, is the help of people who understand what real life is like in our desperately underfunded and often very dangerous public schools. They need the help of people who can respect the wisdom those school people as working stiffs have derived from their everyday experience in those schools. They need help from people who respect the ideas practicing teachers have about improving public schooling, people who will help them develop and implement the good and interesting ideas the school people have about how better to conduct teaching and learning under the difficult conditions of real life in those schools.

They need people working alongside them who see the same problems they see and can help them find workable solutions to those problems, and people who can help them assess whether what they are trying is succeeding.

But, first and above all, the people in our schools need a complete revision of the entire apparatus by which scholarly educational research is conducted and used. We need to take Sanz de Santamaria's and William Coplin's words very much to heart and essentially reverse the authoritarian, antidemocratic power arrangements of the standard academic model of educational research.

Is There Any Hope?

Thankfully, there *is* hope. We do have at least one dramatic example of a pathbreaking educational study conducted in 1991 and 1992 by the Institute for Education in Transformation at the Claremont Graduate School. This research began when faculty members at the graduate school became dissatisfied with what they themselves were doing and began asking themselves some of the tough questions raised in this book.[2]

They wanted, they said,

> to reconnect our graduate education programs with the real life of the schools, to get outside the ivory tower and look at the daily issues that confront students, teachers, administrators, and support staffs inside the public schools of this nation. For us, these projects began as an effort to make our own graduate education programs more relevant, particularly our graduate teacher education internship program. Through our daily work in teacher education and inside schools, it became increasingly clear that there was a tremendous gulf between life inside schools and the perceptions of that life by academicians, policy makers, media, and community leaders.

Two leading members of the graduate faculty, Mary Poplin and Joseph Weeres, were also not completely happy with the various "educational reform" reports that had been emerging over the past fifteen or so years, beginning with *A Nation at Risk*. While agreeing with the position of most of the reports that a crisis did exist in the schools, they were not sure that they were correct in identifying the basic problems of American schooling as being "the serious problem of student underachievement [and students dropping out], [the problem] that there are many children whose home environments make learning difficult, [the problem] that a significant number of teachers are not adequately trained in today's conditions, and [the problem] that these problems and others are exacerbated by the changes that have been, and still are, taking place in the general society outside of our schools."

Even with the very preliminary research they were conducting inside schools, "it was our experience that the best educational practitioners were those most disappointed by these reports, not because they did not believe there was a crisis, but because these reports either missed critical issues or named problems that were only marginally related to those experienced inside schools."

In order to explore these questions more thoroughly, the researchers designed a collaborative, participatory action research project to name and describe the real problems of schooling from the inside. This project would make the actual people living and working inside four typical California elementary and secondary schools the project's active researchers—the students, teachers, day care workers, custodians, secretaries, cafeteria workers, school nurses, administrators, parents, security guards, and counselors. It would be these inside people who would define the problems, conduct the research, and assess the results, not the university people who would be there only to organize and assist the efforts of the insiders.

The four schools selected for the study "had the profile of many schools in this country—low standardized test scores, in middle to lower socioeconomic areas, with students from multiple ethnic and linguistic groups, and faculties who (with the exception of one school that was new) had been in place many years and were largely Euro-American."

The school people conducting the research spent a full year, holding over 160 meetings and four retreats, gathering twenty-four thousand pages of transcriptions, essays, drawings, journal entries and notes, eighteen hours of videotapes and eighty hours of audiotapes. Only after that full year and another six months assessing their findings were they ready to make those findings public in a publication called *Voices from the Inside*.

As Poplin and Weeres put it,

> No one was more surprised by the results of this report than those of us on the outside. We, like the authors of previous reports on schooling and teacher education, would have predicted issues such as what to teach, how to measure it, how much a teacher knows and choice of school would have surfaced; they did not. . . . Indeed, we fear that much of what academicians and policy makers now suggest for the improvement of our schools may actually complicate and exacerbate the problems identified here. At best, their suggestions may not change the situation inside classrooms at all.

The study's report begins by noting one interesting fact and one overall conclusion. The interesting fact is that over the course of the study's eighteen months "the adult participants increasingly understood and came to agree with their students' perceptions of what was wrong with the schools," including one student's devastating statement that "this place hurts my spirit." The overall conclusion is, "Currently, the education system in the U.S. is one in which deeply committed people inside schools feel incapable of acting on their own values. The result is that participants inside schools, from students to administrators, feel unable to meet responsibilities, expectations, and goals for themselves and for others."

The report then laid out the seven basic issues uncovered in the course of the study, none of which involved low academic achievement, dropping out, poor home environments, inadequately trained teachers, or changes in the general society outside of the schools. Rather the real, underlying issues (in condensed form) were the following.

Relationships

The participants felt that the crisis inside schools is directly linked to human relationships and the barrenness, the poor quality, of those relationships. Everyone wanted relationships with individuals who care, listen, understand, respect others, and are honest, open and sensitive. (Nel Noddings has pointed this out in Chapter 8.) Teachers reported that "their best experiences in school are those where they connect with students and are able to help them in some way." They also reported, however, that there is precious little time during the day to seek out individual students. Students also noticed teachers' lack of time to speak to them individually. Parents said they want an honest dialogue between themselves and their children's teachers. Even more important, many parents feared that poor relationships between teachers and their children damage their children's sense of confidence and vitality. When relationships in schools are poor, fear, name calling, threats, or incidents of violence, as well as a sense of depression and hopelessness, exist. This theme was prominently stated by participants and so deeply connected to all other themes in the report that it is believed this may be one of the two most central issues in solving the crisis inside schools.

Race, Culture, and Class

Many students of color and some Euro-Americans perceive schools to be racist and prejudiced, from the staff to the curriculum. Some students doubt the very substance of what is being taught. Many students in public education, especially but not exclusively students of color, are raised in poverty, also creating a myriad of mismatches with school design and expectation. Their prior experiences are often not understood by teachers whose personal experiences have been very different.

Values

While many people think that people of color or poor people in general hold different basic values from those of the dominant culture, the report stated, "our data hold no evidence that people inside schools have significantly different fundamental values. Our data suggest that parents, teachers, students, staff, and administrators of all ethnicities and classes value and desire education, honesty, integrity, beauty, care, justice, courage, and meaningful hard work. . . . However, very little time is spent in classrooms discussing these issues and a number of restrictions exist against doing so."

Teaching and Learning

Students, especially those past fifth grade, frequently report that they are bored in school and see little relevance of what is taught to their lives and their futures. Teachers feel pressured to teach what is mandated and sometimes doubt the appropriateness for their students. Teachers also are often bored by the curriculum they feel they must teach. Students from all groups, remedial and advanced, high school to elementary, desire both rigor and fun in their schoolwork. They express enthusiasm about learning experiences that are complex but understandable, full of rich meanings and discussions of values, require their own participation, and offer some choice. According to student descriptions, the most boring and least relevant schoolwork includes activities that stick closely to standardized materials and traditional teaching methods. Students want more participation in important choices inside classrooms. Teachers feel a need for time to rethink curriculum and instruction and to form honest dialogues with one another regarding teaching. A good deal of knowledge about how to make teaching better already exists, but there is little time to learn or share such knowledge. Many of the students of color bring knowledge from their communities that they do not see represented in school curriculum. This makes them doubt the curriculum and not feel validated.

Safety

Related to disconnected relationships and to not knowing about one another's differences is the issue of safety. Very few school people or parents feel schools are safe places. Teachers, students, and staff fear physical violence. The influence of drugs, gangs, and random violence is felt by students. An alarmingly large number of elementary students feel they may not live to be adults.

Physical Environment

Students want schools that reflect order, beauty, and space, and that contain rich materials and media. The desire for clean, esthetically pleasing, and physically comfortable space is expressed by all groups in schools.

Despair, Hope, and the Process of Change

Many participants felt a hopelessness about schools. Paradoxically, hope seemed to emerge following honest dialogues about the collective despair. Participants were anxious for change and were willing to participate in change they see as relevant. "We have strong indications that change inside schools might best be stimulated through participatory processes. In these self-driven research processes, participants come openly to discuss their hopes and dreams. Through this process, we understood that there were shared common values around which we could begin to imagine a more ideal school."

Here, at least and at last, we have some genuinely democratic, contextualized, personal but still intellectually rigorous research that is abstracted from a welter of first-hand information but abstracted only to a degree that leaves in all of the human elements, all of the human pain and confusion that are the home territory of any decently humane educational enterprise. We need more such research. But most of all, we need to take the next steps and begin the arduous process of translating these findings into genuine, meaningful plans and policies for creating those better elementary and secondary schools—and better colleges, universities, and schools of education.

Notes

1. *A Nation at Risk, The Imperative for Educational Reform* (Washington, D.C.: U.S. Office of Education, 1983).

2. All quotations are from Mary Poplin and Joseph Weeres, *Voices from the Inside: A Report on Schooling from Inside the Classroom* (Claremont, Calif.: Institute for Education in Transformation, 1992).

11

University-Assisted Community Schools and Strategic Academically Based Community Service

IRA HARKAVY AND JOHN PUCKETT

The problems of the American city have increasingly become the problems of the urban college and university. There is no escape from the issues of poverty, crime, and physical deterioration that are at the gates of urban higher educational institutions. The choice is to return to the mythic image of the university on the hill, and suffer for it, or to become engaged in an effective and proactive fashion.

No urban university has developed *the* model for working effectively with its environment. A number of excellent experiments are being undertaken, but they all represent partial attempts that do not mobilize the broad range of university resources and expertise.

Partial attempts simply will not do for either the university or society. A full-hearted and full-minded effort is needed—one that defines the problem of the city as the strategic problem for the American urban university. Ernest Boyer's extraordinarily influential call for creating the New American College has relevance here. Deploring the crisis in our public schools and the desperate condition of our cities, Boyer challenged American higher educators to change radically their priorities and to act effectively to meet their civic and societal responsibilities: "Do colleges really believe they can ignore social pathologies that surround schools and erode the educational foundations of our nation?" Specifically, Boyer called for creating a "New American College . . . [which takes] special pride in its capacity to connect thought to action, theory to practice. . . . The New American College, as a connected institution, would be committed to improving, in a very intentional way, the human condition." [1]

Calling for creating the New American College is one thing, creating it is something else indeed. To put it mildly, it is very hard to do. After World War I, a strong tradition developed that separated scholarly research from the goal of improving the human condition in the here and now. Disconnection from, rather then connection to, society became the operational style of the vast majority of America's colleges and universities.[2]

After 1945, of course, higher education did connect. It connected, however, to distant, not local, problems. The Cold War became the defining issue that led to the development of the vast American university system. Propelled by fear of, and competition with, the Soviet Union, American politicians, with significant support from the American public, unquestioningly accepted requests from the "military-industrial-academic complex" for increased aid and support to higher education.[3] The collapse of the Berlin Wall in 1989 and the crack-up of the Soviet Union in 1991, however, signaled the end of the "Big Science Cold War University." Long-ignored internal problems, including those Boyer identifies, could be ignored no longer. Over forty-five years of looking outward had its costs as unresolved domestic problems developed into unresolved, highly visible crises.[4]

But crises alone will not undo a history of nearly one hundred years of universities' functioning as if they were in, but not of, their communities. Moreover, the ignoring of pressing societal problems was accompanied by a fragmentation of mission that separated service from research and teaching, and spurred the development of self-contained, self-referential disciplinary communities, making effective engagement all the more difficult.[5]

Tradition and fragmentation are certainly significant barriers to creating connected institutions. An additional barrier, however, may be even more formidable: a fundamental contradiction in the structure of the American research university itself, a contradiction built in at its very creation. Daniel Coit Gilman, the founder of Johns Hopkins and central architect of the nineteenth-century research university, claimed that one of his proudest accomplishments was "a school of science grafted on one of the oldest and most conservative classical colleges."[6] Although referring specifically to the merger of the Sheffield Scientific School with Yale College, Gilman felt that this achievement exemplified his contribution to American higher education.

As a product of a merger of the German research university and the American college, the American research university was bound to develop severe tensions and contradictions from a joining of two markedly different entities. The research university was dedicated to specialized scholarship, and the university provided service through specialized inquiry and studies. For the American college, on the other hand, general education, character building, and civic education were the central purposes. The college provided service to society through cultivating in young people, to use Benjamin Franklin's phrase, "an *Inclination* join'd with an *Ability* to serve."[7] The research university has, of course, dominated this merger, creating an ethos and culture that rewards specialized study rather than more general scholarship and the education of the next generation for moral, civic, and intellectual leadership.

The Center for Community Partnerships and Strategic Academically Based Community Service

The Center for Community Partnerships of the University of Pennsylvania was founded on the notion that the vast range of resources of the American university, appropriately and creatively employed, can help us figure out how best to proceed. At Penn, over the past number of years, we have been working on the problem of how to create modern cosmopolitan, local communities. It is within the American city that the need for communities based on face-to-face relationships and exemplifying humanistic universal values is most acute. The problem of the city is the strategic problem of our time. As such, it is a problem most likely to advance the university's primary mission of producing, preserving, and transmitting knowledge. This resonates with Dewey's claim that real advances in knowledge occur through a focus on the central problems of society.[8]

A strategic real-world and intellectual problem Penn and all other urban universities face is what should be done to overcome the deep, pervasive, interrelated problems affecting the people in their local geographic environments. This concrete, immediate, practical, and theoretical problem requires creative, interdisciplinary, interactive scholarship. It is a problem that can help science, and scholarship in general, to transcend traditional boundaries and achieve a level of mutual understanding, innovation, and cooperation among disciplines rarely achieved in the past.[9]

The Center for Community Partnerships was founded in 1992 to achieve the following objectives:

- Improve the internal coordination and collaboration of university community service programs.
- Create new and effective partnerships between the university and the community.
- Strengthen a national network of institutions of higher education committed to engagement with their local communities.

The center is an outgrowth of the Penn Program for Public Service, which was created in 1989 to replace and expand the Office of Community-Oriented Policy Studies in the School of Arts and Sciences.[10] The center's director reports both to Penn's Vice President for Government, Community, and Public Affairs and to the Provost (the university's chief academic officer). Through the center, the university currently engages in three types of activities:

- Academically based community service
- Direct traditional service
- Community economic development

Most central is the development and extension of strategic academically based community service, which has as a primary goal contributing to the well-being of people in the community both now and in the future. It is service rooted in and intrinsically tied to teaching and research, and it aims to bring about structural community improvement (e.g, effective public schools, neighborhood economic development, strong community organizations) rather than simply to alleviate individual misery (e.g., feeding the hungry, sheltering the homeless, tutoring slow learners). In Penn's case, the primary site for strategic academically based community service is the university's local environment of West Philadelphia.[11]

Specifically, the center focuses on two strategic academically based community service activities:

- It develops and supports undergraduate and graduate seminars, courses, and research projects. By the academic year 1998–1999, approximately 80 courses had been developed that supported Penn's work in West Philadelphia. (Forty-two of them were offered over the spring and fall semesters.)
- It coordinates internships for students to engage intensively in work in the community, especially in the public schools. The following programs are of particular note.

Public Service Summer Internship

This is a twelve-week multifaceted summer program that engages undergraduates in a seminar with the center director. Its title is Action Seminar in Faculty-Student Collaborative Learning and Research: Toward Overcoming the "Savage Inequalities" Within America's Schooling System; What Should Urban Universities, Public Schools and Communities Do? Penn–West Philadelphia as an Experiment in Progress.

Additionally, the students work as assistant teachers, helping to develop and teach community-focused, problem-solving curricula to middle-school students at one of several summer institutes in West Philadelphia public schools.

Program to Link Intellectual Resources and Community Needs

This program enhances undergraduate education at Penn by providing students with research and work on collaborative community projects that aim to make structural improvements in the West Philadelphia community in the program's three project areas: culture and community studies, environment and health, and nutrition and health.

The program, supported by the W. K. Kellogg Foundation, provides support for the development and implementation of academically based community service courses linked to work at West Philadelphia Improvement Corps (WEPIC) schools. The curricular themes of the program not only organize the faculty participation at Penn but also reflect and support curriculum initiatives that are being mutually developed at the local WEPIC public schools.

The program also sponsors annual conferences that report on the academically based community service projects developed during each academic year. The projects are co-presented by Penn faculty and students as well as the public school teachers and students. The conferences are attended by university faculty and students, public school administrators, teachers, and students, community members, city officials, and other interested colleagues from across the region and country.

Program in Nonprofits, Universities, Communities, and Schools (PNUCS)

This program develops academically based community service to improve theory and practice in the nonprofit field. The program activities engage the community in active, full participation at all stages and incorporate joint problem solving. Faculty members from five of Penn's schools play a leadership role in developing the program within their schools.

The key project activities include (1) community asset mapping; (2) restructuring current courses and development of three new academically based community service courses each year; (3) development of two new programs in the School of Social Work, including a certificate program in nonprofit management and an interdisciplinary master's program in community-based nonprofit administration; (4) technical assistance from Penn staff and faculty teams to small West Philadelphia nonprofits to address short-term needs (grant writing, computer training) and longer-term needs on issues of public policy and program development; (5) development of a public school–based youth leadership development program to foster the next generation of community leaders of West Philadelphia; and (6) creation by the Graduate School of Education of classes for West Philadelphia teachers and administrators on how to effectively engage the community with the public schools. A community advisory board guides the program and helps define needs. The program is supported by the W. K. Kellogg Foundation.

Program in Universities, Communities of Faith, Schools, and Neighborhood Organizations

This program brings the Penn community, together with the leaders of West Philadelphia schools and neighborhood organizations, into dialogue with religious leaders of all faiths in West Philadelphia. Through this dialogue, program leaders seek to break down long-standing barriers. The program also draws these groups into jointly determined and mutually beneficial action that addresses community needs such as literacy and education projects. Other related activities include the development of new Penn courses that engage Penn faculty and students in the work of the program. Project leaders have the opportunity to visit other programs across the country that are engaged in similar dialogue and action. Penn also hosts several conferences on these issues. The program is supported by the Jessie Ball duPont Fund.

Community Outreach Partnership Center (COPC)

This program involves a collaboration among faculty, staff, and students from Penn's School of Arts and Sciences, Graduate School of Education, Graduate School of Fine Arts, School of Social Work, the Wharton School, and Penn's Morris Arboretum. This interdisciplinary program works in partnership with Penn's community in West Philadelphia, particularly in the West Philadelphia Empowerment Zone. Penn's COPC addresses issues defined by its community advisory board: (1) minority entrepreneurship; (2) infrastructure issues such as brownfields and urban flooding; (3) education and job training for school-age youth as well as adults; (4) access to information about West Philadelphia; (5) use of technology to develop further community-initiated programs; and (6) capacity building of local nonprofits and community development corporations. The program is supported by the U.S. Department of Housing and Urban Development.

WEPIC Replication Project

This project developed from the significant interest in Penn's university-assisted community school model. In 1995, with DeWitt Wallace–Reader's Digest Fund support, three universities were funded for three years to develop WEPIC-type programs. In 1998 renewed funding from the fund as well as new support from the Corporation for National Service led to support for nine universities and colleges to adapt the WEPIC model to their own settings: University of Kentucky–Lexington, University of Alabama at Birmingham, Clark Atlanta University, University of New Mexico at Albuquerque, Community College of Aurora (Colorado), Bates College, University of Dayton, University of Denver, and the University of Rhode Island.

The WEPIC Replication Project also hosts yearly national conferences on university/school/community collaboration and publishes a journal, *Universities and Community Schools*.

Link to Learn and Technology Challenge Grant

Link to Learn, a project of the Pennsylvania Department of Education, and the School District of Philadelphia Technology Challenge Grant, a project of the U.S. Department of Education, maximize the use of technology to improve educational outcomes for children in grades K–12 through real-world, action-oriented projects. Teachers and students involved in this initiative are provided technology training, materials, and hands-on support by Penn students and staff.

Philadelphia Higher Educational Network for Neighborhood Development (PHENND)

This is a consortium of colleges and universities housed at the Center. Formed in 1988 to encourage area universities and colleges to engage their faculty and students in projects in their local communities, PHENND currently involves thirty-five higher educational institutions. Earlier PHENND programs included Summer of Service (1993), a children's health outreach and immunization program, and the Pennsylvania Service Scholars (1994–1997), a campus-based AmeriCorps program.[12] In 1997 support from the Corporation for National Service allowed for expansion of the PHENND Coalition and development of the following programs at member institutions: course development grants to support academically based community service in the Philadelphia region; and grants for community-initiated projects, technical assistance, and seminars for faculty and students; and a regional conference.

WEPIC and University-Assisted Community Schools: Learning from Schooling History

The WEPIC community schools project provides the on-site catalyst and integrative mechanism for strategic academically based community service. A school-based school and community revitalization program, WEPIC represents a coalition of Penn faculty, staff, graduate and undergraduate students; West Philadelphia teachers, students, and school administrators; and community organizations and government agencies. This coalition's goal is to produce comprehensive, university-assisted community schools that serve, educate, and activate all members of the community, revitalizing the curriculum through a community-oriented, real-world problem-solving approach. WEPIC seeks to help develop schools that are open year-round and function simultaneously as the core building for the community and as its educational and service delivery hub.

WEPIC was formed in the spring of 1985 and gained momentum in the aftermath of the notorious MOVE fire on Osage Avenue. The original project involved one West Philadelphia school—the Bryant Elementary School—where WEPIC focused on organizing school and neighborhood beautification projects and developing youth employment opportunities (high school students also worked on the projects). In 1989 the coalition adopted the community school idea as a general strategy and took concrete action to create a community school in West Philadelphia. That year the Commonwealth of Pennsylvania, Scott Paper Company, the Mott Foundation, and the Department of Health and Human Services funded extended-day and weekend components of a WEPIC-sponsored community school effort at the John P. Turner Middle School. The University of Pennsylvania also began publication of its journal, *Universities and Community Schools,* as a vehicle "to help establish an international, informal 'visible college'—or network—of academics and practitioners working, in different places and ways, to increase the contribution universities make to the development and effectiveness of community schools."[13]

Although aware of the community school idea through John Dewey's work[14] and other sources, WEPIC planners first began to explore the potential of the community school idea in 1989, in a seminar of school practitioners and academics. Informal discussions among university faculty colleagues in the seminar pointed to the need for research that would look backward critically to earlier comprehensive efforts to use schools as catalysts and centers for social regeneration. Presumably a careful historical study would illuminate and guide the process of creating and sustaining fully realized community schools in the present situation of West Philadelphia. Intrigued by this prospect, several university faculty members associated with WEPIC began to investigate the history of the community school idea. Two case studies central to this historical study—the community school experiments of Elsie Ripley Clapp in Central Appalachia and Leonard Covello in East Harlem, in the 1930s—helped define and shape a critically important role for the University of Pennsylvania in WEPIC.

A protégé of John Dewey, Clapp created two short-lived but significant community schools, the Ballard School in Jefferson County, Kentucky (1929–1934), and the Arthurdale School in Preston County, West Virginia (1934–1936). Clapp's experiment in Jefferson County explored the development of a community-centered curriculum; the Ballard School resembled Dewey's Laboratory School at the University of Chicago with an emphasis on experiential learning and curricular spiraling of an integrative theme at increasing levels of complexity—in Dewey's case, social occupations and American economic development; in Clapp's case, Kentucky life and history. By 1934, after five years at the Ballard School, Clapp had begun to envisage the rural school as a mechanism for social change (she now called it a "socially functioning school"), an idea she carried to a more ambitious project in Arthurdale, a federal subsistence homestead located near Morgantown, West Virginia, at the center of the Monongahela Valley coal industry. The Arthurdale School marked a strategic advance over the Ballard School as Clapp gave the new school a significant social reconstructionist component lacking in the earlier experiment—a curriculum that revolved around occupations and concerns related to actually creating the Arthurdale community. Yet it was short-lived. At the behest of Arthurdale's private donors and state advisory committee, Clapp concluded the experimental phase of her program in 1936 and transferred administration of the Arthurdale School to West Virginia state and county authorities. In the absence of sustained institutional support—neither government nor private funding was forthcoming after another year—the Arthurdale community school lost its community focus; as progressive teachers left Arthurdale, they were replaced by traditional teachers.[15]

In a vastly different setting, another pioneering community school also opened its doors in 1934. The first high school of any type in East Harlem, Benjamin Franklin High School was the brainchild of its first principal, Leonard Covello, who directed the community school from 1934 to 1956 (the key years of community school activity were 1934–1942). Although Franklin was not a cult of personality, it was nevertheless virtually inseparable from Covello, indelibly stamped by his charismatic leadership and unstinted devotion to the high school and East Harlem. Covello's immigrant background and his prominent career as an educator of second- and third-generation Italian-Americans at DeWitt Clinton High School in central Manhattan were seedbeds that nourished Covello's social and political acuity, and pushed him inexorably to undertake the social regeneration of East Harlem through the agency of a community high school. Greatly influenced by New York's settlement movement, he conceptualized the community high school as a kind of publicly funded social settlement that would provide extra-hours educational, social, health, and recreational services to Franklin students and East Harlem residents.

Covello organized the high school into three spheres of activity: community center, day school (regular curricular and extracurricular activities), and adult school. The primary catalyst for community improvement was the pioneering Community Advisory Committee (CAC), which over the years comprised an assortment of school/community committees, each assigned to a specific problem area in East Harlem; the CAC's finest achievement was the East Harlem Housing Campaign, which spearheaded construction of the East River Houses, the district's first low-income housing project. Covello also introduced "street units" (several research bureaus, an alumni club, an adult social center) and a program of multicultural education. A key element— perhaps the essential factor—in the early success of Franklin's enormously popular community programs was the Works Progress Administration, which supported the labor force for these programs in the 1930s; indeed, the demise of the WPA was a major factor in the decline of the community high school in the 1940s.[16]

For those involved in WEPIC's work, the experience of Clapp and Covello illustrated that sustained institutional support is a sine qua non of community schools. In 1936 philanthropic funding for the Arthurdale School ended, and the state of West Virginia refused to continue the project. Divested of its progressive teachers and community program, Arthurdale became an ordinary rural school. In East Harlem, the resource problem was underscored by the withdrawal of the WPA, which staffed key components of Benjamin Franklin High School. Indeed, the WPA is a focal point for hard thinking about this particular lesson of community school history. What functional substitute for the WPA is available to inner-city community schools of the twenty-first century? That question has helped us and our colleagues to think long and hard about the role of the university in helping to create, develop, and sustain community schools.

Elsewhere we have proposed a radical rethinking of the urban university along lines suggested by Jane Addams and the early settlement movement. In 1929, near the end of her extraordinary career, Addams wrote that the social settlement served the same function as the university, but the settlement's impact encompassed a broader and needier population:

> It was the function of the settlements to bring into the circle of knowledge and full life, men and women who might otherwise be left outside. Some of these men and women were outside simply because of their ignorance, some of them because they led lives of hard work that narrowed their

interests, and others because they were unaware of the possibilities of life and needed a friendly touch to awaken them. The colleges and universities had made a little inner circle of illuminated space beyond which there stretched a region of darkness, and it was the duty of the settlements to draw into the light those who were out of it. It seemed to us that our mission was just as important as that of either the university or the college.

The key challenge today, however, is not to have social settlements function as universities but rather to have universities function as perennial, deeply rooted settlements, providing illuminated space for their communities as they conduct their mission of producing, preserving, and transmitting knowledge to advance human welfare and to develop theories that have broad utility and application. As comprehensive institutions, we would argue, universities are uniquely qualified to provide broadly based, sustained, comprehensive support. The community school project itself becomes the organizing catalyst, enabling the university to function as a new form of social settlement—one innovative, humanistic strategy to better perform its traditional mission—as well as to better perform its role as a cosmopolitan civic university.[17]

University-assisted community schools and the related concept of academically based community service—teaching and research intrinsically rooted in service—provide a strategy to help overcome the resource obstacle of community schools. This strategy involves a significant redirection and integration of the academy's historic missions of teaching, research, and service, helping to rectify the "false trichotomization and fragmentation inherent in treating teaching, research, and service as distinctly separate activities carried out at a common university site."[18]

To a significant extent, it is the work of Addams' colleague John Dewey that led us to extend the concept of strategic academically based community service. The concept, we discovered, could be understood as a component of Dewey's brilliant theory of instrumental intelligence.

Dewey's Work As the Basis for Integrating Academics, Service, and Community Schools

According to Dewey, genuine learning only occurs when human beings focus their attention, energies, and abilities on solving genuine "dilemmas" and "perplexities." Other mental activity fails to produce reflection and intellectual progress. As John E. Smith has written about Dewey's theory of instrumental intelligence, "Reflective thought is an active response to the challenge of the environment."[19] In 1910, Dewey spelled out the basis of his real-world, problem-driven, problem-solving theory of instrumental intelligence as follows:

> Thinking begins in what may fairly be called a *forked-road* situation, a situation which is ambiguous, which presents a dilemma, which proposes alternatives. As long as our activity slides smoothly along from one thing to another, or as long as we permit our imagination to entertain fancies at pleasure, there is no call for reflection. Difficulty or obstruction in the way of reaching a belief brings us, however, to a pause. . . .
>
> *Demand for the solution of a perplexity is the steadying and guiding factor in the entire process of reflection* . . . a question to be answered, an ambiguity to be resolved, sets up an end and holds the current of ideas to a definite channel . . . [emphasis added].
>
> [In summary] . . . the origin of thinking is some perplexity, confusion, or doubt. Thinking is not a case of spontaneous combustion; it does not occur just on "general principles." There is something specific which occasions and involves it.[20]

Employing Dewey's theory of instrumental intelligence is, of course, only a starting point. There are an infinite number of perplexities and dilemmas for universities to focus upon. Which problem or set of problems is significant, basic, and strategic enough to lead to societal as well as intellectual progress? In 1927, in *The Public and Its Problems,* Dewey unequivocally identified the existence of "neighborly community" as indispensable for a well-functioning democratic society: "There is no substitute for the vitality and depth of close and direct intercourse and attachment. . . . Democracy must begin at home, and its home is the neighborly community." In the same book, he also noted that creating a genuinely democratic community is "in the first instance an intellectual problem."[21] Seventy-two years later, we still do not know how to create democratic neighborly communities. Events in Bosnia and Kosovo, the states of the former Soviet Union, South Africa, France, Germany, Northern Ireland, and so on, indicate that this very practical and core theoretical problem of the social sciences is more than an American dilemma. The problem of how to create these communities is the strategic problem of our time. As such, it is the problem most likely to advance the university's primary mission of producing, preserving, and transmitting knowledge to advance human welfare.

The particular strategic real-world and intellectual problem urban universities face is how to overcome the deep, pervasive, interrelated problems of their local environments. This concrete, immediate, practical, and theoretical problem requires creative, interdisciplinary interaction. Urban universities encompass the range of human knowledge needed to solve the complex, comprehensive, and interconnected problems found in the city. To actually solve the problem, however, will require universities to change and increasingly become organizations that encourage and foster a Deweyan approach of "learning by strategic community problem solving and real-world reflective doing."

Applying a Deweyan Approach: Case Studies in Progress

It is, of course, infinitely easier to call for a Deweyan approach than to actually put that approach into practice. As we have discussed, for fourteen years faculty, students, and staff from the University of Pennsylvania have been participating in a partnership (WEPIC) with public schools, community groups, and other organizations to create university-assisted community schools in Penn's local environment of West Philadelphia. WEPIC has identified the university-assisted community school, which functions as the center of education, service, and engagement for all residents of a specified locality, as the vehicle for creating face-to-face, neighborly communities in an area plagued by urban blight, poverty, and decline. The university, through its Center for Community Partnerships, has contributed to creating university-assisted community schools through a series of communal participatory action research projects.

As an institutional strategy, communal participatory action research is different from traditional participatory action research (PAR). Both research processes are directed toward problems in the real world, concerned with application, and obviously participatory. They differ in the degree to which they are continuous, comprehensive, beneficial, and necessary to the organization or community studied and the university. For example, traditional PAR is exemplified in the efforts of William Foote Whyte and his associates at Cornell University to advance industrial democracy in the worker cooperatives of Mondragón, Spain.[22] Its considerable utility and theoretical significance notwithstanding, the research at Mondragón is not an institutional necessity for Cornell. By contrast, the University of Pennsylvania's enlightened self-interest is directly tied to the success of its research efforts in West Philadelphia, hence its emphasis on communal participatory action research. In short, proximity and a focus on problems that are institutionally significant to the university encourage sustained, continuous research involvement; problem-focused research, in turn, necessitates sustained, continuous partnerships between the university and its geographic community. A crucial issue, of course, is the degree to which these locally based research projects result in general knowledge. The center's position is based on a Deweyan orientation that local does not mean parochial and that the solution to local problems necessarily requires an understanding of national and global issues as well as an effective use and development of theory.

Two Penn seminars focused on advancing community school development—Anthropology 210 and Sociology 302—have made particularly significant contributions to teaching, research, and service. Both strategic academically based community service seminars have at their core communal participatory action research projects that involve public school students as well as Penn undergraduates as active problem solvers who contribute to knowledge. A sketch of each seminar's evolution also illustrates how Dewey's theory of instrumental intelligence might be applied in practice.

Anthropology 210

Anthropology 210 focuses on the relationships between "Anthropology and Biomedical Science."[23] An undergraduate course, it was developed to link premedical training at Penn with the Anthropology Department's program in medical anthropology. The course has always emphasized deepening students' awareness and knowledge of health and disease as rooted within human biological variability, human evolutionary history, and the synergism between human biology and culture. That orientation has remained constant. In 1990, however, the course was revised significantly after Professor Francis Johnston, who teaches it, decided to participate actively in the project to help the Turner Middle School in West Philadelphia (a school in which over 84 percent of the students come from low-income families) transform itself into a community school.[24]

From 1990 to date, students in Anthropology 210 have carried out a variety of activities at Turner focused on the interactive relationships among diet, nutrition, growth, and health. Reading and class discussions in Anthropology 210 deal with theories of health and disease; concepts of population health; the evaluation of health, nutrition, and growth status at the aggregate level; and the formulation, application, and evaluation of intervention programs following the model of participatory action research. Beginning in 1990 these more theoretical aspects of the course have been applied in practice through an interrelated set of semester-long student group projects carried out at the Turner School, spanning a range of research and service activities.

Since its 1990 revision, Anthropology 210 has been explicitly organized around strategic academically based community service and communal participatory action research. Students are encouraged to view their education at Penn as preparing them to contribute to the solution of societal problems through service to the local community, and to do so by devoting a large part of their work in the course to a significant human problem, in this case, the "nutriture" of disadvantaged inner-city children. (*Nutriture* is defined as "the balance between the intake and expenditure of energy and nutrients by an organism.") Direct linkage between students' work in the field—a long-standing tradition in anthropology—and their readings and class discussion helps them put their practical experience into a framework of theory and generalizable knowledge. The students conceive and conduct their projects as rigorous investigations of problems (in both the human and scientific senses), which require careful attention to the methods of scholarly investigation. Moreover, because their projects deal with different aspects of a single significant and complex problem and are carried out as group activities, the students come to better understand the complexity of societal problems, and the advantages and difficulties of collaborative attempts to solve them.

In effect, since Anthropology 210 was reoriented and reorganized in 1990, its members have worked with teachers and students at the Turner School to construct a real-world "nutrition laboratory" in West Philadelphia. Part of that laboratory's work has been to design and carry out the Turner Nutritional Awareness Project. Among other goals, that project aims to enhance the nutriture of Turner students by providing them with the framework for making informed decisions about diet, nutrition, and health. To help achieve that goal, Penn students have worked closely with Turner students and teachers and conducted a variety of projects grouped in four main categories: (1) teaching nutrition, (2) evaluating nutritional status, (3) recording and evaluating the actual diets of Turner students, and (4) studying nutritional ecology, i.e., observing behavior in the school lunchroom, mapping sources of food in the Turner neighborhood, and recording the types of food featured and sold in them.

To carry out these four types of projects, Penn and Turner students engage in a variety of activities that require systematic research, data collection, and data analysis and interpretation. That is, in accord with John Dewey's precepts, the Penn and Turner students collaborate in learning by real-world doing about significant real-world problems and *reflecting* on what they are doing. As a result, according to Professor Johnston, Anthropology 210 is working better for Penn students than it ever has; he finds the course continually more stimulating, enlightening, and enjoyable to teach; and the Turner students seem highly motivated to work seriously on the subjects involved in the nutritional awareness project. Moreover, the descriptive data produced in Anthropology 210 have been presented at university seminars and scholarly meetings, and published in the scientific literature. These data focus on aspects of the quality of the Turner students' diets and on the high prevalence of obesity—among the highest yet reported for American youth of any ethnic group. These data have also stimulated at least one doctoral dissertation, which examined the dietary and cultural correlates of obesity and developed programs to decrease the prevalence of obesity through community-based strategies.

Sociology 302

Approximately five years ago, Frank F. Furstenberg, Jr., Penn's Zellerbach Family Professor of Sociology and Research, began a communal participatory action research project at University City High School. Adjacent to Penn's campus, University City High School had consistently been placed near or at the very bottom of Philadelphia's high schools. (Some marked improvements have been recorded in recent years.) As of 1994, with 88.5 percent of its students from low-income families, 50 percent of its students receiving a D or an F in at least one course, an average combined SAT score of 643, and the eighth worst suspension rate and seventh worst absentee rate among Philadelphia's public high schools, University City High School was (and still is) visible testimony to Penn's need to do more and better in its work with West Philadelphia.[25] Furstenberg was the first of approximately fifteen faculty members to connect his or her academic work with University City High School. This "wave" of Penn involvement was the direct result of efforts by James H. Lytle, an extraordinarily able, progressive, Deweyan principal, who was first assigned to the high school in 1995–1996. (Lytle subsequently became Superintendent of Schools in Trenton, New Jersey. He has been replaced at University City High by another extraordinary educator, Florence Johnson.)

A scholar of the family, Furstenberg has published widely on teenage sexuality, pregnancy, and childbearing as well as divorce, remarriage, and stepparenting. In recent years, Furstenberg's work has focused on the family in disadvantaged urban neighborhoods, with particular attention to adolescent sexual behavior, changes in the well-being of children, and urban education.

Ira Harkavy has known Furstenberg since 1967, when Furstenberg was a new assistant professor and Harkavy was a sophomore at Penn. Since the early 1990s, Harkavy had "made the case" to Furstenberg that he turn his research and teaching toward West Philadelphia. A grant from the Ford Foundation to the Center for Community Partnerships and the College of Arts and Sciences to develop academically based community service courses in sociology as well as three other departments provided an additional incentive for Furstenberg to pilot a West Philadelphia seminar. Since he cared deeply about the dreadful condition of public schooling in Philadelphia and wanted to do something to reverse those conditions, and since he found the University City High School to be in particular need of assistance and advantageously located for serious sustained engagement, Furstenberg focused his attention on that high school.

Wanting both to study and to help reduce teenage pregnancy, Furstenberg designed his project to be participatory action in design from the outset. At the core of Furstenberg's work was a two-semester senior thesis seminar, Sociology 302, Community Research and Community Service. Seminar students worked with teachers in four small learning communities (schools-within-schools designed to break up large impersonal schools into smaller, more learning-friendly units) to incorporate a teenage pregnancy prevention project into the curriculum.

Sociology 302 was also divided into task forces working to design a proposal for reducing teenage pregnancy at the University City High School. One task force focused on designing a sexuality education program for teenagers; another on the transition from high school to the workforce; and a third on the transition from high school to college. Each task force produced a paper and presented it to a group of elementary and secondary teachers who had been meeting regularly with Furstenberg to discuss how to reduce the pregnancy rate in the high school, increase attendance, and lower the dropout rate.

Each Sociology 302 undergraduate also wrote an individual research paper based on his or her experiences at University City High. Papers focused on such topics as race relations, school culture, teenage fatherhood, and the impact of work. Finally, Furstenberg, his students, and University City students conducted a baseline survey of the school, collecting data on teenage parents and demographics of the school population in general. This information will be used to develop a more comprehensive intervention designed to reduce teenage pregnancy at University City High.

Reports from the field and the seminar have been exceedingly positive thus far. Furstenberg has described this work as the "most electric teaching I have done in nearly thirty years at Penn." He also expanded the project to a public school located in North Philadelphia, and plans to develop a comparative project involving both sites during the 1999–2000 academic year.

Furstenberg's and Johnston's seminars are two of approximately eighty academically based community service courses that work with the Center for Community Partnerships and WEPIC to create university-assisted community schools. During the 1998–1999 academic year, moreover, forty-one graduate students and 202 undergraduates received support from the center. The community school project also contributed to the Urban Agenda named as one of

Penn's top six academic priorities by the president and provost. These developments notwithstanding, a Platonic/anti-Deweyan academic culture continues to hold sway at Penn, as it does across American higher education.

Conclusion

We have argued that for intellectual, societal, and moral reasons, the American urban university needs to devote full-hearted and full-minded attention to the problem of the American city. Specifically, we have argued for an approach that focuses academic resources on solving the problems of the university's local environment. Even more specifically, we have highlighted work to create, develop, and sustain university-assisted community schools in Penn's local environment of West Philadelphia as illustrative of a potentially useful approach for improving scholarship, schooling, and society. We described the community school work of Elsie Clapp and Leonard Covello, both to illustrate an inspiration for those efforts and to highlight the need for an anchor institution to sustain a community school over time.

Although we have been working with WEPIC and its university-assisted community school project for more than fourteen years, we see that work as just emerging from its infancy. In spite of our best efforts and those of our many colleagues, and in spite of Penn's increased focus on improving conditions in its local environment, the schools and communities of West Philadelphia have actually deteriorated since 1985. We are certain that this scenario is similar to that in other cities, whether or not they have experienced increased engagement from their local universities. Wider societal forces, including job and population loss, federal and state policies forsaking the cities and their residents, globalization of the economy, and illusory incremental efforts that fail to address the underlying causes of America's chronic urban crisis are among the various reasons that conditions have deteriorated. Most of these forces are, of course, not immutable; change is indeed possible. For change to occur, however, requires that the American university (as the institution primarily responsible for creating new knowledge, educating tomorrow's leaders, and shaping the American schooling system) overcome its own learned helplessness and take the lead in helping to solve the seemingly intractable problems of our urban schools and communities.

Our position in many ways echoes Derek Bok's, as stated in his highly influential book, *Universities and the Future of America*. Arguing that "the modern university is the central institution in postindustrial society," and "higher education in the United States has no peer," Bok, in effect, posed this central question: If American universities are so great, how come American society has such great and growing problems? To quote him directly,

If universities are so important to society and if ours are so superior, one might have thought that America would be flourishing in comparison with other industrialized countries of the world. *Yet this is plainly not the case. . . .* [The "great challenge facing industrialized societies" is] . . . how to build a society that combines a healthy, growing economy with an adequate measure of security, opportunity, and well-being *for all its citizens.*[26] [emphasis added]

That challenge can only be successfully met with the active participation of the American research university. Moreover, if the university takes that challenge seriously, it will, we are convinced, more successfully advance its mission of advancing, preserving, and transmitting knowledge to advance human welfare.

Notes

1. Ernest Boyer, "Creating the New American College," *Chronicle of Higher Education,* March 9, 1994, p. A48.

2. For discussion of these trends, see Ira Harkavy and John L. Puckett, "Toward Effective University–Public School Partnerships: An Analysis of a Contemporary Model," *Teachers College Record* 92 (1991): 556–581, and "Lessons from Hull House for the Contemporary Urban University," *Social Service Review* 68 (1994): 301–321.

3. The quoted phrase is taken from a speech by Senator J. William Fulbright printed in the *Congressional Record,* December 13, 1967. For a discussion of the functioning of the military-industrial complex during the Cold War, see Stuart W. Leslie, *The Cold War and American Science: The Military-Industrial-Academic Complex at MIT and Stanford* (New York: Columbia University Press, 1993).

4. A discussion of the effects of the ending of the Cold War on the American university can be found in Lee Benson and Ira Harkavy, "School and Community in the Global Society," *Universities and Community Schools* 5, no. 1–2 (1997): 16–71.

5. For a more extended discussion, see Harkavy and Puckett, "Toward Effective University–Public School Partnerships"; and Ira Harkavy, "The University and Social Sciences in the Social Order: An Historical Overview and 'Where Do We Go from Here?'" *Virginia Social Science Journal* 27 (1992): 1–8, 17–19.

6. Daniel Coit Gilman, *University Problems in the United States* (1898; reprint, New York: Garret, 1969), iii.

7. Albert H. Smyth, ed., *The Writings of Benjamin Franklin* (New York: Macmillan, 1907), 2: 38.

8. We are indebted to our colleagues Lee Benson and Robert Westbrook for advancing our understanding of Dewey. See Robert Westbrook, *John Dewey and American Democracy* (Ithaca, N.Y.: Cornell University Press, 1991).

9. For discussion of the positive effects of problem-focused research, see David Hamburg, "Education for Conflict Resolution: Can We Learn to Live Together?" in *Carnegie Corporation Annual Report* (New York: Carnegie Corporation, 1994).

10. For more details of this development, see Harkavy and Puckett, "Toward Effective University–Public School Partnerships"; Lee Benson and Ira Harkavy, "Progressing Beyond the Welfare State," *Universities and Community Schools* 2, no. 1–2, 1–25.

11. A district of 14.2 square miles, West Philadelphia is bounded on the east by the Schuylkill River (which separates the district from the center city), on the south by the Media–West Chester railroad, on the west by Cobbs Creek, and on the north by City Line Avenue. The University of Pennsylvania rises above the Schuylkill River in the eastern sector of the district. Comprising nine "neighborhoods," West Philadelphia has a total population of 219,713, according to the 1990 Census (13.9 percent of the city's total); the district's racial/ethnic composition is 72 percent black, 24 percent white, 3.3 percent Asian, and 1.1 percent Hispanic origin. The current poverty rate is 18 percent, just above the city average. From 1989 to 1993, the number of the district's residents receiving welfare assistance increased by approximately 25 percent. Philadelphia City Planning Commission, *The Plan for West Philadelphia*, 1994.

12. AmeriCorps is the central program in President Bill Clinton's effort to develop and extend national service. The Corporation for National Service is the federal administrative entity responsible for AmeriCorps and other national and community service programs.

13. Mission statement, *Universities and Community Schools* 1, no. 1 (1989): 1.

14. John Dewey, "The School as Social Centre," *Journal of the Proceedings of the National Education Association* (1902): 373–383.

15. The major sources for the Ballard and Arthurdale community schools are Elsie R. Clapp, *Community Schools in Action* (New York: Viking Press, 1939), and *The Uses of Resources in Education* (New York: Harper, 1952). Other useful sources are Stephen E. Haid, "Arthurdale: An Experiment in Community Planning, 1933–1947," Ph.D. dissertation, University of West Virginia, 1975; and Daniel Perlstein, "Community and Democracy in American Schools: Arthurdale and the Fate of Progressive Education," *Teacher's College Record* 97 (1996): 625–50.

16. These paragraphs on Covello and Benjamin Franklin High School draw freely upon the Covello Papers, Balch Institute for Ethnic Studies, Philadelphia. The following published sources are also useful: Leonard Covello, *The Heart Is the Teacher* (New York: McGraw-Hill, 1958), "A High School and Its Immigrant Community— A Challenge and an Opportunity," *Journal of Educational Sociology* 9 (1936): 331–346, "Neighborhood Growth Through the School," *Progressive Education* 2 (1938), "A Community-Centered School and the Problem of Housing," *Educational Forum* 7, no. 2 (1943), and *The Social Background of the Italo-American School Child* (Totowa, N.J.: Rowman and Littlefield, 1972); Robert W. Peebles, *Leonard Covello* (1967; reprint, New York: Arno, 1980); Robert A. Orsi, *The Madonna of 115th Street* (New

Haven, Conn.: Yale University Press, 1985); Gerald Meyer, *Vito Marcantonio* (New York: New York University Press, 1989).

17. Harkavy and Puckett, "Lessons from Hull House," 312. The Addams quotation is from her book, *The Second Twenty Years at Hull-House: September 1909 to September 1929, with a Record of Growing World Consciousness* (New York: Macmillan, 1930), 405.

18. Lee Benson and Ira Harkavy, "1994 as Turning Point: The University-Assisted Community School Idea Becomes a Movement," *Universities and Community Schools* 4, no. 1–2 (1994): 7.

19. John E. Smith, *The Spirit of American Philosophy* (Albany: State University of New York Press, 1993), 124.

20. John Dewey, *How We Think* (New York: 1910, reprint, Boston: D. C. Heath, 1990), 11–12.

21. John Dewey, *The Public and Its Problems* (1927; reprint, Alan Swallow Denver, Colo.: 1954), 147, 213.

22. See William F. Whyte and Kathleen Whyte, *Making Mondragón: The Growth and Dynamics of the Worker Cooperative Complex* (Ithaca, N.Y.: ILR, 1988); Davydd J. Greenwood and Jose Luis Gonzáles Santos, *Industrial Democracy as Process: Participatory Action Research in the Fagor Cooperative Group of Mondragón* (Assen / Maastrich, The Netherlands: Van Gorcum, 1992).

23. For a fuller discussion of Anthropology 210 and its implications, see Lee Benson and Ira Harkavy, "Anthropology 210, Academically Based Community Service, and the Advancement of Knowledge, Teaching, and Learning, An Experiment in Progress," *Universities and Community Schools* 4, no. 1–2 (1994): 66–69, and Ira Harkavy, Francis E. Johnston, and John L. Puckett, "The University of Pennsylvania's Center for Community Partnerships as an Organizational Innovation for Advancing Action Research," *Concepts and Transformations*, no. 1 (1996): 15–29.

24. School District of Philadelphia, *School Profiles* (1995), http://partners.upenn.edu/wp/k12/turner/profile.html.

25. School District of Philadelphia, *School Profiles* (1995), http://partners.upenn.edu/wp/k12/uchs/profile.html.

26. Derek Bok, *Universities and the Future of America* (Durham, NC: Duke University Press, 1990), 3–4.

12

Audaciously Preparing for Uncertainty and Change

A New Vision for American Education?

EVANS CLINCHY

So now we have explored some of the problems confronting the American system of education from kindergarten through graduate school and have begun to suggest some possible solutions to these problems. We have also attempted to spell out a few productive directions in which we should be heading.

Among this array of problems and possible solutions several clear and common themes emerge. Perhaps the most obvious and important of these are the three concerns raised or at least touched upon by every contributor to this book, each of them revolving around the central issues of social equity and the proper role of higher education in a democratic society.

The first of these is the problem of competitive selectivity. As matters stand at present, entrance into our colleges and universities is achieved only after years of strenuous academic competition beginning in kindergarten and extending through high school. This is a process that gradually winnows out the "acceptable" portion of the student population—less than one half of the total number of students—on the basis of their ability to meet the narrow academic standards of the various postsecondary admissions requirements. An even smaller percentage is admitted to our prestigious colleges, research universities, and graduate schools. And given the dropout rates at colleges and universities (about 50 percent), an even smaller group actually makes it over the academic hurdles and ends up with leadership positions and financial success in this competitive capitalist society.

No matter how we may try to justify this system as one that only rewards achievement and merit, we know perfectly well that this is not the case. The best predictors of success in school and college are still race (white and, increasingly,

Asian), social and economic class, and previous educational level of one's parents. It is a system, as Pat Shannon has pointed out, in which few are called in the first place and even fewer are chosen to be the winners in this society's rigged and artificially rugged educational marathon.

Insofar as this is the case, we have allowed ourselves to create and maintain an educational system that is unjust and inequitable. It is a system that even in its most benign and caring form is still based upon Western capitalist society's vicious "survival of the fittest" practices in their current neo–Social Darwinian (or, more accurately, neo-Malthusian) form.

The second great problem mentioned by the contributors is closely related to the first. This is that profound dilemma, Sanz de Santamaria says, of the totalitarian structure of our systems of higher and elementary and secondary schooling. This is a structure governed

> by the alienating assumption that one [the institution] has the knowledge the other [the student] lacks and has to learn. . . . Since in our educational institutions . . . it is always assumed—even in many of those institutions that theoretically reject this assumption—that the teachers . . . know and the students [and their] . . . communities don't know, the students and communities are never given the opportunity to express and describe their own experiences and knowledge in their own ways and their own words. The . . . objective [of the education process] is rather the opposite: to teach the students and the communities to express themselves in the professors' . . . ways and words, since they are, by assumption, "the ones who know."

It is interesting to think about what might happen if a large number of the people belonging to this society's underclass—some of those people, both young and old, who can barely read and write, who could never pass a high school graduation exam or get more than a combined score of 200 on the SATs—were suddenly admitted to Harvard or Yale or Stanford or Berkeley? Since it would make no sense to conduct the conventional information transmission, lecture, and listening process or to make the usual reading and writing assignments, what on earth would the faculty do with these tough young people and hard-pressed adults from the streets of Harlem or Camden, New Jersey, or East St. Louis or the projects on the near West side of Chicago or the Watts district of Los Angeles?

How would the academic scholars go about conveying to them what it is that they as the faculty know? And would such knowledge have any relevance at all to the lives this huge number of people live? Is it possible that the faculty might then be compelled to *listen* to these peculiar students, to give them "the opportunity to express and describe their own experiences and knowledge in their own ways and their own words?" Might the faculty thus be required to try to find out what was going on in the heads of these students and to discover whether what the colleges and universities know has any meaning whatsoever for the lives those students have led and are still leading or to the communities from which they come? Or, to take a slightly different tack, what might those odd students do *to* and *in* the staid, orderly, disengaged, abstracted courses of study they would find themselves subjected to? Might they force the academic scholars to rethink what they are doing and how they are doing it?

The contributors to this book have also raised the question that immediately follows any such thinking about the nature of the scholarly enterprise, the question of the *disconnection* between what goes on in our colleges and universities and what goes on in the larger society (and thus a lack of *responsibility* for what goes on in that society).

There are, of course, a host of further connected problems that flow from these concerns. In Sanz de Santamaria's view, the elitist system of selection for admission, the totalitarian nature of the process of education, and the disconnection from the real world are antidemocratic. If this is so, we are then faced with the failure of our present systems of elementary and secondary and higher education to educate children and young people to live in, work in, care about, and work for the improvement of the quality of life in a democratic society. This is especially a failure to make that society work for every human being in it, most crucially for the young, the poor, the homeless, the elderly, and all those in need.

Indeed, what we have at present is a system of schooling from elementary school through graduate school that in all too many ways promotes precisely the opposite result. It is a system that supports and maintains a society based upon self-centeredness, as Bill Coplin writes, a society that not merely permits but actually encourages and applauds the enormous and growing disparities of wealth between "the few and the majority" described by Pat Shannon. It is a society that permits one-third of its children to be born and to live in poverty, a society that allows the few to earn millions of dollars per year while children are starving on our streets and their schools are crumbling around them. It is a society that proposes to spend 150 billion dollars on a new and dubiously necessary fighter plane while saying that we are too poor to provide a social security system or a health care system or an educational system that serves all Americans. It is, further and finally, a society that actually allows and even encourages corporate entrepreneurs to make a profit out of caring for the sick and educating the young, a society that even proposes the making of corporate profits out of operating prisons and neo-Dickensian orphanages for abandoned children.

But Noddings, Coplin, Harkavy, Puckett, and others also take our present educational system to task for what they see as a *moral* failure, its ingrained difficulty in assisting children and young people in their task of becoming decent, caring human beings. The system, they say, routinely ignores the existence of students' homes, families, and local communities in favor of concentrating on conventional academic learning. The system does not consider it a part of its educational responsibility to prepare students to become good fathers and mothers, committed family members who care for and about their children and their elderly, and contributing members of their local communities.

In addition to this failure, there are now the intertwined hurdles of money and the Supreme Court's rejection of specialized ethnic and race-based admissions to colleges and universities. Similar judgments are being applied as well to the elementary and secondary school student assignment and desegregation policies, thus essentially negating *Brown v. Board of Education* and potentially returning the country as a whole to the segregated neighborhood schools and the segregated schooling we already have in many of our inner cities because of the Supreme Court's continued refusal to allow compulsory urban/suburban integration plans.

When these kinds of policies are combined with the costs of attending college—ranging from around $1,600 a year at a two-year community college to $30,000 a year at an Ivy League institution—it is clear that most young people and their families, especially poor and minority groups, will be unable to afford to attend those institutions. This means that access to higher education—and thus to positions of power and authority in this society—increasingly will be restricted once again to the majority white and relatively well-to-do part of the population. Hardly a wise or pleasant—and certainly not a just or fair—state of affairs.

A Most Immodest Proposal—Stage One

To raise at the very least a possible antidote to all of these dire predictions, suppose for a minute that we take seriously Deborah Meier's proposal that the best way to begin to solve some of these problems is to make the developmental, Deweyan, progressive principles of kindergarten the basis of a new and quite different educational system running from kindergarten through graduate school. If we do this, it immediately becomes obvious that the changes we are asking for in our institutions of elementary and secondary and higher education are truly staggering. They would require us to rethink and reshape *all* of our educational institutions from the primary grades up and most especially to design a new organizational structure for our entire system of K–12 public education and our colleges and universities.

Therefore, the two practical questions that now face us are whether such massive changes are possible and, if we decide they are or might be, how we might bring them about.

Seymour Sarason, the eminent psychologist and educational reformer, has written several revolutionary books describing the ills of our present educational system, including *How Our Schools Should Be Governed and Why*, as well as a chapter in my previous edited collection, *Creating New Schools: How Small Schools Are Changing American Education*.

In these works, Sarason has eloquently raised the question of what our public school systems—most particularly that much needed *new* K–12 school system—should be like and how they should be governed. In thinking about this question, Sarason was reminded of the Constitutional Convention conducted by the emerging United States of America in 1787:

> That convention was called to repair the inadequacies and dangers of the Articles of Confederation. It became evident, especially to James Madison, that the articles were unrescuable, and rather than engage in an effort of repair, they started, so to speak, from scratch. Over several hot, steamy months in Philadelphia they fashioned a historically momentous document. (Slavery was a fateful blind spot, of course.) It was not easy. The issues—historical, moral, political, organizational, economic, geographic, slavery, and variations in the size of the colonies—were complex, indeed, and they had the wisdom to include a self-correcting mechanism, i.e., the amending process.
>
> I refer here to the 1787 convention for two reasons; one is a glimpse of the obvious, the other somewhat less so. Both have direct bearing on my conviction that in regard to a new governance system of education nothing will ever happen unless and until the national-political leadership convenes the equivalent of a constitutional convention—in size comparable to that of 1787—to critique the existing governance of our educational system and to propose changes or a new system. Let me just add at this point I have asked scores of individuals and groups this question: If you were starting from scratch, would you come up with the existing system? No one has ever said yes.
>
> The most obvious feature of the 1787 convention was that its participants may well be the most mature, intelligent, probing, dedicated group that has ever been assigned a crucial public task. . . . The related but less obvious feature is that they did not want or need a staff of experts to help them analyze and define the issues. By virtue of direct experience they knew the issues, which is not to say that they did not, initially at least, have dramatically different views about how to deal with those issues. And by virtue of education and an unexcelled interest in and grasp of moral-religious, political history, they were the experts. They were not chosen for purposes of window-dressing, i.e., putting their imprimatur on a final report written by

others. For them, the convention was not a part-time activity. At great personal cost to themselves and their families (given what transportation was like in those days) they gave their all. And they had the courage to depart from what was and to sail on truly uncharted seas. They did not do this with complete confidence, they knew the risks and uncertainties of what they were proposing. But they also knew that what was could never be a basis for forging a nation.

My call for a presidential-congressional appointed commission on the governance of education will understandably engender sardonic laughter in those familiar with the history of such commissions. Those familiar with President Reagan's commission which gave us *A Nation at Risk* could claim, as I do, that with friends like that education need never worry about having enemies. It is a report containing pallid generalities, and a sense of urgency and crisis followed by nothing resembling a concrete idea or proposal. It was a pretentious sermon. But then again it is par for the course for politicians (and other well-meaning individuals) to talk about educational reform in ways that confirm Mencken's maxim that for every important public problem there is a simple answer that is wrong. They also confirm the adage that it is hard to be completely wrong. (1999)

Sarason goes on to point out that there have been in the past two federally sponsored commissions or groups that have been exceptions to the general failure and insipidness of such bodies, one during World War II (the G.I. Bill) that gave us our present system for admitting war veterans, and the other a mental health commission that dramatically changed our state mental health programs. Sarason writes,

Why did the plans of these two groups break new ground?

1. There was recognition that drastic changes were in order, not only in the professional communities but, crucially, *at the highest layers of political authority and leadership.* (That, of course, was the case in 1787.)

2. The groups were comprised of people with long, *direct* experience with the problems with which they had to deal. (Again, like 1787.) There was little or no selection of participants in terms of window dressing. It was obvious, at least to me, that most were chosen because of their dissatisfaction with the past system and its practices.

3. They did not focus on considerations of cost but rather on the overarching question: What needs to be done to improve the quality of care? (In the case of the 1787 convention the question front and center was how to harmonize central power and authority, on the one hand, with individual liberty on the other hand.) They did not need to do extensive studies to demonstrate the obvious: the existing system was dramatically costly, the costs would escalate, quality would not improve.

4. Precisely because of the level of political sponsorship of the groups and of the social and economic climate of the early postwar years, the groups had a reason to believe their proposals would be widely diffused. (1999)

If we are to begin Sarason's task of creating a new governance structure for our system of public education and simultaneously to accept Deborah Meier's proposals for lasting change from preschool through graduate school, we need to recognize the necessity to work simultaneously at every level of the total educational system. While the new governance structure and the developmental principles of kindergarten at each of those levels are suggested here, we need always to pay attention to how the various levels interact and how the transitions from level to level can be smoothly and justly managed.

It is especially important that colleges, universities, and schools of education be among the prime movers of any such enterprise. No change of any importance is going to happen in our elementary and secondary schools until there are vast changes in what colleges and universities do and how they conceive their part of the educational enterprise. This is most particularly true of our schools of education, for it is there that most of the professionals in the new schools will be prepared, even if we move—as we should—to a much greater reliance on carefully mentored apprenticeships out in the real educational world of the schools themselves.

What we are thus immodestly proposing here as the first stage in this process of massive reconstruction is the conduct not of another Einsteinian thought experiment but a real-life modern educational version of Sarason's 1787 constitutional convention aimed at reconstituting our entire educational system from the bottom to very top.

For this first stage, we need to tackle not only the complete revision of our approach to the preschool through graduate school curriculum but a complete revision of the preschool through graduate school governance system. We are proposing to do this by convening as our constitutional convention a representative sample of the people actually involved in the enterprise of schooling from all levels of the system. If we are to follow the Sarason 1787 example, these would have to be people with a broad mix of qualifications.

One set of qualifications would be that some of them would be people who are recognized manifestly as the "most mature, intelligent, probing, dedicated," eminent, and highly respected people in their fields, people who are convinced that the educational system must be rethought and re-created from kindergarten through college and university. These would be people who had considerable educational and political clout but who were in no way "window dressing." But other people would be school practitioners selected to represent all of those actual, day-to-day working people included in the Claremont study—especially principals and teachers, of course, but also school secretaries, teacher aides, custodians, cafeteria workers, bus drivers, and, above all, parents and students.

A second important qualification would be that they would be people who, as was the case with the convention of 1787, understood that they were there "to repair the inadequacies and dangers of" the present system of American education by starting from absolute scratch, people who could answer Sarason's question, "If you were starting from scratch, would you come up with the existing system?" with a resounding "No!"

The third qualification would be that these people (adapting Sarason's description)

> would not want or need a staff of experts to help them analyze and define the issues. By virtue of direct experience, they would know the issues. . . . And by virtue of education and an unexcelled interest in . . . educational history, they would be the experts. They would not . . . put their imprimatur on a final report written by others. For them, the assigned activity would not be a part-time activity. . . . And they would have the courage to depart from what was . . . [because they] . . . would know that what is could never be the basis for forging a new system of education.

This commission, then, would include not only leading civic-minded citizens but leading representatives of each of the scholarly disciplines and leading curriculum designers from each of the relevant elementary and secondary school curriculum associations in each of those present "core" subject matter compartments. These representatives would be joined by representatives of the previously mentioned "Claremont study" groups. All of these people would know that they were there "to repair the inadequacies and dangers of" the present system of American education by starting from absolute scratch. They would be charged with five tasks.

1. Every scholar and curriculum specialist in each discipline would together be asked to explain to the group as a whole the ways in which and the extent to which their discipline fulfills (for higher education) Ben Franklin's rationale that its purpose is the development and application of knowledge to improve human welfare through a threefold mission of research, teaching, *and public service.* The elementary and secondary school people would be asked to explain how they and their subject matter departments prepare students to live in, work in, and improve a democratic society.

That is, each scholar and curriculum specialist would be asked to describe in detail how the men and women engaged in teaching that discipline not only advance the study of the discipline itself but also contribute to the betterment of the larger, nonscholarly world and human welfare in general. Or, if their discipline does not now fulfill that rationale, how would they propose that it should do so in the future?

This would necessarily include an explanation of why *any* student should be required or encouraged to study that particular discipline or school subject. That is, how would the student's developing intelligence and the social and moral quality of that student's life in the real, nonacademic world be enhanced by studying that discipline and that subject?

2. At the same time, the members of the "Claremont study" groups would be called upon to take the results of the Claremont study and spell out the changes they see as necessary in the governance and conduct of the schooling process if that process is no longer to "hurt the spirit" of everyone involved in it.

The two groups would then be asked to join together and respond to the results of each other's deliberations. They would proceed *jointly* to answer the following question: Based upon the conclusions at which all of you have arrived, are there some great, overarching, all-inclusive intellectual *questions* (not answers, but questions) that occur in, reoccur in, and are fundamental to *all* of your disciplines and to the ways you now think that the schools should be organized and governed? That is, can you identify a small set of interdisciplinary philosophical queries—let's say, ten such queries—that underlie *all* of your various educational pursuits? These would be questions that are of such crucial importance that *every* human being would be well advised to explore them, to grapple with all their implications for a successfully examined life and an improved human world.

These would be questions to which students should be able to construct at least tentative but increasingly intellectually sophisticated and personally satisfying answers as they move through our new, radically transformed preschool through graduate school educational system. These would also therefore have to be questions that students already have in their own heads and are wondering about, or questions that, once broached by the adult staffs of their schools, would immediately appear to students as vitally important to their own lives.

Many of these questions would, of course, be the questions that have perplexed and bedeviled humankind, especially humankind's great philosophers and thinkers, since the dawn of human consciousness some two million years ago: What is the "good" life? What is a "good" human being? What is a "good and just" society? Where did the universe come from and how does it work? Where did life come from and how did it begin? Why are a few people rich and so many people poor? Why do some human beings do such horrible things to other human beings? Why are there so many different kinds of plants and animals and how did they get to be so different? In the end, is there any point to it all?

This would *not* in any way be an exercise in the setting of academic "standards" in the sense of "what all students should learn and remember" or "what all students should know and be able to do," matters with "right" answers on which all students would be tested in order to graduate from high school or college. Rather, this would be an attempt to develop a small, manageable number of interdisciplinary, transcendently important questions that students and their teachers, *beginning in kindergarten and extending through graduate schools,* could collaboratively explore. As they developed their tentative, always changing and developing answers, they could test those answers out in the real world. Any and all proposed answers to these questions would be sought, not only from books and other typical educational materials but from actually studying and working in that larger world outside of school, from the students' own lives, the lives of their families, and the communities from which they come. The students would therefore become involved in the business of developing their own intellectual constructions, which might prove useful to them as they go about attempting to understand and make sense of life and that world out there.

The standards involved here would be the standards of intellectual rigor and depth: have the students (and their teachers) at all times asked themselves the fundamental epistemological question, How do we know what we think we know? Have they thought deeply and broadly about the questions, considered all of the evidence, and arrived at their own at least tentative explanatory theories? Have they carefully studied perhaps not all but a reasonable amount of the existing thought about these questions contained in books and every other form of stored data, printed or electronic? Have they explored these questions with people out in the larger society and especially in their own local communities?

One of the basic and lasting rules governing the conduct of any such enterprise would be the primary assumption that all such constructions *are and always will be* the creations of fallible human beings living at a particular time and within a particular human culture, and that all such constructions are therefore always open to revision, expansion, and alteration as new evidence comes to light and new thinking occurs.

This new curriculum—this process of students and their teachers asking the questions and creating the resulting constructions or intellectual models—would have to be a process adapted, transformed, expanded to serve a broad variety of students from the very young to the very old and a variety of schools from preschool through graduate school. But the consideration of all such questions would at all times be melded with a broad concern for human welfare and the improvement of human society. Students would never be presented with any set of final great "truths" laid down by the scholarly gods, which they would then be instructed to memorize, but only with those great human questions to be explored and thought about.

3. The assembled commission members would then be asked to design collaboratively in rough, nonconstrictive outline form that new educational/curricular/teaching/learning, question-answering, model-building structure for our systems of elementary and secondary and higher education—the basic operational rules (based upon the results of the first two tasks) by which those educational institutions would actually be conducted. That is, these rules would allow university scholars and subject matter specialists in the elementary and secondary schools to continue their interests and pursuits. But in the new institutions, those pursuits would be arranged and conducted (most likely in a quite interdisciplinary manner) so that their application to the larger, nonacademic society—and therefore their contribution to the improvement of human welfare—would be manifestly part and parcel of the educational practices of all of the institutions, elementary and secondary and higher.

All such institutions would incorporate Meier's ideas of organizing on the kindergarten principles of question asking and model building, and the ideas of Ohanian, Nathan, Noddings, Sanz de Santamaria, Coplin, Shannon, Harkavy, and Puckett as well. They would be institutions that primarily served their students and their society rather than the scholarly academic disciplines. They would be institutions in which the education of young people would be based not simply upon the acquisition of the content contained in the feudal scholarly domains but upon the idea that students must construct *their own* well informed but constantly changing and developing visions of the world. This would therefore be an educational process based not only upon Deweyan and Meieran developmental kindergarten principles but upon Franklin's (and Leland Stanford's) insistence that any institution of education should be based not only on teaching but also on public and community service.

4. The assembled representatives then would be asked to spell out in some detail a new system of educational governance running from preschool through graduate school and including all of the major federal, state, and local players. This system would guarantee that all of the changes spelled out in the first three tasks would be permanently maintained as *the* normal, everyday way our schools, colleges, universities, and graduate schools actually would be run from now on.

5. The assembled representatives would be asked to propose solutions to the money problem at all educational levels. At the higher educational level, it doesn't do much good to make all of the radical changes spelled out as a result of the first four tasks if our public educational institutions are not adequately funded and if, in the case of both public and private colleges and universities, most students will not be able to afford the costs of attending them. So the representatives would be asked to come up with new approaches to make it possible for *any and all* interested students to go to *every* kind of public or private institution of higher education when, as, if, and at whatever age it might be appropriate for each individual student to do so, whether or not they are initially and traditionally considered "suitable" aspirants for higher education.

One radical and possibly outlandish way to start here might be with the design of ways in which higher education students could assume more adult responsibilty for the conduct of their educational lives (and the college curriculum broadened) through students' taking on many of the practical tasks of keeping their institutions going (and making these tasks an integral part of the curricular process). Instead of having everything done for them by expensive older staff, students would now be expected as part of their education to assist in the administrative and business side of their institutions (and to learn about economics and organizational psychology). They could become involved in the maintenance and improvement of their physical facilities (thereby acquiring practical skills in, for instance, electricity, plumbing, carpentry that they will need in maintaining their own future homes) in the preparation and serving of food (thereby acquiring not only the skills of preparing food but, as Nel Noddings suggests, the cultural appreciation of a wide variety of the world's cuisines and of fine wines). They could take part in the landscaping and continued beautification of their rural or urban campuses (and thereby learn about practical botany, environmental design, and gardening), and so on. Every student, rich or poor, would thus become a work-study student and contribute to a broadened conception of what a college education ought to be and to lowering the costs and contributing to the overall quality of life in their college communities. This would also mean that all of the people usually classified as nonacademic staff would become teachers and full-fledged faculty members in this greatly broadened and much more realistic curriculum.

After all, large numbers of college and university students (perhaps most?) now have to work part-time outside their institutions during the school year in order to afford tuition and other educational costs. Why not put that time spent working at McDonald's into working for their own institutions and thereby reducing the amount of money they need to get their education?

At the same time, the group might strongly recommend Meier's suggestion for a higher education voucher system similar to the G.I. Bill that would guarantee access for all moderate-income as well as all poor and minority students whenever during their lives they decided that such access would be wise and appropriate (another good use for the $150 billion *not* spent on that new fighter plane).

At the elementary and secondary education level, there could be similar cost reduction suggestions involving student responsibility for the practical side of their school operations, but the primary recommendation here might well have to be that per pupil spending be equalized for every student in the country at levels equal to the spending levels of our richly endowed suburban school districts.

A Most Immodest Proposal—Stage Two

Once the assembled convention of scholars, school people, and other participants succeeded in fulfilling these five tasks, the second stage of this proposal requires moving from the thinking and generalized design phase into the very real worlds of both elementary and secondary and higher education. This would be the task of testing this new model out by subjecting it to an experimental participatory action research process that would tell us whether this radically different approach is really the kind of educational system we want for the foreseeable future.

What we are proposing here is a greatly expanded, twenty-first-century version of the almost totally neglected Eight-Year Study briefly described by Joe Nathan in Chapter 3, the study that was conducted in the 1930s and early 1940s by the Commission on the Relation of School and College of the Progressive Education Association (PEA).[1]

The problem facing the advocates of progressive education and thus the PEA in 1930 was the problem of college admissions requirements (yes, some things never change). The PEA's executive board appointed a committee "to explore the possibilities of better coordination of school and college work and to seek an agreement which would provide freedom for secondary schools to attempt fundamental reconstruction."

The committee decided that they wished to

work toward a type of secondary education which will be flexible, responsive to changing needs, and clearly based on an understanding of the qualities needed in adult life. We are trying to develop students who regard education as an enduring quest for meanings rather than credit accumulation; who desire to investigate, to follow the leadings of a subject, to explore new fields of thought; knowing how to budget time, to read well, to use sources of knowledge effectively and who are experienced in fulfilling obligations which come with membership in the school or college community.

Yes, it could have been written by any member of Theodore Sizer's Coalition of Essential Schools, or by Dewey himself.

But would such schools be able to get their students admitted to the country's colleges and universities? In order to answer that question, the committee set up an elaborate experiment. Thirty high schools all across the country, public and private, representing a cross-section of the high school population, were selected to develop themselves into the "fundamentally reconstructed" progressive schools they had always wished and hoped to become. Some three hundred colleges were then organized to waive their normal admissions requirements for graduates of these schools. The success or failure of the experiment would then be determined by how well the progressively educated students did in college on a wide variety of criteria.

The assessment team's technique was to set up 1,475 pairs of college students, each consisting of a graduate of one of the study schools and a graduate of some other nonprogressive secondary school matched as closely as possible with respect to sex, age, race, Scholastic Aptitude (now Assessment) scores, home and community background, and vocational and avocational interests.

At the end of the study eight years later, the assessment team, led by the late Ralph Tyler, reported the following results for the students admitted from the thirty progressive schools: they earned a slightly higher total grade average; they displayed a greater degree of intellectual curiosity and drive; they seemed to have developed clearer ideas concerning the meaning of education; they more often demonstrated a high degree of resourcefulness in meeting new situations; they had about the same problems of adjustment to college life as the comparison group but approached the solution to the problem with greater effectiveness; they participated more frequently in organized student groups; they earned a higher percentage of nonacademic honors; they had a more adult orientation toward a choice of vocation; and they demonstrated a more active concern for national and world affairs. All of the results, in short, that just about everyone could possibly hope for.

One might have thought that such results would immediately have a transformative effect on both the nation's high schools and the college admissions requirements. But they did not. The only extenuating circumstance here is that the results appeared in 1942, in the middle of World War II, a time when the nation's attention and efforts were hardly directed at the improvement of its public schools.

An equally persuasive reason for the total ignoring of the study and its results, however, is that *the radically progressive educational changes were limited to the experiment's high schools and were not also required of the colleges and universities.* The higher education institutions were asked only to lift temporarily their usual admissions requirements, not to change themselves into radically progressive colleges and universities. Since those colleges and universities remained for the most part the same old traditional institutions, it must have been all too easy for them not to go to the bother of changing their venerable admissions practices for all schools across the country or to completely revamp their conventional curricular and organizational structures just to satisfy the demands of a few oddball high schools. And this would remain the case even if the graduates of those oddball schools did better in the traditional educational environment and by the traditional academic standards of the colleges and universities themselves.

The success of those progressively educated students might also have suggested, but clearly did not suggest, to the colleges and universities that those students—and, indeed, *all* college students—might do even better in their institutions of higher education if the colleges and universities were themselves transformed into progressive establishments.

And it apparently did not occur to those institutions of higher education to exert pressure on the nation's still traditional high schools to become more progressive, even when the graduates of the progressive schools were doing better in college than the graduates of the traditional schools.

The Eight-Year Study's lack of success in transforming either elementary and secondary or higher education, however, should not be taken to mean that it was a waste of everyone's time and energy or that *another such experiment, conducted this time on a much larger, more comprehensive scale, conducted in Sarason /1787 fashion, would necessarily also fail to produce significant change.*

It is precisely such a study that we are immodestly proposing here. This time, however, the radically progressive changes would not be limited to the elementary and secondary schools but would include carefully selected colleges and universities as well. We are also proposing a longer time period and a careful staging of both the preparation for and the actual conduct of the experiment.

In short, what we are proposing is that a group of carefully chosen early childhood programs, elementary schools, middle schools, high schools, colleges, and universities (or particular pieces of those institutions of higher education) be carved out of our present preschool through college system and organized in such a fashion that a child entering an early childhood program at age three or four would be guaranteed a thoroughly progressive educational experience from that age until graduation from college. (We'll leave the graduate schools until later.) These students (and their parents) would have to be volunteers, since choice versus relative nonchoice is itself part of the experiment. As with the Eight-Year Study, a control group of similar, carefully matched conventional institutions and (probably nonvolunteer and nonchoice) students would also be selected. In order to cover the full and diverse range of students and the full range of possible progressive institutions, we would most likely need at least ten schools in each of our categories for both the experimental and the control groups, that is, ten early childhood programs, ten elementary schools, ten middle schools, ten high schools, and ten four-year colleges in each group, or one hundred schools in all. Assuming an average size of four hundred students for each school, we are talking about something in the neighborhood of 40,000 subjects, depending upon the precise ways in which the designers and evaluators collaboratively decided to conduct the study.

The ideal time period for the such a study would, of course, be twenty-five years (thus dovetailing nicely with a title such as the Twenty-Five-Year Study for the Twenty-First Century). Although there may be good reasons for trying to shorten this period, and ways in which it could be shortened without harm to the results, let's spell out why it would ideally take twenty-five years and just how in very general terms such a full-length study might be conducted. Even though the full study might take twenty-five years, enormous amounts of useful information would be gathered *every* year at *every* stage of the experiment.

The first task, then, is to divide the study into three stages.

Stage One—The First Five Planning and Start-Up Years

Although it might be possible to find a few existing elementary and secondary schools and perhaps even a few existing colleges and universities or pieces of such institutions that would meet the criteria for the study, it is altogether unlikely that there would be enough of these to conduct a meaningful experiment. In any case, no such study could or should be conducted without careful, extensive preparation and planning. Such planning would include not only the design of the study itself but especially the task of making sure that all of the participating schools and institutions are really there, that they are truly reformed, progressive institutions, and that they are committed to being there for the long haul.

Thus the first five years of the study would be devoted to study design and to identifying the full range of institutions who wish to participate and giving them the time (and whatever funding might be necessary) to become the reformed, progressive institutions they would like to be. It is also possible that many of these participating institutions would have to be essentially *new* institutions and would thus need start-up time and experience before launching into the study itself. However, whenever during this start-up period any participant deemed itself ready to accept students, it would proceed to do so.

And, of course, one of the most important aspects of the design process would be the creation of the research/assessment component—defining the criteria for certifying a participant as truly developmental, progressive, demonstrably kindergarten-inspired, and suitably Meierian. And an equally important task: spelling out in considerable detail the human—and humane—attributes of the program's graduates that should be used to judge whether each segment of the preschool through college and university progressive educational program has successfully served its student and parent clientele. And the final task of deciding upon the criteria to be used to decide whether the new system of educational governance is doing the job it was designed to do.

Stage Two—The Nineteen Operational Years

As the various components of the system began their full official operation, all students in the program would be tracked from day of their entry at whatever level they start. Thus an early childhood entrant at age three would have the full nineteen years of the experiment. A child starting in kindergarten at age five would have seventeen years. A student starting middle school at roughly grade 6 would have ten years, a high school student starting at grade 9 would have eight years, a college-level student would have four years. Students could enter between these starting levels if the schools so choose. Thus, although the benefits of the experiment would presumably vary depending upon when a student entered, all students no matter when they entered would be tracked to ascertain the degree of their benefit, if any, by comparison with their control group counterparts. The research group would track and code every student as to year and level of entrance, and so on. The research group would also issue interim reports every year as it analyzed the accumulated data for each previous year.

It would inevitably be the case, of course, that some students would have to drop out because of family movement and other unforeseen circumstances and would have to be replaced. The hope and expectation, however, would be that a sufficient number of students would make it from start to finish for there to be a statistically significant set of results, although *all* of the data on *all* of the students would be clearly useful and important.

Stage Three: The Assessment Year

The final, twenty-fifth, year of the experiment would be devoted to gathering and analyzing all the data of the previous years, writing them all up, and making the results widely known.

The Possible Results of Such an Immodest Proposal

As was the case in 1787, any such undertaking would have to have political and financial support at the highest levels of government and society, and especially at the highest levels of the educational world. (As for the financial part of it, I think we could safely estimate that the cost of this experiment over the full twenty-five-year period would be approximately the cost of *one* of those new fighter planes.) It would also require a commitment to the idea that such rigorous, real-world, longitudinal experimentation is not only well worth conducting but likely the *only* way in which we can even begin to come to any meaningful conclusions about how we should or should not conduct the national enterprise of educating the young.

So here we have one possible way of beginning to answer the questions raised by Meier, Ohanian, Nathan, and all of the other perplexed practitioners in our kindergartens, elementary schools, and high schools. We also perhaps have a way of bringing about the kind of changes in the American system of education, public and private, from preschool through college and university, that many of us would so very much like to see. Such a study might also lead to the creation of a just and humane American educational system from preschool through graduate school, a system that might then enable us to begin the arduous, even daunting task of building a truly just and humane American society of which we could all be proud.

Note

1. This description of the Eight-Year Study is drawn from Lawrence A. Crenin, *The Transformation of the School* (New York: Alfred A. Knopf, 1962), 251–258.

References

Sarason, Seymour. 1999. "Contexts of Productive Learning, Governance, Charter Schools, the Creation of Settings and the Wailing Wall." In *Creating New Schools: How Small Schools Are Changing American Education*, ed. Evans Clinchy. New York: Teachers College Press.

Contributors

Evans Clinchy is Senior Consultant at the Institute for Responsive Education at Northeastern University, Boston, MA. He is the coauthor with Timothy W. Young of *Choice in Public Education* (Teachers College Press, 1992), and editor of a trilogy of books on educational reform including this present book and *Transforming Public Education: A New Course for America's Future* (Teachers College Press, 1997) and *Creating New Schools: How Small Schools Are Changing American Education* (Teachers College Press, 1999).

William D. Coplin is Director and Professor of Public Affairs at the Maxwell School of Citizenship and Public Affairs and the College of Arts and Sciences at Syracuse University. He is also Laura J. and L. Douglass Meredith Professor for Teaching Excellence. He is the author of *You Can Make a Difference: A Guide for Genuine Do-Gooders,* to be published in late 1999 by Routledge.

Ira Harkavy is director of the Center for Community Partnerships and Associate Vice President at the University of Pennsylvania. He teaches in the departments of history, urban studies, and city and regional planning, and is Executive Editor of *Universities and Community Schools* and chair of the Coalition for Community Schools.

Nona Lyons is associate visiting professor of education at Dartmouth College in Hanover, NH. She is editor of *With Portfolio in Hand: Validating the New Teacher Professionalism* (Teachers College Press, 1999). The recipient of a Spencer Fellowship, she was a visiting research scholar at the Wellesley College Center for Research on Women. She is the coauthor of *Making Connections: The Relational World of Adolescent Girls at Emma Willard School* (Harvard University Press).

Deborah Meier, author of *The Power of Their Ideas* (Beacon Press, 1995), founded and directed the Central Park East Elementary and Secondary Schools in East Harlem from 1974 to 1995. She is now principal of Mission Hill School, a public elementary "pilot" school in Boston's Roxbury community and vice-chair of the Coalition of Essential Schools. She began her career as a kindergarten and Headstart teacher. In 1987 she was a recipient of a MacArthur grant for her work in East Harlem.

Joe Nathan has been an award-winning inner city public school teacher and administrator. He is currently Director of the Center For School Change at the Humphrey Center at the University of Minnesota.

Nel Noddings is Lee Jacks Professor of Child Education Emerita at Stanford University and Professor of Education at Teachers College, Columbia University. Her most recent book, coedited with Michael Katz and Kenneth Strike, is *Justice and Caring* (Teachers College Press, 1999).

Susan Ohanian is a teacher, writer, and consultant living in Charlotte, VT. Her most recent book is *One Size Fits Few: The Folly of Educational Standards* (Heinemann, 1999).

John Puckett is associate professor and associate dean at the University of Pennsylvania Graduate School of Education, where he teaches courses on the social forces and contexts of urban education. For the past twelve years he has helped create, and report on, the theory and practice of community schools and academically based community service in West Philadelphia.

Alejandro Sanz de Santamaria is professor of economics at the Centro de Estudios Sobre Desarrollo Economico at the University of the Andes in Bogota, Columbia.

Patrick Shannon is professor of education at Pennsylvania State University in University Part, PA. A former preschool and elementary school teacher, he is the author of nine books.

Index